THE NEW POETRY

Language & Maps.
Transport

THE NEW POETRY

EDITED BY
MICHAEL HULSE
DAVID KENNEDY
DAVID MORLEY

BLOODAXE BOOKS

ISBN: 1 85224 245 0 hardback edition
      1 85224 244 2 paperback edition

First published 1993 by
Bloodaxe Books Ltd,
P.O. Box 1SN,
Newcastle upon Tyne NE99 1SN.

Bloodaxe Books Ltd acknowledges
the financial assistance of Northern Arts.

Cover painting reproduced by kind permission of
Raab Boukamel Galleries Ltd, 9 Cork Street, London W1X 1PD.

Cover printing by J. Thomson Colour Printers Ltd, Glasgow.

Printed in Great Britain by
Cromwell Press Ltd, Broughton Gifford, Melksham, Wiltshire.

CONTENTS

Simon Armitage (*b.* 1963)

PREFACE

This anthology represents what we believe to be the best poetry written in the British Isles in the 1980s and early 1990s by a distinctive new generation of poets. The statement necessarily demands a few words about our methodology. Firstly, we have not included any work by poets who appeared in *The Penguin Book of Contemporary British Poetry* because we wanted to highlight writers who have either come to prominence or have started writing since its publication in 1982. Similarly, we have not included any writers born before 1940; to have done so would have resulted in a very different anthology, one in which we would have had very little space for the younger writers whose work we particularly wanted to represent. Secondly, it is important to stress that within those criteria we have worked with total openness to what is being written. This has involved reading the complete poetry lists of major publishers, specialist poetry publishers and small presses, as well as trawling exhaustively through magazines and pamphlets. Finally, it has meant reducing a list of over 250 writers to the 55 represented here. The inclusion of so many poets reflects the sheer quantity of outstanding poetry currently being written in Britain and Ireland. To all the publishers who sent us books and typescripts, to all the poets who let us see work in progress, to all the friends and families who participated and supported us, we offer our thanks.

Michael Hulse
David Kennedy
David Morley

INTRODUCTION

Every age gets the literature it deserves. As the 20th century opened, the graceful throes of pre-First World War Europe produced a Rilke, the Chicago stockyards an Upton Sinclair, and post-Victorian England the complacency of the Georgian poets but also the turbulent energy of D.H. Lawrence. The seeming exhaustion of classical civilisation produced Dada, Eliot, Cavafy and Gottfried Benn. Throughout the century, the hierarchies of values that once made stable poetics possible have been disappearing. In the absence of shared moral and religious ideals, common social or sexual *mores* or political ideologies, or any philosophy on the conduct of life, plurality has replaced monocentric totemism.

At any period in the century, values have been in a state of flux. In the 1980s, this flux was dramatic. The decade began with the noisy, triumphalist dismantling of the post-1945 liberal consensus in Britain and the USA; it ended with the disintegration of the Soviet Union and the Eastern Bloc. Britain, like Spain and Portugal before it, continued to decline while pretending not to notice. The period witnessed events that were often bewilderingly contradictory: Britain's final loss of place on the world stage versus her involvement in armed conflict in the Falklands and the Gulf; the rise of the New Right and its brutal politics of the balance sheet versus the overall confusion of socialism; the creation of a permanent underclass through rising unemployment versus aggressive *laissez-faire* in the high streets and stock market. Together, these events seemed a black vindication of Mrs Thatcher's famous remark that 'there is no such thing as society'. The British Government, severing its final connections with the ideologies of the Welfare State, was able to perpetrate scams like the 1982 Nationality Act, which, as Salman Rushdie wrote, 'abolished the *ius soli*. From now on citizenship is the gift of government'. In Ireland, the problems of a poor, pro-European nation with its own distinctive dilemmas were not helped any nearer to solution by the pervasive influence of the Catholic Church. And everywhere, growing awareness of environmental issues underlined Western capitalism's ambivalent relationship with science and technology.

This anthology showcases the poetry written by a generation of British and Irish writers who began writing or came to prominence in the 1980s and early 1990s. We believe the poetry collected here confirms what William Scammell has described as 'a flourishing contemporary poetic culture with something of the *brio* and the ambition once thought lost to the novel and to more exciting poets overseas'. The new poetry emphasises accessibility, democracy and responsiveness, humour and seriousness, and reaffirms the art's significance as public utterance. The new poetry highlights the beginning of the end of British poetry's tribal divisions and isolation, and a new cohesiveness – its constituent parts "talk" to one another readily, eloquently, and freely while preserving their unique identities. Thirty years ago, A. Alvarez published his pioneering anthology *The New Poetry*. We make no apology for using his title for an anthology of poetry that is fresh in its attitudes, risk-taking in its address, and plural in its forms and voices.

* * *

Life in post-imperial Britain and the death of the national consensus produced scathing and journalistic work from perhaps the most controversial ironist of the 1980s, Peter Reading. His post-War English childhood is presented as a series of scenes from Betjemanesque metropolitan life:

> Pyrex, a pie-dish, deep-lined with apple lumps,
> deft in the left hand; with the right, flopping on
> pall of white-dusted droopy pastry,
> slicing off overlaps, jabbing steam-vents...

> '52: Mummy paused, wiped a floured hand and tuned in the wireless –
> sad Elgar, crackling, then *death of our King, George the Sixth.*

Gutter comedy, and tongue-in-cheek linguistic registers (the *Boys' Own*/Biggles Exclamatory), are used to smuggle scathing comments on delusions of British political grandeur:

> '56: going home from the Juniors,
> I read the headlines **Suez** and **Crisis Point** –
> crikey! I thought, there must be something
> terribly wrong with the nation's toilets;

> soon if the Government didn't act there'd be all kinds of nasties
> gushing up out of the drains, Britain would be [is] engulfed.

By the 1980s, Britannia had long ceased to rule the waves; those in power, however, found it difficult to accept the fact. 'Inglan is a bitch', wrote Linton Kwesi Johnson: for Britain's blacks and Asians, the period was sometimes a lethal reminder that the old British superiority complex was dying a hard death. Peter Didsbury, sick of England in his English garden, found that the aptest image for that hard, slow dying, and for the post-colonial Englishman's need to ignore its grip, was

that blasted elm, that rocks to your fingers
and threatens to fall. It would lie across
half the garden. I estimate its height
and step that far away, before I go.

Eighties Britain grieved observers. Reading's sequence *Perduta Gente* contrasted have-nots sleeping rough outside the Royal Festival Hall and the haves listening to Sibelius within. His anger was shared by many. Glyn Maxwell, though he ends 'Helene and Heloise' with a refusal to be self-righteous, feels compelled to record his awareness that only a mile or so from the slick stylish girls he is watching there is 'a squad/ Of infuriated coldly eyeing sons/ Kicking the screaming oath out of anyone's'. Urban violence – racial, brutal – prompted some of Reading's most arresting work. His attraction to the stuff of which seamier headlines are made struck his sterner critics as relentless. But Reading's retort stated the classic position of those who feel it is impossible to address social injustice in genteel, sanitised work: 'He don't *invent* it, you know'.

Poems in this book by Eavan Boland, Charles Boyle and Harry Clifton take a broader, historical view, but insist on the political and historical meanings of the personal and domestic. Shorter, polemically pointed, but equally powerful views are taken by Duncan Bush in his responses to the 1984 Miners' Strike; by Paul Durcan in his broadsides against the power of Irish Catholicism; by David Dabydeen and Sujata Bhatt in their exploration of racial identity; or by Robert Crawford and W.N. Herbert in their promotion of Scottish *inter*-Nationalism. The post-Romantic tradition in the British Isles has perpetuated the belief that poetry and political concerns are incompatible. In fact they are inseparable: it hardly needed Tom Paulin to remind us that the subtext in Larkin, even when his subject was horses at grass, rarely strayed far from the political decline of England. Work in this anthology by John Hartley Williams, Ciaran Carson, Sean O'Brien, Michael Hofmann, Fred D'Aguiar and others shows that political poetry is now unembarrassed by the constraints of Romantic first-person lyricism.

The strengths on display in the writing of Carol Ann Duffy or Jackie Kay, of Ian McMillan or Geoff Hattersley, are located in a tension between ironic social naturalism and confrontational political work. Duffy has been exemplary in re-energising a feminist, public voice in poetry. Her habitual use of the dramatic monologue gives her poetry attack and access, and enables her to popularise complex ideas about language and its political role and meanings. 'Poet for Our Times' is a bitterly funny indictment of the Thatcher years, and of the abuses that come with a debasement of language and syntax. It is written (like Reading's work) out of a conviction that poetry must get its hands dirty if it is to take on the enemy and help preserve a liberal society and humanist culture. The title's use of 'for' instead of 'of' is almost a warning in itself that we get what we deserve.

Jackie Kay inhabits much the same territory as Carol Ann Duffy, but takes the older poet's procedures further by extending the monologue to dramatic forms. Kay's personal circumstances as a black Briton adopted and raised by a white Scottish family may be taken as an extreme example of what Terry Eagleton has termed 'the marginal becoming central'. A multicultural society challenges the very idea of a centre, and produces pluralism of poetic voice.

The idea of a centre is particularly fraught for those who feel marginalised. Arguably it is now more an idea than a reality; Donald Davie (himself, like Ian McMillan, from Barnsley, a working-class northern town with no claims to be the citadel), has expressed astonishment that the Anglo-Saxon centre, 'allegedly located in London and Oxbridge mostly, is supposed to be deeply satisfying to the English themselves'. But the need of those traditionally on the periphery to define their identity against "the centre" continues, and does much to explain similarities of strategy or tone between certain black and women writers, Scots and Caribbeans, Irish poets and Welsh. The imagery and frank address shared by Grace Nichols and Michèle Roberts are an example of this phenomenon. We believe the prevalence of such connections undermines conceptions of culture based on ideas of isolated achievement and originality. Similarly, the ease with which a Nichols, David Dabydeen or Fred D'Aguiar move between Caribbean and standard English is mirrored in the use of both English and Scots in the work of Robert Crawford, Liz Lochhead and W.N. Herbert. These affinities can attract a cynical brand of criticism (one observer described Herbert's Scots poetry as the poetic equivalent of 'blacking up'), but they may nonetheless have complex roots; Alan Riach has drawn attention to the Scottish influence on Caribbean language and writing, noting Kamau Brathwaite's 'explicit recognition of the Scots linguistic component in Creole'.

Dabydeen's deliberate engagement with Creole – his attempt to uncover 'its potential as a naturally tragic language', and his conviction that it 'is capable of expressing the full experience of its users, which is a very deep one, deep in suffering, cruelty, drunken merriment and tenderness' – reflects his awareness of the multicultural realities. 'In the 1970s and 1980s,' Dabydeen has pointed out, 'Britain became the third largest West Indian island after Jamaica and Trinidad: there are nearly a million of us living here.' This insight is never absent from Afro-Caribbean poetry's sense of being in a culture but not *of* it. D'Aguiar's poetry, like Dabydeen's, draws strength from a sense of exile; it is the achievement of their work that it does not seem estranged from family and home. Both poets, and Grace Nichols, have rejected validation from the outside and made their own way, knowing that if language is to articulate cultural identity there is no alternative. That stance at its most assertive has made Linton Kwesi Johnson a major figure in black British writing. The question raised for every reader of a poem like 'Mekkin History' is: what sort of society are we all conniving in if everyday violence continues to be the shared experience of a significant proportion of its citizens? It can come as no surprise that the work of Johnson and other black writers is "creolised"; if standard English is considered unequal to the task of recording the everyday bitterness of black suffering (as Johnson's 'Mekkin History' suggests), the choice of a non-standard dialect becomes a political decision – and arguably the first unpatronising use of non-standard English since Shakespeare. Johnson's own poetry, and his example as a public figure, have provided an invaluable model for younger writer-performers such as Lemn Sissay and Benjamin Zephaniah. Drawing for his dub poetry on oral usage, music, and poetic models of widely divergent kinds, Johnson has established the legitimacy of form-in-flux, of unsophisticated and fiercely targeted work that articulates the restlessness of the black diaspora. If 'Bass Culture' uses reggae as a means of investigating culture and language as a place of struggle, behind that approach in some sense are Marxist commentators such as Marcuse, with their assumption that the status quo is not monolithic or fixed.

A need to find alternatives to the real or imagined English centre vigorously informs the current resilience of Scottish writing. Robert Crawford and W.N. Herbert take their lead from Hugh MacDiarmid's belief 'in the possibility [of] the act of poetry being the reverse of what it is usually thought to be; not an idea gradually shaping itself in words, but deriving entirely from words'. Herbert has glossed this: 'It is also precisely in this way that writers such as Crawford and Kinloch are reconceptualising Scots. Yet, like the work of the Language poets, which offers among other things a critique of bankrupt vocabularies of capitalism, this is not merely aestheticism. Such exper-

imentation, because of Scotland's historic record of linguistic
subjugation, must always carry a political overtone. These are
necessary stages in the creation of an independent speech, the
S=C=O=T=S of a *nazione in liberta.*'

It is this ideological background that energises Crawford's and
Herbert's best writing. Both poets deploy science and its vocabu-
laries. In Crawford's case this is allied with the "talking up" done
by 'the MacAvantgarde'. A poem entitled 'Scotland' begins:

> Semi-conductor country, land crammed with intimate expanses,
> Your cities are superlattices, heterojunctive
> Graphed from the air, your cropmarked farmlands
> Are epitaxies of tweed.

Even allowing for the presence of MacDiarmid in that passage, the
radical nature of the contemporary Scottish scene, and the way it
uses many of the practices of Modernism as the bases for further
experiment, may be discerned in the fact that many of these words
have never appeared in an English poem before or in some of these
combinations. 'Scotland' and a similar poem like 'Alba Einstein',
which imagines a whole cultural industry springing up around the
confirmation of Einstein's Scottish origins, are wickedly asking *And
why not?* At the same time, they are sapping preconceptions of new
Scotland as 'silicon Glencoe', and old Scotland as shortbread in
tartan tins. It is a refusal to be put in one's place that has a num-
ber of meanings. Herbert's work in Scots plays with ideas of a
classless language that is a liberation not only from the constraints
of English but also from expectations of poetic subject.

A willingness to challenge the centre, to write poetry recognisable
as social discourse, is a hallmark of many northern English poets –
Peter Didsbury and Sean O'Brien, both closely associated with the
importance of Hull as a literary centre, and others loosely centred
on Huddersfield, among them Simon Armitage, Geoff Hattersley
and Ian McMillan. Armitage enjoyed phenomenal success with his
first volume *Zoom!* which sold over 6000 copies. His demotic rhy-
thms, his Larkin-Amis eye for everyday English life, and his use of
cliché, pun and wisecrack, make his work immediately accessible;
but beneath the streetwise, user-friendly surface is a poetry that
remains obsessive about the circumstances of its own making and
self-consciously alert to its effects. The habitual laconic tone func-
tions, in fact, as a way of behaving-in-language which has been
borrowed and refined from American writers like O'Hara, Kees
and Lowell. Geoff Hattersley's work is more obviously "cultured"
or "in a culture". Where Armitage's personae often seem loath to

stray too far from the semi-literate there is something almost "book-ish" about Hattersley's work and its interiors. As with Michael Hofmann, Hattersley's poetry enacts tensions and movements between room and street, and this is further mirrored by what Hattersley himself has called 'the subconscious working with the conscious in an odd balance'. As the narrator of 'Eccentric Hair' puts it:

> ...I'd no idea what I wanted,
> other than to be able to relax
> and see the funny sides of things again.

This passivity is a pose that allows a shifting perception of the connections between citizen and state, micro and macro. The residual urban paranoia in some of the poems is another version of this, a concern about role and appropriate behaviour in a particular culture and in the world at large. Hattersley's work, like Armitage's, is essentially a poetry of domestic moments and oblique responses to larger events. Ian McMillan's work is a unique combination of stand-up comedy and surrealism, in which language is treated with a healthy, postmodern disrespect. Indeed, language is itself part of the subject; McMillan likes to use lines as sign-posts, repeating or inverting, attaching unfamiliar words to familiar phrases. Words and syntax, as with Maxwell, are used "directionally" as well as descriptively. McMillan has written directly about the political struggle surrounding the dismantling of the coal industry and the destruction of working-class life in his native South Yorkshire and, in this light, it's possible to read his approach to language "politically" as a kind of revenge or guerrilla warfare on one of the instruments of authority. At the same time, however, McMillan together with Armitage, Hattersley, and Peter Sansom – whose longer poems we would like to have represented had there been more space – exemplifies the way in which many writers in the 1980s and early 1990s have come to poetry as something unfixed and have written without the need for any external, legitimating voice.

It would be possible to define the poetry this anthology documents as possessing at heart a new complexity in the available voices, syntax and language of poetry, and thus of its processes of perception. At a simple level this appears, in the early 1980s, in John Hartley Williams' 'Song of the Grillbar Restaurant'. Williams writes: 'I kept an eye on myself/ in the pink mirror/ & the eye kept an eye on myself'. This is not merely a recognition of the fiction-making inherent in all poetry but also a questioning of ideas about poetic authority, sincerity and authenticity. Behind Williams stand Olson, cummings and Zukofsky. In fact, American presences in the newer British and Irish writers are many: Robert Lowell in Michael Hofmann and Simon Armitage, Louis Simpson in Charles Boyle, John Ashbery in Peter Didsbury and John Ash, Frank O'Hara in Geoff Hattersley, James Merrill in David Hartnett, Anthony Hecht in George Szirtes, C.K. Williams in Ciaran Carson, $L=A=N=G=U=A=G=E$ poetry in Robert Crawford. In Hofmann there is also Hans Magnus Enzensberger; in Charles Boyle, Miroslav Holub; in Stephen Romer, Jean Follain. A willingness to look beyond the British Isles for affinities and kickstarts has been the hallmark of this period – contemporary figures such as Joseph Brodsky, Les Murray, Allen Curnow or Sharon Olds, and older writers such as Montale, Pessoa or Mandelstam (and in David Constantine's case Hölderlin). These writers have been real presences for many of the poets in this anthology, and underwrite the many challenges to poetic practice, form, and modes of meaning.

Glyn Maxwell's poetry exploits the possibilities of an untrustworthy "I" and a passive narrator – the narrator of one poem, not collected here, refers to himself as a 'mild citizen/ of what's suggested' – to powerful and far-reaching effect. His work is remarkable for a self-conscious wit and an attack derived, paradoxically, from a relentless conceptualising of language that plays with misreadings, tautologies, insecurities and qualification. Maxwell's is a re-emphasised and re-directed syntax that, in mimicking the evasions and non-sequiturs of everyday speech, reminds us that language is always debased currency. In one sense, of course, Maxwell is only asking us to do what all original writers ask us to do: to reconsider the relationship between reading and writing and, through it, the workings of the imagination. However, this is something that goes much deeper than the merely literary. Maxwell's work is perhaps the most obviously radical phrasing and answering of another set of questions that many of the poets collected here could be said to have asked themselves: what does the British poet write about? How is it to be written? How can it escape the negative inheritance of British poetry: its ironies, its understatements, its dissipated energies? It is this that underlies the fact that, read aloud, Maxwell's poetry is instantly recognisable as something that has its roots in everyday urban speech. Similarly, reflections on the role of the modern English poet inform Maxwell's habitual use of the mock heroic form and his allusions to and borrowings from the vocabularies of martial politics, the Bible, nursery rhymes, sport, commerce, advertising and the media.

Maxwell's mixing of registers, idioms and thematic provenances is shared by some of the strongest writers of the period. Peter Reading, in this a true postmodern, is happiest when he can manipulate reader expectation by contrasting tonality and subject, lofty style and squalid nastiness. This is true not only of his socio-political work but also of his writing on everyday human pain. 'You find the Limerick inapposite?' demands Reading. 'Try the pretty Choriamb?' The question that underlies these provocatively ironic demands touches upon the very relation of rhetorical form to experience. The same enquiry was the mainspring of Selima Hill's book-length poem *The Accumulation of Small Acts of Kindness*, with which she won the Arvon International Competition. The narrative takes the form of diaries written by a young woman before, during and after an extended stay in a psychiatric hospital. It highlights elements in Hill's work that give her a centrality in the new poetry that has not yet been sufficiently acknowledged. In charting personal development and the enactment of self-knowledge, her poems are radically anarchic in conception, moving between poles of fragility and stability and exploiting linguistic tensions between the narrative first person and a lack of active or decisive verbs. There is a similar recognition of passive registers in the work of the Huddersfield poets, but Hill goes further in her exploration of sensation and of the provisionality of selfhood. Hill can be read for her emotional impressionism, and for an exoticism which recalls Flaubert and that English desert eccentric Lady Hester Stanhope. Her radical contribution is to marry this to a sense of the "I" that seems Lacanian rather than Freudian, and to a contingent narrative sense schooled on Philip Roth, Virginia Woolf and Max Frisch rather than on any "great tradition".

Doubts about authenticity of self and narrative authority has informed poetry throughout this period. Some of the poets in *The New Poetry* – notably Paula Meehan, Sujata Bhatt and Jackie Kay – preserve a relatively uncontaminated singleness in the first person, but for others the pronominal act is itself a risk. Like Selima Hill, John Ash is fascinated by the sweeping gestures of purple, elevated styles, with the excitements of the senses, and with social bizarrerie. He has rarely found it possible to locate a stable self in his work. In poems such as 'Casino' he charts the terrain of cultural debris across which postmodern first persons, singular or plural, acting or narrating, have to make their way:

There were always big sailing ships –
magnificent coldly maternal women

> – or I should say there was always
> the large idea of sailing ships
>
> the anachronism of mysterious departures
> into a world too thoroughly discovered.
>
> In those days we came to the coast in winter,

This flamboyantly bathetic misprision of *The Waste Land* set the main Ash tone, and his cultural spoofery often reappeared in Peter Didsbury, Frank Kuppner and Ian Duhig. Postmodernism, notoriously elusive, can in part be seen as a relish for cumbersome cultural props for their totemic presence alone, without much attempt to see causal connections between larger cultural ideas and the facts of everyday life. Modernism posed Cognitive Questions (asked by most artists of the 20th century, Platonic or Aristotelian, till around 1958): 'How can I interpret this world of which I am part? And what am I in it?' Postmodernism poses Postcognitive Questions (asked by most artists since then): 'Which world is this? What is to be done in it? Which of my selves is to do it?' As in the work of Paul Muldoon, a presiding figure for many of the poets included here, this is more than the relativism that is still gaining currency. It is a realisation that ideas of meaning, truth and understanding are in themselves fictions determined by the rhetorical forms and linguistic terms used to express them.

That realisation graphically informs the work of Frank Kuppner, and interestingly licks at the edges of Pauline Stainer's poetry. Kuppner is an individualist with few discernible affinities. In a single quatrain from his off-beat masterpiece *A Bad Day for the Sung Dynasty* –

> Something something something something something;
> Something something something smiling something;
> Something smiling something something something;
> The old scholar finds himself involuntarily smiling.

– Kuppner contrives to burlesque academia, kneejerk reader response, and the mechanics of rhetoric. His anarchic humour may owe debts to sources as different as *Monty Python* and Alasdair Gray, but the heart of it is always a wariness of the Romantic self. In Pauline Stainer's work that wariness is refracted through a deeply English perspective informed by Victorian art, stained glass and church architecture, and seems often unsure of the degree to which it is genuinely committed to the metaphysical and sacred. The scientific empiricist in her withdraws from substantial avowal: it is this that produces the quirkily unstable frissons in her work and generates her attempts at scientific demonstrations of the sacred and vice versa. This places her at the forefront of a loose grouping of writers which includes W.N. Herbert, Robert Crawford, Jo Shapcott and Lavinia Greenlaw, who are making fruitful explorations of science as both subject and method. For example, Maggie Hannan's poetry withdraws the "I" almost completely and replaces it with strict, Ian McEwan-like rules of observation. 'The Prism', a section of her sequence 'The Vanishing Point', provides an apt image for the way she breaks a subject down and reassembles it with unusual synonyms and bony rhythms.

Poetry in the 1980s and early 1990s in England, Scotland and Wales has been largely about writers "making their own luck" and, finding themselves uncomfortable with authority and orthodoxy, seeking out new models and positions. In the process, they have discovered a new pluralism and are starting to define a believable role for poetry. The situation in Ireland – to English observers – presents, at first sight, an enviable contrast. 'Ireland,' wrote Gerald Dawe introducing *The New Younger Irish Poets*, 'is a visibly literary culture... Indeed, poetry has a curious public life in Ireland that often gives a misleading notion of just how central it actually is in Irish society'. The situation with anthologies might be a case in point: major undertakings from Faber, Oxford and Penguin as well as volumes from smaller, native presses devoted to the work of women poets and poets writing in Irish. So too, is the virtual pop star status enjoyed by Paul Durcan and Brendan Kennelly. All of these seem inconceivable if transposed to other parts of the British Isles.

However, beneath this bright surface, Ireland – all of its counties, north and south – works through its own singular dilemmas. Dawe has written elsewhere, almost bitterly, of poetry being given 'media coverage' at the expense of 'any reasonably detailed literary evaluation', and of its becoming 'a life-style in Ireland'. The example of Patrick Kavanagh continues to be both enabling and hindering in its implications for poetry's – and the poet's – public role and, in the course of compiling this anthology, we failed to find a single collection that was not larded with hyper-praise. The new Irish poets we have included here have been chosen because they confront the dilemmas of modern Ireland while at the same time recognising its position on the European and world stage, and the universality of the Irish experience.

Paul Durcan shares many of the concerns of non-Irish poets in this period: his declamatory style and his worldwide reputation as a reader of his own poems are, for example, another instance of the

blurring of the page and performance we find elsewhere. His work
is exemplary for its attack and its willingness to engage in the public
arena. Similarly, when he writes – in a poem not included here –
'I am the centre of the universe', the statement is intensely politi-
cal in its dramatic self-obsession when viewed not only against the
background of contemporary Ireland but also against a wider per-
spective of political change and uncertainty.

Dermot Bolger and Ciaran Carson display a determination to
remind us – in the face of powerful traditions to the contrary –
that a component of the Irish experience is iundeniably urban. In
this, they mirror the backdrop to new Irish film-making. Both poets
are adept at bending the long line and extended form to the service
of a novelistic and hallucinatory social realist discourse. Where
Bolger, however, rarely gets beyond portrayals of paranoia and
urban blight, Carson's relation to Belfast is a love affair with every
brick of every street, a compendium of stories, a time machine of
moments, smells and music. Carson has studied traditional oral
narrative forms, and this informs his particular gift for locating
anecdote and history in each other. Eavan Boland's poetry is marked
by a similar insistence. A black lace fan becomes a way of recaptur-
ing a past that 'is a empty café terrace'. Boland's poetry re-peoples
that terrace with the figures, usually women, who have been erased
and forgotten. The enabling radicalism of Boland's enterprise is
confirmed by her discernible influence on a younger poet, Paula
Meehan, who shares a concern with interiors and seemingly mun-
dane objects.

The work of Nuala Ní Dhomhnaill is typical of the rise and con-
solidation of women poets. At first sight, its Irish context might
seem to render here poetry particular and localised. But a closer
examination of its particular "moment" reveals that Irish poetry
has not been immune to some of the shifts that have occurred
elsewhere in our period.

Ní Dhomhnaill is the most prominent woman of a generation of
poets who emerged in the early 1970s and came to be associated
with the periodical *Innti*. This grouping was initially perceived to
be radical: its project, a refutation of the late Máirtín Ó Cadhain's
assertion that 'These days there is little left for poetry to do. Noth-
ing is left to poetry in Irish but brief lyrics...' The implication
was that the future lay with prose. The date of Ó Cadhain's state-
ment – 1970 – is significant in as much as English poetry was felt
to be in a similar state of disarray and largely overshadowed by the
novel after the excesses of the 1960s. And yet, the early 1970s would

see first collections from figures such as Muldoon, Harrison and Fenton, and the wider recognition and influence of Dunn, Heaney and Mahon.

A revitalisation occurred in Irish poetry – the achievements of Michael Hartnett should not be understated in this context – and through Ní Dhomhnaill and others associated with *Innti*, the Gaelic lyric was shown to be contemporary and responsive to a wide range of issues. Their poetry reflected and fed off the many social changes in Ireland at the time. The result was a shift in both writers and audience: from old to young, from rural to urban, from conservative to radical. As we have seen throughout the 1980s and 1990s, the poetry created its own audience.

These changes of emphasis probably explain much of the attraction Ní Dhomhnaill's poetry continues to have for translators, and we have chosen her work precisely because of this level of access. The number of major poets who have been moved to translate her represents not only a recognition of her importance but also a rediscovery of the importance of Gaelic traditions in Irish poetry. We hope that the readers of this anthology will appreciate Ní Dhomhnaill's poetry for itself, and will find it an intriguing and inviting entrance to a different poetic tradition, notable for its emotional enlargement and use of language uninfected by class positions.

* * *

A recent editorial in *Poetry Review* (London) comparing Britain and Ireland, complained that:

> To turn the spotlight on Britain we see that canon-making has collapsed into hectic pluralism and specialist interest serving. Despite the chorus of criticism that greeted Morrison and Motion's *Penguin Book of Contemporary British Poetry* in 1982, the dissent has not spawned a serious rival; instead, the key anthologies have been on women's poetry and Westindian-British poetry. An anthology like *The New Younger Irish Poets* seems unthinkable in Britain; instead we have the many introduction anthologies, the Gregories, the Bloodaxe *New Women Poets* etc.
>
> This loss of the sense of the canon has weakened British poetry. There is an audience beyond the insiders, who would like to know what is happening in poetry – it is no use saying there's any amount of it scattered around: a few key anthologies are essential.

It would be absurdly presumptuous of us to claim *The New Poetry* is in any way definitive but it is, we hope, "defining". Where others perceive pluralism as on the one hand hectic, and on the other serving special interests, we would argue that in the case of the former this signifies health as opposed to further decline; and in the case of the latter, such highlighting is long overdue in a culture which persistently ignores or marginalises the voices and achievements of a significant number of its people.

The work collected here documents poetry in the British Isles at last responding to the imperatives of the times. It is writing that is alert to the fact that British poetry's prevailing modes – in our period, social and realist – are species of fiction like any other and that, consequently, the "truth" or "understanding" promised of poetry are largely fictional too. Nearly seventy years ago, in an essay entitled 'A Prophecy or a Plea', Laura Riding asserted that 'the function of the poet, of the poetic mind, is inductive rather than deductive. Life needs proving in poetry as well as in science'. Similar convictions underlie the poetry in this anthology. It is a poetry which understands that before it is moral, representational or empirical, it is above all *sceptical;* whose defining presences are, consequently, most often to be found in John Ashbery, W.H. Auden, Elizabeth Bishop and Derek Mahon; and which represents an exhilarating re-discovery of the freedom of the imagination. Or, as Paul Muldoon wrote of Nerval:

> ...he hanged himself from a lamp-post
> with a length of chain, which made me think
>
> of something else, then something else again.

THE EDITORS
Sheffield / Cologne

PUBLISHER'S NOTE: The poetry of Michael Hulse has been included in this anthology at the wish of the other editors.

PAULINE STAINER

Sighting the Slave Ship

We came to unexpected latitudes –
sighted the slave ship
during divine service
on deck.

In earlier dog-days
we had made landfall
between forests of sandalwood,
taken on salt, falcons and sulphur.

What haunted us later
was not the cool dispensing
of sacrament
in the burnished doldrums

but something more exotic –
that sense
of a slight shift of cargo
while becalmed.

The Ice-Pilot Speaks

I

No such thing
as a routine death –
in *ultima thule*
the shaman stretches
the throat of a walrus
over his drum.

It is Ascension week;
the men wear black crêpe veils
against snowblindness,
the ship's astronomer
is given four ounces
of raven;

sterna paradisaea
is caught with ordinary cotton;
a number of snowy owls
are shot,
one thawing its prey
against its breast.

O terra incognita –
the tundra is silk-crewel work;
polar bears sweat
through upturned paws,
the ship's figurehead
warm as from the furnace

the sagas redden –
on tinted lantern slides
Amundsen drives
five of his dogs
to death
Language, open the sacred quarry.

II

I dream of your body
when there is no open water
and the Inuit women
soften foxskins
with their teeth.

It was like drawing
without looking
at the paper
as I ran my hand
between your breasts

but you remembered the nuns
at the silk farm
blanching the cocoons,
teasing out
the single thread

raw silk running

III

i

Like Quakers
the icebergs recline
their nudes

the light from their viscera
so blue, addicts can
no longer find the vein.

ii

Gymnopédies
Satie seeking
the antique whiteness

the estuary
swinging its mirrors
at right-angles

a looking-glass quadrille,
pistons counselling
perfection.

iii

Disquieting muses –
subtext
of the deep keels

the bisque-doll
on the seabed
mouthing the Titanic.

IV

Is it minimalist –
the music
for a northern light

fleece growing along
a sheep's spine, lava slowing
under high pressure hoses

the ship's surgeon cutting flesh
from between the ribs of the dead
to feed the living?

What is the sound
for such interstices –
the Piper Alpha wailing

fenders on the Silver-Pit
blistering at
the golden scenario

those two divers on the spiderdeck
underwater
at the time of explosion?

V

The high scree makes one dream –
ptarmigan hunters
use the snow as reflector
where they roost unseen,
the eight Inuit mummies,
one with Down's syndrome.

The blood-group of mummies
can be determined;
so what is this slippage
when you put them up darkly,
the white dead
already meditating flight

and the hunters are silenced
not by the muzzle-flash
from a gun
but by that sense
of encounter
with their own coffin?

VI

What is song
when the shroud
is left unlaced at the mouth
and the arctic tern
has a radio transmitter
lashed with fuse-wire
to its leg?

What are footings?
Reindeer kneel
to the cull;
in Eller Moss
was found the skeleton
of a stag
standing upon its feet

At the magician's house
I carve ivory noseplugs
in the shape of a bird
with inlaid eyes.
What is the spirit
at gaze

the deerness of deer?

VII

St Brendan's monks
sail through the eye
of the iceberg.

At first, they ran
with the shadow of the land
through light bluish fog

later, by moonlight,
the ship caulked
with tallow, shamans

clashing over the Pole
as if to earth
any dead in the rigging,

and at dawn,
floes gliding by,
chesspieces in lenten veils

the sea a silver-stained
histology slide,
the O of the iceberg

whistling like Chinese birds
with porcelain whistles
on their feet.

Even in prayer
they could never replay it –
the purity of that zero

Varèse, playing
the density of his flute's
own platinum

the intervening angel
bearing a consignment
of freshwater.

VIII

Pestilencia!

The living wear
the black death
like windroses,
red for the quarter,
green for the half-winds.

Who says plague
is monotonous?
Christ turns
on Yggdrasill
under the strobe lights

I am my beloved's
his desire is toward me
and the dead stiffen
under their many eiders.

IX

In the North West Passage
William Newton, ice-mate,
hallucinates:

under the mosquito net
Marguerite
braids her hair

*We sleep apart
as if we were dead*

*but o the searching
tongue of the sea*

*each time the muslin
billows the bed*

*a leopard coughs
in the camphor tree.*

X

Up she rises –
the sunken softwood ship
with her dissolving
cargo of sugar,
fainter than
the eight hooves
of Sleipnir
on the albumen print
of the glacier.

Pittura metafisica
the mistletoe shafting
Balder; Borges
feeling the pillar
in his hotel room
at Reykjavik,
the Euclid of childhood
flowing through him
like serum.

One waterfall is extraordinarily like another
but for lovers
who kneel at its lip
and drink from
an unspilled moon
the source is altered
utterly,
until the painter,
erasing their figures

draws 5 strings
down the canvas
and hears from behind
the golden mean
the rasp of the salt-lick
as on the evening
of the first day
a man's hair
comes out of the ice.

XI

Sfumato!

The blue whales are flensed
by steam winch;
local reds
boil from the heart.

The whalers could be
gods, butchering
Balder's horse against
the midnight sun.

Loki is bound
with his own entrails
but who will wear
this smoking scarlet?

XII

We are close-hauled;
the narwhals hang
belly to belly
in the water.

I run my finger
through your menstrual blood
and put it to my mouth –
O Sigurd, who understood

the speech of birds
and slit the mailshirt
grown into her flesh
as Sigrdrifa slept

not a drop runs over,
but there is no room for another
and outside
the warm ice rafting.

XIII

They had no faint object camera –
whether they saw pack-ice or fog-bank
or mirage, will never be known

the weather not quite reliable,
leprosy
that white list in the sky.

So what made our love-making
the palimpsest
for all successive acts

when in the sedge-meadow
the gods are discovered
at chess

and give over
on their marvellous boards
the game that must be lost?

JOHN HARTLEY WILLIAMS

Lament for the Subotica-Palić Tramway

Let's have a lament for things past.
It's easy to do & it costs nothing:
Let's get down to how things
      really ought to be.

On a Sunday afternoon the trams used to run
Out along the edge of the maize-fields
With windows open, so that the dark men in
      white shirts
And the softly-interior-smiling women with
      high-button'd necks
Could feel the breeze, the aromatic air, as
      it soothed their sweat.
And the tram used to roll along its weedy track
At ten miles an hour; the chocolate-brown tram
That came to a halt every two hundred yards
And sat in the patient silence of emptiness
While others climbed aboard. How different this was
From the modern horror, the ghastly contemporary
      totalitarian ear-drum pounder,
The never-silent always-polluting high-tyred
           motor-bus!

When the tram stopped, everything stopped.
And then you would hear the clunky sound of the bell,
Halfway between a ding & a thud,
And the tram would slip backwards a little,
          preparing itself,
And then clout you in the back with enormous
          electric acceleration
Till it reached a speed somewhat above walking pace!
The people loved it, for it always stopped for them.
It carried fat ladies ten feet & then placed
      them down on the earth again
With their bags & double-chins & the worries
      that fat ladies have.
And the conductor would sometimes let it go on
      to the next stop

While he finished a conversation with a friend
      encountered in the street.
Then, with a jolting run, his dull-colour'd
      mechanical clipper
Knocking his breast-bone, he would rejoin
      the ship!
And the tram would go thru the town in its
      special sanctuary of track,
Along an aisle that had been laid down for it,
Rather as a file of monks, in a religious age,
Might pass with regularity, quite unobserved,
      thru a busy populace.
And the people in the street could hear its
      vibrato-less bell
As it went by, a reminder of gentle motion, of
      the agreeable flux of affairs,
Without turmoil or passion or agitation.

After the tram ran the school-children, or hung
      off the back step,
Or clustered in the standing place round the doors,
Never deigning to occupy the narrow & immensely
      polished wooden seats,
But rolling with the warps in the track, feeling
      the sensation of something precarious but solid.
And it was a single-track line, that tramway,
With passing places, at every third stop.
You waited while the contrary tram came
      slowly up the line to meet you,
Its big beetle front swaying & glittering,
Taking, O an appreciable swathe of time from
      the fortunate afternoon,
Until it swung alongside & you gazed at the
      contrary people, sitting in silence,
Smiling, perhaps, at their own absurd contrariety,
      until
With a bound you were off again
      down that track.

And leaving the town in the summer, the air was
      heavy with the dust of crops.
People with huge water melons sat, leaning forward,
      gazing across the flatland.

And sometimes, I've been told, the chocolate tram would derail,
        at its usual unspectacular pace,
And plough gently into the maize, nesting its large
        iron buffers
In the stiff green-shirted plants, with their pale
        yellow cobs.
And the whole tramway of the town would come to a
        stop,
While an extraordinary breakdown wagon, of cables &
        winches, & a small crane,
Would come out of the house where all the trams
        spent the night
And wallow towards the crisis point, with officials·in uniform
Standing on either side. Meanwhile the rest of the trams
        did not move.
They could not advance or retreat, & so people
                        would say:
'The tramway's broken down!'
And the occupants of each tram would step out
        & conversation would flower under the plane trees
In the centre of the town. And some would decide to walk,
But others would not be so pressed.
And even in the case of a winter's day
People would warm themselves with talk,
        remaining inside,
And feel themselves pleasantly marooned.

Of course the old tramway grew old.
New buses came from Sweden & gave the streets
        a new look.
But it was not long before they appeared
        dusty & grubby & somehow chewed-up.
And it seemed that they were always late, or you had just
        missed one,
Or they were impossibly crowded. And between each
        stop
Was a huge distance,
So that the fat ladies were carried almost as far
        on the wrong side
As they got on the right side.
And finally they closed the tramway altogether
Which, I believe, was a cause even for tears
        among some folk,

To see those old chocolate beetles stacked like so
      many boxes
In the single-roomed mansion from which they had once
      so proudly lumbered forth
To serve the people. And nobody really knew what
      to do with them,
So they are still there to this day, rusting & rotting,
With the wood ripped away & the windows shattered,
All their once priceless character now derided,
And even the landmarks of their route
Are torn up, except
For a few strands of track, embedded here & there
      in the cobbles.

It was a woeful day
When they closed the tramway, & I wish to sing
Of my deep surprise & astonishment,
(And of my deeper knowledge that this
      is always so,
But nevertheless to sing)
Of my profound sadness, my uneasiness of mind,
That we should leave fat ladies standing at the tram-stop
      gazing sadly into distant rain.

And I will sing…

Song of the Grillbar Restaurant

here is a song that i sang that was
sung in a place that was not song
which few are   & i kept an eye on myself
in the pink mirror
& the eye kept an eye on myself   & the coats

for here we had a glove with fingers
cruelly cut off   and here we had
pockletless coat, brimless hat, scarf with no throat
which I sang as follows
to be apart from you is death

i sang to this, the mantra of a folded mac,
O never do desert me, to the hooks
O see me thru the worst, to walls of stale cream
i leave you now
& in the precious body of the cloakroom girl

i'll find a garmentless & maimed reprieve

On the Island

All around the National Gallery
are Poles selling their inheritance to Turks.

'This samovar cost me 22 marks!' says one Turk
leaving, to another arriving.

It's Tuesday. Even if the rest of the week
doesn't happen, you can walk out to Krumme Lanke

look at the nudists, take yr clothes off yrself,
if you feel like it, or fall in love again at the Polish market

& have me tell you the story of Henry Rivers,
(at the Polish market),

who had a yellow balloon, in which he breasted the hill
to the next valley, wherein lived his inamorata, Elvira Cigarettepaper,

and he, unable to land, pulled her up into the basket
& as they went up...down came their underthings.

This you can do in Westberlin as you walk between the objects
which Polish people have set out for sale:

a ceramic rolling pin, a large glass horse...
some matching ceramic-handled spoons...

And bearing in mind how long these people have travelled,
over what roads, bearing what documents, speaking to what officials,

the beauty of the city seems to reside in that horse
in which I see reflected the buttons on yr shirt,

& my fingers, too fast for the buttons, & the eyes
of the Polish vendor's daughter, from Katowice or Osnowiec.

Not far away, you can hear fleets of yellow buses
as they plough the Street of the Seventeenth of July.

I am Henry Rivers. This is my balloon.
You my *geliebte* Elvira, my little *Eck-kneipe*,

my Brücke der Einheit across which spies are exchanged,
you are my summer residence by Friedrich Schinkel,

out of Hohenzollern summers & Prussian flatness, you are
the *treffendes Angebot* I find whenever I take a step, & the Polish
    merchant

heads me off into the corners & squares on a city map,
where haggling wears an unpronounceable name, like love. And I
    want to tell him:

'Beware!'

'On Fasanenplatz I saw a lighted bus reversing into darkness!
It was full of elderly people, tense & trembling,

& I saw that the driver was frightened & had lost his way,
as he eased his bus silently into the shadow & disappeared from
    existence

like a man who realises the only way out of a hopeless parking
    situation
is to move in a direction formerly considered impossible!'

Well, it's true that the parking situation has become acute,
so let me recommend to you the midnight dancing cruise:

Northwards over the Wannsee holding yr glass horse in one hand,
my fingers undoing yr blouse with the other, while the trumpets
    stagger about like drunks,

& a Man from the East buries his stubble in yr blue-veined throat,
as if it were truly possible to have a *Wirtschaftswunder* on the dance
    floor.

'*Forward in disorder!*' cry Elvira & Henry, those famous Berliners,
wastrels of the post-war years, making uneconomic miracles

out of the simple plot of vanishing when they are wanted,
rising into the night beneath the pregnant belly of their *Luftschiff,*

yellow stretch marks creaking into warm summer darkness, as
a spiritual breeze unfastens their transparent silk garments,

& they taste one another, gingerly, on the inside of each other's thighs
while the jazz band below crashes around & finally falls into the water,

& the Polish girl slips her fingers into my zip, & draws me toward
        her car
murmuring: '*Das gläserne Pferd ist unbezahlbar, einfach nicht zu
        bezahlen...*'

The Palace of Sophie Charlotte crumbles at her experienced touch,
& the Pomeranian crows are turned to crystal in midflight,

that slow, beating, sinister flight of the hooded grey,
which Henry reaches out from the basket & firmly takes hold of,

letting it cool & harden in his hand, feeling the cables groan,
as Elvira (for his sake) tries to be as naked as she can...

Dawn Beach

From here to the turn of the century
is hardly a mile

as the bat flies, zig-zag, thru pitch
nothingness.

They seem so pleased with themselves over there.
It must be better than it is now. Or was:

cities fouled, mud & dullness
kicking their heels round the outskirts,

poor numbskulls throttled for a penny,
waifs abused, mis-used...

Now we have brilliant golf-balls
of lucid & sinister harmony

& later a curious blackness
so near you can reach out & touch it.

It will be hot, like an animal that
has been sleeping on the refrigerator,

or an arm that twists out of darkness
around you, deliberate with desire.

Luckily, trains run out to the edges of the city,
taking me with them.

Nothing has changed much here. Chickens scratch.
Sprouts flower. A few sheds tumble quietly.

From here to the future
is but a few clods of earth.

And beyond that
is the pallor of wasteland in the early dawn.

Huge pylons tramp the cow-flecked grass.
Some trees echo of forests. History is flat.

And across it, vibrating & buzzing,
hurtle the illuminated trucks, carrying wealth.

Consignments of money pass by on the high road
above our stooped backs, where we inspect for worms –

the reassuring sight of worms,
slithering, concertina-ing.

I believe I should engage my neighbour in conversation,
but he has walked some distance off, absorbed.

He is glancing a spade at the Metazoic,
sheer & clean, the downward layers of the future.

How does it look to him? Or to me, for that matter?
What one can immediately comprehend, I mean?

Sounds of a radio come from the lighted window
of his caravan. Frying smells in the morning air.

My neighbour's wife. Her breasts. Her warm tongue.
I am lapped on an invisible shore,

something restless, cast up, willing to be sucked back,
willing to go forward, struggling against the idea of it.

It is in that moment I know she is God.
She does not even bother to undress properly.

God remains cloaked for want of time, as we know.
And it is not long from here to there.

What shall we say? The city blazes to my right.
She is at my elbow.

When I come finally to the door, & look out
I see the twenty-first century as clearly as a cat.

It is moving along the wall, slinking, & stops.
It faces me, its pre-historic head, its green eyes:

A look of such incomprehensible significance
I can only nod, half-bemusedly. And it vanishes.

A god too, perhaps? I hear her behind me, rustling.
The stroke of nyloned legs. The voice of invitation: 'Come.'

And the rule of sunlight pitches up above the skyline
like the beginning of some new & terrible game.

The Ideology

Germaine Greer has a thing
        about the consumerist couple
prolonging active orgasm
        '*die Pflicht der Freude*'

                        you might say, &
                        therefore
                        French knickers in grey
                        champagne silk
                        and all
                        the paraphernalia

necessary for
'man's inordinately long life'.

I think of this
as we enter *Hennes & Mauritz*
                        to purchase
the sd garment
& I walk from the
                trying-on room
                back
to the rail
for a smaller size

                        'man's inordinately
                        long
                        journey across
                        the lingerie department'

holding
that small thing
made in
Shanghai

                        to the imperial
                        delight of
                        severed fingertips...

Later, in bed, I pull
out the three studs
at the crotch, like water

                        you are, pleased,
                        running thru my palm
                        as we dawdle out
                        high above the bar '*Zum Ambrosius:
                        Ein Begriff in Berlin*'
                        toward pleasure...

Ah, society's
inordinately long
sub-fertile

                        wandering
                        in sweet sateen...

Until at 3 a.m.
we hear the cops
placate a fracas
in the joint

EAVAN BOLAND

The Black Lace Fan My Mother Gave Me

It was the first gift he ever gave her,
buying it for five francs in the Galeries
in pre-war Paris. It was stifling.
A starless drought made the nights stormy.

They stayed in the city for the summer.
They met in cafés. She was always early.
He was late. That evening he was later.
They wrapped the fan. He looked at his watch.

She looked down the Boulevard des Capucines.
She ordered more coffee. She stood up.
The streets were emptying. The heat was killing.
She thought the distance smelled of rain and lightning.

These are wild roses, appliquéd on silk by hand,
darkly picked, stitched boldly, quickly.
The rest is tortoiseshell and has the reticent,
clear patience of its element. It is

a worn-out, underwater bullion and it keeps,
even now, an inference of its violation.
The lace is overcast as if the weather
it opened for and offset had entered it.

The past is an empty café terrace.
An airless dusk before thunder. A man running.
And no way now to know what happened then –
none at all – unless, of course, you improvise:

The blackbird on this first sultry morning,
in summer, finding buds, worms, fruit,
feels the heat. Suddenly she puts out her wing –
the whole, full, flirtatious span of it.

The Journey
(for Elizabeth Ryle)

> *Immediately cries were heard. These were the loud wailing of infant*
> *souls weeping at the very entrance-way; never had they had their*
> *share of life's sweetness for the dark day had stolen them from their*
> *mothers' breasts and plunged them to a death before their time.*
> — VIRGIL, The Aeneid, Book VI

And then the dark fell and 'there has never'
I said 'been a poem to an antibiotic:
never a word to compare with the odes on
the flower of the raw sloe for fever

or the devious Africa-seeking tern
or the protein treasures of the sea-bed.
Depend on it, somewhere a poet is wasting
his sweet uncluttered metres on the obvious

emblem instead of the real thing.
Instead of sulpha we shall have hyssop dipped
in the wild blood of the unblemished lamb,
so every day the language gets less

for the task and we are less with the language.'
I finished speaking and the anger faded
and dark fell and the book beside me
lay open at the page Aphrodite

comforts Sappho in her love's duress.
The poplars shifted their music in the garden,
a child startled in a dream,
my room was a mess —

the usual hardcovers, half-finished cups,
clothes piled up on an old chair —
and I was listening out but in my head was
a loosening and sweetening heaviness,

not sleep, but nearly sleep, not dreaming really
but as ready to believe and still
unfevered, calm and unsurprised
when she came and stood beside me

and I would have known her anywhere
and I would have gone with her anywhere
and she came wordlessly
and without a word I went with her

down down down without so much as
ever touching down but always, always
with a sense of mulch beneath us,
the way of stairs winding down to a river

and as we went on the light went on
failing and I looked sideways to be certain
it was she, misshapen, musical –
Sappho – the scholiast's nightingale

and down we went, again down
until we came to a sudden rest
beside a river in what seemed to be
an oppressive suburb of the dawn.

My eyes got slowly used to the bad light.
At first I saw shadows, only shadows.
Then I could make out women and children
and, in the way they were, the grace of love.

'Cholera, typhus, croup, diphtheria'
she said, 'in those days they racketed
in every backstreet and alley of old Europe.
Behold the children of the plague.'

Then to my horror I could see to each
nipple some had clipped a limpet shape –
suckling darknesses – while others had their arms
weighed down, making terrible pietàs.

She took my sleeve and said to me, 'be careful.
Do not define these women by their work:
not as washerwomen trussed in dust and sweating,
muscling water into linen by the river's edge

'nor as court ladies brailled in silk
on wool and woven with an ivory unicorn
and hung, nor as laundresses tossing cotton,
brisking daylight with lavender and gossip.

But these are women who went out like you
when dusk became a dark sweet with leaves,
recovering the day, stooping, picking up
teddy bears and rag dolls and tricycles and buckets –

love's archaeology – and they too like you
stood boot deep in flowers once in summer
or saw winter come in with a single magpie
in a caul of haws, a solo harlequin.'

I stood fixed. I could not reach or speak to them.
Between us was the melancholy river,
the dream water, the narcotic crossing
and they had passed over it, its cold persuasions.

I whispered, 'let me be
let me at least be their witness,' but she said
'what you have seen is beyond speech,
beyond song, only not beyond love;

remember it, you will remember it'
and I heard her say but she was fading fast
as we emerged under the stars of heaven,
'there are not many of us; you are dear

and stand beside me as my own daughter.
I have brought you here so you will know forever
the silences in which are our beginnings,
in which we have an origin like water,'

and the wind shifted and the window clasp
opened, banged and I woke up to find
the poetry books stacked higgledy piggledy,
my skirt spread out where I had laid it –

nothing was changed; nothing was more clear
but it was wet and the year was late.
The rain was grief in arrears; my children
slept the last dark out safely and I wept.

That the Science of Cartography is Limited

– and not simply by the fact that this shading of
forest cannot show the fragrance of balsam,
the gloom of cypresses
is what I wish to prove.

When you and I were first in love we drove
to the borders of Connacht
and entered a wood there.

Look down you said: this was once a famine road.

I looked down at ivy and the scutch grass
rough-cast stone had
disappeared into as you told me
in the second winter of their ordeal, in

1847, when the crop had failed twice,
Relief Committees gave
the starving Irish such roads to build.

Where they died, there the road ended

and ends still and when I take down
the map of this island, it is never so
I can say here is
the masterful, the apt rendering of

the spherical as flat, nor
an ingenious design which persuades a curve
into a plane,
but to tell myself again that

the line which says woodland and cries hunger
and gives out among sweet pine and cypress,
and finds no horizon
will not be there.

Distances

The radio is playing downstairs in the kitchen.
The clock says eight and the light says
winter. You are pulling up your hood against a bad morning.

Don't leave, I say. Don't go without telling me
the name of that song. You call it back to me from the stairs:
'I Wish I Was In Carrickfergus'

and the words open out with emigrant grief the way the streets
of a small town open out in
memory: salt-loving fuchsias to one side and

a market in full swing on the other with
linen for sale and tacky apples and a glass and wire hill
of spectacles on a metal tray. The front door bangs

and you're gone. I will think of it all morning while a fine
drizzle closes in, making the distances
fiction: not of that place but this and of how

restless we would be, you and I, inside the perfect
music of that basalt and sandstone
coastal town. We would walk the streets in

the scentless afternoon of a ballad measure,
longing to be able
to tell each other that the starched lace and linen of

adult handkerchiefs scraped your face and left your tears
falling; how the apples were mush inside the crisp sugar
shell and the spectacles out of focus.

FROM *Outside History*

IX. *In Exile*

The German girls who came to us that winter and
the winter after and who helped my mother fuel
the iron stove and arranged our clothes in wet
thicknesses on the wooden rail after tea was over,

spoke no English, understood no French. They were
sisters from a ruined city and they spoke rapidly
in their own tongue: syllables in which pain was
radical, integral; and with what sense of injury

the language angled for an unhurt kingdom – for
the rise, curve, kill and swift return to the wrist,
to the hood – I never knew. To me they were the sounds
of evening only, of the cold, of the Irish dark and

continuous with all such recurrences: the drizzle in
the lilac, the dusk always at the back door, like
the tinkers I was threatened with, the cat inching
closer to the fire with its screen of clothes, where

I am standing in the stone-flagged kitchen; there are
bleached rags, perhaps, and a pot of tea on the stove.
And I see myself, four years of age and looking up,
storing such music – guttural, hurt to the quick –

as I hear now, forty years on and far from where
I heard it first. Among these salt-boxes, marshes and
the glove-tanned colours of the sugar-maples, in
this New England town at the start of winter, I am

so much South of it: the soft wet, the light and
those early darks which strengthen the assassin's
hand; and hide the wound. Here, in this scalding air,
my speech will not heal. I do not want it to heal.

*   *   *

XII. *Outside History*

There are outsiders, always. These stars —
these iron inklings of an Irish January,
whose light happened

thousands of years before
our pain did: they are, they have always been
outside history.

They keep their distance. Under them remains
a place where you found
you were human, and

a landscape in which you know you are mortal.
And a time to choose between them.
I have chosen:

out of myth into history I move to be
part of that ordeal
whose darkness is

only now reaching me from those fields,
those rivers, those roads clotted as
firmaments with the dead.

How slowly they die
as we kneel beside them, whisper in their ear.
And we are too late. We are always too late.

DAVID CONSTANTINE

Eldon Hole

They fastened a poor man here on a rope's end
And through the turbulence of the jackdaws let him down
To where everything lost collects, all the earth's cold,
And the crying of fallen things goes round and round
And where, if anywhere, the worm is coiled.

When he had filled with cold they hauled him up.
The horrors were swarming in his beard and hair.
His teeth had broken chattering and could not stop
Mincing his tongue. He lay in the rope and stared,
Stared at the sky and feared he would live for ever.

Like one of those dreadful fish that are all head
They saw him at his little window beaming out
Bald and whiskerless and squiddy-eyed
He hung in the branches of their nightmares like a swede.
They listened at his door for in his throat

Poor Isaac when the wounds in his mouth had healed
Talked to himself deep down. It was a sound
Like the never-ending yelps of a small stone
Falling to where the worm lives and the cold
And everything hurt goes round and round and round.

The Door

Yes, that is the door and behind it they live,
But not grossly as we do. Through a fine sieve
Their people pass the incoming air. They are said
To circulate thoughtfully in walled gardens, the aged –
And they live long – wheeling in chairs. They exchange
Nothing but traditional courtesies. Most strange
However is their manner of dying, for they know the hour,
When it comes, as old elephants do. They devour

Their usual breakfast of plovers' eggs and rise
Then or are lifted by the janitors and without goodbyes
They step or are borne aloft through that door there –
And thus they end. For of course meeting the air,
The air we breathe, they perish instantly,
They go all into dust, into dead dust, and Stanley,
The Sweeper, comes with his brush and shovel and little cart
And sweeps them up and shovels them not apart
But into one black plastic bag with dimps, dog-shit
And all our common dirt. But this they intend and it
Signals their gracious willingness to reside
In the poor heart of life, once they have died.

'In the ocean room'

In the ocean room, in the history of voyaging,
The best he showed me was the giant nautilus.
We were cheek by cheek, pressing against the glass,
When one or other of us began imagining
Sleep underwater and the old way of breathing.

He was the pearly nautilus and I
Allowed my body to the way he rocked.
So we tolled forward and with my fingertips
I read the scrimshaw: poems, fables, the log
Of landfalls, idle beautiful lines

As long as thong but flowering queerly
And becoming another creation. Couched on him
I read and silvery tickling bubbles
Hurried from my mouth. In the next case
There was a photograph of a savage man

All mapped out, he wore the fabulous
Whole world, not an inch of him was free,
And he wore it under the skin that rubs away.
His wife (I read) with the point of her tongue
And nails at night had inked and coloured him in.

Watching for Dolphins

In the summer months on every crossing to Piraeus
One noticed that certain passengers soon rose
From seats in the packed saloon and with serious
Looks and no acknowledgement of a common purpose
Passed forward through the small door into the bows
To watch for dolphins. One saw them lose

Every other wish. Even the lovers
Turned their desires on the sea, and a fat man
Hung with equipment to photograph the occasion
Stared like a saint, through sad bi-focals; others,
Hopeless themselves, looked to the children for they
Would see dolphins if anyone would. Day after day

Or on their last opportunity all gazed
Undecided whether a flat calm were favourable
Or a sea the sun and the wind between them raised
To a likeness of dolphins. Were gulls a sign, that fell
Screeching from the sky or over an unremarkable place
Sat in a silent school? Every face

After its character implored the sea.
All, unaccustomed, wanted epiphany,
Praying the sky would clang and the abused Aegean
Reverberate with cymbal, gong and drum.
We could not imagine more prayer, and had they then
On the waves, on the climax of our longing come

Smiling, snub-nosed, domed like satyrs, oh
We should have laughed and lifted the children up
Stranger to stranger, pointing how with a leap
They left their element, three or four times, centred
On grace, and heavily and warm re-entered,
Looping the keel. We should have felt them go

Further and further into the deep parts. But soon
We were among the great tankers, under their chains
In black water. We had not seen the dolphins
But woke, blinking. Eyes cast down
With no admission of disappointment the company
Dispersed and prepared to land in the city.

PAUL DURCAN

Priest Accused of Not Wearing Condom

A forty-two-year-old parish priest – Fr Francey Mulholland –
Was charged yesterday in the Circuit Criminal Court
With not wearing a condom, and with intent
To cause an unwanted pregnancy.
Fr Mulholland pleaded guilty to both charges.
Pleading for leniency, counsel for Fr Mulholland
Stated that the priest was ignorant in the use of condoms,
Coming as he did from a farming background,
And that if he had known how to operate a condom
He would most certainly have operated a condom.
Sentencing the accused to two years' hard labour
Judge Gemma FitzGerald stated that it was disturbing
In this day and age, and in this progressive country,
That a priest should contemplate not wearing a condom
And when it was a case of a young, virile, parish priest
Like Fr Mulholland, it was doubly disturbing
And not only doubly disturbing but singularly scandalous.
She recommended that while serving his sentence
Fr Mulholland should be given access to condom therapy.
Perhaps – she commented – he is lacking in condom consciousness.
Leave to appeal was granted, as was bail
On condition that Fr Mulholland satisfied the Gardai
That he was in full possession of, and at all times,
The Joy of Sex by Dr Alex Comfort,
The devotional sex manual recently banned by the State Censorship.
Judge Gemma added that it was gallant of the bailswoman,
Fr Mulholland's girlfriend, to go bail for the priest,
Considering the gravity of the offence to her person.
The bailswoman, Ms Liz Graves, stated that Fr Mulholland
Had promised her never again not to wear a condom.
The couple left the courtroom
To the rousing applause of their families and their friends,
Not to mention three or four stalwart bishops cheering meekly in
      the distant background.

Martha's Wall

Her pleasure – what gave her pleasure – was to be walked
Down her wall, the South Wall, a skinny, crinkly, golden-stemmed
      wall
That contracts and expands, worms and unworms, in and out of
      Dublin Bay,
Across the sea's thighs pillowing in, besotted, under daisy-gartered
      skies.
She'd curl her finger around my finger and I'd lead her out on to it.
She liked it when the flowering sea was shedding spray across it.
She'd tense up with delight to see me get wet
And wetter still, and wetter – the wetter it was
The better she liked it, and me – and she wanted always
To get down, away down, to the very end of it
Where there is a deep-red lighthouse, and the deep-red lighthouse
Was hers also, hers, and we'd sit down on a bench under it
And she'd put her arm around my neck and we'd stop needing to
      speak
And we'd sit there, breathless, in silence, for a long time.

At the Funeral of the Marriage

At the funeral of the marriage
My wife and I paced
On either side of the hearse,
Our children racing behind it...
As the coffin was emptied
Down into the bottomless grave,
Our children stood in a half-circle,
Playing on flutes and recorders.
My wife and I held hands.
While the mourners wept and the gravediggers
Unfurled shovelfuls of clay
Down on top of the coffin,
We slowly walked away,
Accomplices beneath the yew trees.
We had a cup of tea in the graveyard café
Across the street from the gates:

We discussed the texture of the undertaker's face,
Its beetroot quality.
As I gazed at my wife
I wondered who on earth she was –
I saw that she was a green-eyed stranger.
I said to her: Would you like to go to a film?
She said: I would love to go to a film.
In the back seats of the cinema,
As we slid up and down in our seats
In a frenzy of hooks and clasps,
The manager courteously asked us not to take off our clothes.
We walked off urgently through the rain-strewn streets
Into a leaf-sodden cul-de-sac
And as, from the tropic isle of our bed,
Chock-a-block with sighs & cries,
We threw our funeral garments on the floor,
We could hear laughter outside the door.
There is no noise children love more to hear
Than the noise of their parents making love:
O my darling, who on earth are you?

Crinkle, near Birr

Daddy and I were lovers
From the beginning, and when I was six
We got married in the church of Crinkle, near Birr.-
The Irish Independent photographed the wedding.
My mother gave me away.
My sister was best man.
He was forty-two and a TV personality in Yorkshire,
Close to his widowed mother in Mayo,
Always having his photograph taken,
Always grinning and polite and manly and coy and brittle,
Checking the stubs of his chequebooks,
Tying up his used chequebooks in elastic bands,
Putting money away for a rainy day,
Making gilt-edged investments.
It was in the days before he became a judge.
He compèred boxing fights and women's beauty contests

In an accent that was neither English nor Irish nor American.
It was known as the Athlone accent.
When he spoke of Athlone
Listeners were meant to think
Of a convent in the middle of a dark forest
To which the speaker was chaplain.

We went on our honeymoon
To Galway, the City of the Tribes.
We stayed in the Eglinton Hotel in Salthill.
For breakfast we ate grapefruit segments and toast
And the manager bowed, the waiters goosing around us.
We stood on the Salmon Bridge counting
Squadrons of salmon floating face down in the waters below,
Waiting to go upstream to spawn.

In the afternoons we spawned our own selves in our hotel bedroom
Listening to cricket.
The West Indies were playing the MCC at Lord's.
We lay in bed listening to Rohan Kanhai batting for a double century
And Garfield Sobers taking six wickets for forty-five runs.
O Owen of the Birds,
That is what it meant to be Irish and free –
To be father and son in bed together
In a hotel in the City of the Tribes
Listening to cricket on the BBC Radio Third Service.
After dinner we walked on the pier at Spiddal,
Holding hands, watching schools
Of porpoises playing in the apple-light of the Western sea.
One night after dinner we drove to Gort,
Where Daddy let his hair down
And we played a game of cricket
In the back garden of another father-and-son couple.
When Daddy bowled, I was his wicketkeeper.
He fancied himself as Ray Lindwall
And I fancied myself as Godfrey Evans –
Godders jackknifing over bails and stumps.
When we returned to the hotel, we entered
By the fire escape, feeling in a mood to be secretive,
Black iron staircase flicked up against white pebble-dash gable.
Daddy divided the human race
Into those who had fire escapes and spoke Irish

And those who had not got fire escapes and did not speak Irish.
Another night we sat in a kitchen in Furbo
With a schoolteacher hobnobbing in Irish
Exotic as Urdu, all that rain and night at the windowpane.

The marriage lasted five years.
On a summer's night in Newcastle West
After a game of cricket with boys my own age
I came back into the house without my school blazer.
'Where have you left your school blazer
Which you should not have been wearing in the first place?
School blazers are not for wearing.
School blazers cost money.'
I had left it on a fence in the field.
When I went to retrieve it, it was lolling out of a cow's mouth,
One arm of it.
Daddy took off his trousers belt,
Rolled it up in a ball round his fist,
And let fly at me with it.
In a dust storm of tears I glimpsed
His Western movie hero's eyes stare at me.

When I was twelve, I obtained a silent divorce.
Ireland is one of the few civilised countries
– And the only country outside Asia –
In this respect, that while husbands and wives
Can only at best separate,
Children can obtain a silent divorce from their parents.
When I look back at the years of my marriage to Daddy
What I remember most
Are not the beatings-up and the temper tantrums
But the quality of his silence when he was happy.
Walking at evening with him down at the river,
I lay on my back in the waters of his silence,
The silence of a diffident, chivalrous bridegroom,
And he carried me in his two hands home to bed.

Chips

I am sitting alone in the window of the Kentucky Grill,
Staring out at O'Connell Street in the night,
Shoving chips into my mouth.
Girls in paper hats are mopping up floors all around me.
Presently they are mopping up my feet.
'Excuse me' – I listen to myself say to them
As I hold up my feet to accommodate their mops,
Shoving a last chip into my mouth.
On the bin at the door it says:
FEED ME.

When Daddy died I gazed upon his chips
– I mean, his features –
While a priest poured a bottle of ketchup over him.
I thought it strange
And I walked out of the hospital into the city of night.

When I was seven and he took me to see
Charlie Chaplin in City Lights
In the Regal Rooms,
After the film was over we walked all the way home
From Hawkins Street to Leeson Street
Through streets that were dark and wet and cold and homelier
Than any landscape I was to see again,
Until after your death to Newfoundland I came
To give one quick, brief,
Received-in-boots-of-woolly-warmth-
By-fishermen's-wives
Recital of my verses.

There is no one in my life
Whom I disliked so submissively,
Yet whom I loved so mercilessly,
As you, Daddy. To me
You were at once saint and murderer.
When you raised your right hand
To smash in my face,
I saw the face of the murderer.
When you spoke the name

Of a belovèd townland or parish,
Keelogues or Parke,
I saw the face of a saint.

You were the artist of artists,
Ur of the Chaldees;
Priest of priests,
Melchisedech of the Ox;
Storyteller of storytellers,
Homer of Nephin;
Piper of pipers,
Carolan of the Moy;
Poet of poets,
Raftery of Turlough.
That's it –
I've had my chips.

Antwerp, 1984

We are keeping silent vigil at the window
Of the train from Amsterdam to Brussels,
Sitting opposite one another,
An agèd judge and his middle-aged son,
Shooting the dykes
Into flashfloods of oblivion
At the bottom of a vertical sky.
We are travelling at speed
Through the suburbs of Antwerp.
I am staring at a poplar tree
Quivering in a November breeze
When I glimpse your face in the window
And you glimpse mine.
In the high-speed window
Our eyes meet, each of us
Yearning for what the other yearns:
To be a tree – that tree.
By the time the message
Arrives in my brain
The train is a half-mile past

The level crossing
Where we glimpsed one another
In the poplar tree.
You elect to break the silence.
'My favourite poem' – you announce –
'Is "Trees" by Joyce Kilmer.'
'My favourite poem' – I reply –
'Is "The Brook" by Lord Tennyson.'
That is all we have to say
To one another.
I look at you
As you are
In your train seat,
Not as you were
A moment ago in the window,
Your own limbs are unleafing
And quivering
With Parkinson's,
All your roots
Heaped up in bundles
On your lap,
The dark floor beneath your feet
Gone, vanished.
You have five years to live.
I gaze up at your treetops
– Your glazed eyes underpainted with moonlight –
And I pledge that when they fell you,
While they will sell you for firewood,
I will give logs of you
To a woodcarver in Sligo,
Michael Quirke of Wine Street,
Butcher turned woodcarver,
Out of which to magic statuettes
Of the gods and goddesses of Ireland,
The Celtic Deities.
I will wash your body
In linseed oil and turpentine.
I will put you in the window
Of his butcher's shop in Wine Street.
I will call you by your proper name,
Mac Dhuarcáin,
Son of the Melancholy One.

As we approach the crossing of the Rhine
No man could look more melancholy
Than you – Melancholy Daddy.
God took out a Stanley Knife,
Slashed the canvas of life,
Called it a carving of your face,

Called it you.
As we crawl over the Rhine
I put my hand on your knee,
Your quivering knee,
The pair of us gazing down into the wide river far below.

JOHN ENNIS

The Croppy Boy

It's no use, your wild nightly haggle, horse-pissed over me
At Passage by the Suir or maudlin down in Duncannon stoned.
The piked suns shine on ever more cruelly watery.
Winy streets we littered are innocently crimsoned.

On wet cobbles to the sweaty rope, you'll halo me. Naïve,
O yes, my blond teenage hair is styled like the French.
I'm not crying. To ladies, prance of Hessians, I clench
My bony dream, walk on. My ignorant head's a beehive.

From their suite rooms the yogurt mouths of hypocrites
Spit me out like bile. No lusty Patrick sucks their tits.

Rousing Christ, ladies do with me what they please.
While I die, blackbirds sing up the fat-arsed trees.

Mother. It's cruel, Yeomen bar us any last goodbye.
Yesterday I danced, tapped a jig. Noon, see me die.

Alice of Daphne, 1799

I am Alice of Daphne, and my heart clogs for John Pounden.
As the stag cornered by pitch-forks, so antlered his thought against
     the Croppies.
As the Jonathan amongst scented trees of the orchard, so rose my
     sweet back in Daphne. I knew a tender spot down under
     his branches, basked long among his juicy apples.

He rushed me the road to Enniscorthy. I was far gone, awkward
     with our loving:
Bed me with slovens, madden me with fiddles, I grow big now,
     sick for Daphne.
His trunk leant gently onto mine, for I was fourteen years of age.

*

And I said, Never. Never shall we be torn asunder or cut off from
   petalled Daphne, though our green hills crawl back with Croppies
   like flies, for I will not unloose that daft chase wreathing our
   laurels up the sloped white blossoms.
I grafted and shall graft, Jonathan, my virgin bones to yours.
McGuire, good tenant, coffined you when we stank Enniscorthy
   where Croppies piked the brave Orange.

John was twenty-one under the fruiting tree. I played the skittery
   dove after his apples.
Look, my lovelies, the mason plumbs our Wall! You can walk by
   the Slaney!
Crocus open on the Spring Lawn. On Vinegar Hill Providence
   stooped and smiled and picked but a few of the Croppies.

The Black Prince plum blooms early this March for my dears,
   Mary, John Colley, Jane, Patrick, Fanny.
But poor baby Joshua is down with the fits.

TOM LEONARD

FROM *Ghostie Men*

would thi prisoner
in thi bar
please stand

fur thi aforesaid crime
uv writn anuthir poem
awarded thi certificate of safety
by thi scottish education department

fit tay be used in schools
huvn no bad language
sex subversion or antireligion

I hereby sentence you
tay six munths hard labour
doon nthi poetry section
uv yir local library
coontn thi fuckin metaphors

FROM **Unrelated Incidents**

1

its thi lang- wij a thi guhtr thaht hi said its thi langwij a thi guhtr	thi langwij a thi intillect hi said thi lang- wij a thi intill- ects Inglish
awright fur funny stuff ur Stanley Bax- ter ur but luv n science n thaht naw	then whin thi doors slid oapn hi raised his hat geen mi a fare- well nod flung oot his right

fit boldly n
fell eight
storeys
doon thi
empty
lift-shaft

2

ifyi stull
huvny
wurkt oot
thi diff-
rince tween
yir eyes
n
yir ears;
– geez peace,
pal!

fyi stull
huvny
thoata lang-
wij izza
sound-system;
fyi huvny
hudda thingk
aboot thi dif-
frince tween
sound
n object n
symbol; well,
ma innocent
wee
friend – iz
god said ti
adam:

a doant kerr
fyi caw it
an apple
ur
an aippl –
jist leeit
alane!

3

this is thi
six a clock
news thi
man said n
thi reason
a talk wia
BBC accent
iz coz yi
widny wahnt
mi ti talk
aboot thi
trooth wia
voice lik
wanna yoo
scruff. if
a toktaboot
thi trooth
lik wanna yoo
scruff yi
widny thingk
it wuz troo.
jist wanna yoo
scruff tokn.
thirza right
way ti spell
ana right way
ti tok it. this
is me tokn yir
right way a
spellin. this
is ma trooth.
yooz doant no
thi trooth
yirsellz cawz
yi canny talk
right. this is
the six a clock
nyooz. belt up.

4

sittn guzz-
lin a can
a newcastle
brown wotchn
scotsport hum-
min thi furst
movement a
nielsens thurd
symphony – happy
iz larry yi
might say;

a wuz jist turn-
in ovir thi
possibility uv
oapnin anuthir
can whin thi
centre forward
picked up
a loose baw:
hi huddiz back
tay thi
right back iz
hi caught
it wayiz in-
step n jist
faintn this way
then this
way, hi turnd
n cracked it;
jist turnd n
cracked it;
aw nwan move-
ment; in ti
thi net.

5

at thi grand
theological
tennis match
bitween thi
orthodox awl
crocks n
thi
trendy all-
stars, a
rammy
irruptid whin
a yung
trendy bov-
yir boy tellt
hiz mate
who hid an awl
crock scarf
roon hiz shoodirz,
thit he wuz in
a flaigrint
state uv
non-being-fur-
uthirz; tay
which thi
awl crock rep-
lied, why doant
yi shut yir
trap n wotch
thi gemm in
peace; its no
a gemm, hiz
trendy frend
replied,
naithur um a
wotchn it;
a um here ti
witness a
persn-ti-persn
encounter, bi-
fore thi umpire
iz meaninful

symbol,
fur thi umpire-
abuv-thi-
umpire; tay
which thi awl
crock replied:
thaht izza
loada pish.

mirabile dictu,
it startid
pishn; and in
thi troo spirit
a christian
bruthirhood, thi
pair sat miz-
zribly wotchn
thi empty
court,
undir thi wan
umbrella.

KIT WRIGHT

I Found South African Breweries Most Hospitable

Meat smell of blood in locked rooms I cannot smell it,
Screams of the brave in torture loges I never heard nor heard of
Apartheid I wouldn't know how to spell it,
None of these things am I paid to believe a word of
For I am a stranger to cant and contumely.
I am a professional cricketer
My only consideration is my family.

I get my head down nothing to me or mine
Blood is geysering now from ear, from mouth, from eye,
How they take a fresh guard after breaking the spine,
I must play wherever I like or die
So spare me your news your views spare me your homily.
I am a professional cricketer.
My only consideration is my family.

Electrodes wired to their brains they should have had helmets,
Balls wired up they should have been wearing a box,
The danger was the game would turn into a stalemate,
Skin of their feet burnt off I like thick woollen socks
With buckskin boots that accommodate them roomily
For I am a professional cricketer.
My only consideration is my family.

They keep falling out of the window they must be clumsy
And unprofessional not that anyone told me,
Spare me your wittering spare me your whimsy,
Sixty thousand pounds is what they sold me
And I have no brain. I am an anomaly.
I am a professional cricketer.
My only consideration is my family.

The Boys Bump-starting the Hearse

The hearse has stalled in the lane overlooking the river
Where willows are plunging their heads in the bottle-green water
    And bills of green baize drakes kazoo.
    The hearse has stalled and what shall we do?

The old don comes on, a string bag his strongbox.
He knows what is known about Horace but carries no tool-box.
    Small boys shout in the Cambridge sun.
    The hearse has stalled and what's to be done?

Lime flowers drift in the lane to the baskets of bicycles,
Sticker the wall with yellow and powdery particles.
    Monosyllabic, the driver's curse.
    Everything fires. Except the hearse

Whose gastric and gastric whinnies shoot neutered tom cats
In through the kitchen flaps of back gardens where tomtits
    Wizen away from the dangling crust.
    Who shall restart the returned-to-dust?

Shrill and sudden as birds the boys have planted
Their excellent little shoulders against the lamented
    Who bumps in second. A fart of exhaust.
    On goes the don and the holocaust.

Characters of Light

One afternoon in Barnes
I saw how light is never
Statement but the question
To which all things cry answer,
Making their lives and names
By error, how the mindless
Heart has nowhere to go
But learns by touch in the dark.

Centuries agonised
In disbelieving earth,
The pigeon's ragged yew tree
Gives of itself the best
Account it can in the light
Of circumstance: the light:
Demanding its final, only,
Uneven grey-green reply.

A ragged tree and a ragged
Man in a walled garden
Trying the weight of April
Crises, all-imploring
Limbs of almond, magnolia
Moving from bullet to sheath
To bell in dumb explosion,
Forsythia naming the sun,

Knowing his own life
As every other man's
An exact displacement of that
Character of light
He would spend it trying to find,
Knowing the task impossible,
Coming one step closer
One afternoon in Barnes.

The Pinscher Metamorphosis

I was dining with Doberman Pinscher,
Art critic of exquisite malice,
When over what was, I confess,
An unusually forward young *Chambertin*,
I enquired of him, 'Candidly, Doberman,
What do you think of *life*?'

Now Pinscher's talk, as you know,
Moves onward from brilliance: he glints
In the light of quicksilver reflections:
His insights flash like the muzzles
Of sudden guns, his acuity
Dazzles as sun on the sea.

That evening at home in, I must say,
My not unamusing flat, wit
Spun on a sixpence, truth leapt
In the net of his gleaning thought,
He became himself an aphorism
Surpassing his best *bon mot*.

He rippled with brilliant particulars.
The visual arts joined hands
To dance for him, charmed by that music
Of Higher and Lower Criticism –
And then it was that I put to him
'What do you think of life?'

At first I thought he misheard me.
Attuned to a stinging, delicious
And instant response, I sat coyly
Braced for his *aperçu*.
None came. I repeated, 'Candidly,
What do you think of *life?*'

No answer. And then I noticed
Pain enter his widening eyes
And crinkle his forehead, his hand
(Loose-poised for the throw-away gesture)
Blur, roughen, scrape down as its fellow
Slammed down from the arching back

On the table slopped by a
Wide coarse tongue that dawdled
In slobbering varnish, chair crashed
As he sprang from the house in the loud
Free smell of himself and he howled,
Howled, howled in the long street night.

You never can tell with a *Chambertin*.

SELIMA HILL

The Significance of Significance

She was worried he couldn't be happy
just loafing about by the river,
like she liked doing.
Plans, and plans about plans, and sex,
was *his* idea of happiness.
He wore a floppy hat.
She felt so lonely!

Another thing, she couldn't spell.
Laborinth. Itiniry. Elann.
She cooked him cockles
in a thick orange sauce,
and bought him a suitcase –
'for the Great Man'.

They sat on a rocky mountain
dressed in leather.
Sardines and beer.
Parois vertigineuses.

Their children were his books.
She understood that.
O *Significado De Significado,*
lecture notes.

'The blissfully well-run nursing-home'
is now public knowledge –
her little lump, like longing,
prised from her oesophagus;
her crawling from the hut
on her knees.

A tortoise-shell comb,
embroidery,
The Crack.
A lovely moth.
'The nurse is a crashing bore'
... poking about among her mysteries.
God bless you, Patty.

The Graceful Giraffe of Clot Bey

When I ascend the terrace steps of Potsdam
between the yew trees clipped to look like polyps,
or a colony of polyps, by cold water,
with no one about on the steps except myself,
having no language but this –
I certainly need you.

When I hear the risen storks,
the cries from whose long coiled throats
can't help sounding mournful,
as if entire courts together with their kings
are slain, dismembered and buried
in valleys that now lie barren –
I certainly need you.

When I say goodbye
with the same dejected air
I imagine Giacometti would wear
if, torn from his work
and his beautiful brother Diego,
he was set on the deck of a ship
bound for an island inhabited by nothing but tortoises
lumbering about on volcanoes
like abandoned radiators;

when I wave
like sallow mutants discarding limbs
in twilit marshland settlements
where only the rats survive;

when my eyes blur
like the graceful giraffe's of Clot Bey
who continued to gladden the hearts of Parisians
for sixteen years before she died,
mute and majestic,
sunk on her bed of straw –
I certainly need you.

When the telephone,
like a bricked-up cathedral,
refuses to ring;
like a one-hundred-fingered ice-encrusted orchestra,
primed,
beribboned,
and triumphant,
which refuses to strike up and play
without its seraphic conductor –
I certainly need you...

Baby clams wilt in yellow brine.
Van Gogh's ear wilts in a jar in a police station.
My heart, equally forsaken,
wilts in the screw-top jar of your not coming.

Orchids

The aeroplane must have been there
for several weeks. A few birds
were absent-mindedly picking through
the mangled remains of small children,
and a gold dog ran in and out
of the empty cabin, cradling
a spotted quince in its mouth.
The man we were looking for
was lying on a day-bed
under a red tree.
He seemed to be having some problem
with his skin, and was wearing
a pair of white silk gloves
and a white blood-stained hat.
He was the only survivor able to speak
and even he was too weak to talk
for more than a few minutes at a time.
He was an ex-oil-pipe-contractor
and a millionaire
who had been looking for a place
to breed orchids...and as he spoke

he lay back on the bleached canvas
of his ancient bed,
his eyes beginning to run,
his limp white penis
resting in the sunlight
on his glove. While my colleague
went in search of a blanket,
I listened to the gunfire
from the valley,
where my daughter lay awake
behind closed curtains
guarded by sweet machines
like a rare flower.

The Tablecloths

She's looking at me like a doctor
sadly looking at a swollen ear.
Don't move.
Her husband's in the garage making cakes,
his solitude a kind of lamentation
for all the people he has never known.
He wears a scarf.
He hears the blackbirds singing.
He said he was a tablecloth. (It's true –
they called him Tablecloth
because his shirt was checked!)
'I said *don't move!*'

I hear the little inn's sheets quietly flapping.
Black shoes of snow-white children tap the street.
At four o'clock their pride and joy
comes home.
She puts a baked lasagne on to heat.
'Are you in love *right now?*
How can you tell?'
Her mother is a painter
painting me.

She's working with the sea waves in her eyes
and two curled shrimps
inviting me to swim.

The little dog is like a bungalow
waiting for her mistress to come home.
She's growing up to find her caring ways
treated with contempt, the little dog
lying on the landing's sun-pink rays.
I feel so cold.
Stuff paper down her shirt!
The greyness of the sea her mother drowned in
is lapping at our feet like a kitten.
I am a flower.
I am a piece of meat.
She's looking at my face like a mortician.

Don't Let's Talk About Being In Love

Don't let's talk about being in love, OK?
– about *me* being in love, in fact, OK?
about your bloated face, like a magnolia;
about marsupials,
whose little blunted pouches
I'd like to crawl inside, lips first;
about the crashing of a million waterfalls
– as if LOVE were a dome of glass beneath a lake
entered through a maze of dripping tunnels
I hoped and prayed I'd never be found inside.

At night I dream that your bedroom's crammed with ducks.
You smell of mashed-up meal and scrambled egg.
Some of the ducks are broody, and won't stand up.
And I dream of the fingers of your various wives
reaching into your private parts like beaks.
And you're lying across the bed like a man shouldn't be.
And I'm startled awake by the sound of creaking glass
as if the whole affair's about to collapse
and water come pouring in with a rush of fishes
going *slurpetty-slurpetty-slurp* with their low-slung mouths.

Much Against Everyone's Advice

Much against everyone's advice,
I have decided I must not be put off any longer
from coming into the yard
and telling you the truth, as best I can.
There's something I've got to tell you I will say.
Yes, I have been practising, you see –
you would be proud of me.
Alone in this ridiculous café,
with stiffened hair,
holding your last letter
like a penitent teenager
stranded on a cliff
who clutches the Bible
thank God she remembered to bring,
I have been practising.

Do you remember the boat
that dropped from the sky
right into Granma's garden,
just as two little girls,
never to visit fairyland again,
strayed out of the pecan grove?
And Granma turned over in her sleep
and saw a blond young pilot
who looked like Jesus
gazing into her eyes
from just about the level of her bedroom window?
Who ran his hands backwards and forwards
along his glossy cockpit
as if it were a prize bull
and not a stunted machine
that had ruined our lives for ever;
who looked down at the boat
as if she were a dancer, in perfect order,
and not a boat
creaking among squashed roses in our border?

All year he had been practising for this,
and I have too.
Much against everyone's advice,
I have decided to tell you everything
– poor worm.

Not All the Women of England

At the top of the bank
a blond airman
is doing sit-ups
in the tenderest
of early-morning sun.
I want to squash him flat.
He's like my Uncle Pat's
gold cigarette-case
that flies open
when you touch it.

You cruise along the fence
with your elbow
on the rolled-down window-edge.
Everything you come near
falls to bits.

The cattery sells bedding-plants
and runner-beans.
Someone has been up here
to mow a tiny lawn,
and hang a sign above it,
opposite the fence I mentioned,
and the bank, before the airman came.

The way the green brim
of your Chinese sun-hat's
been turned up –
it's like the tail
on a bulldog's bum.
Help me to take no notice,
holy flowers!

The passenger, the passenger,
I don't want to be the passenger.
Please can we stop at the Trout Lakes.

You came into my bedroom
carrying a duck,
and we lived together happily
for five years.
(She was so tame,
they wrote about her
in the *Whitby Gazette*.)
And now you're driving a saloon
I've come to hate
round and round the camp
like a bum.
I think I'm going to say
I want to leave you.
I want to leave you.

The hearts on the shutters
make the houses look like
cuckoo-clocks, or little chalets –
can you hear the cow-bells tinkle?-
where Mother Bear and Father Bear
eat fondue. They overlook
the fence and the bank.

The airman walks away
to living-quarters
we can't see
like a zoo animal.
He polishes his boots.
He's far from home.
Deep in trout lakes on the other side
trouts' dreams of flies
come true...

Not all the women of England
are boiling kettles
by the tall gates
but I love them all.

They shelter in the oaks
on the soft verges
where the airman lights up
his king-size cigarette.

Monkeys

This is the bed
that I became a woman in,
that I lay naked on on tepid nights,
after my grandmother's scaly-fingered gardener
half-marched, half crept in here and mended it
(like a man mends a cage in a zoo,
with excited reluctance);
I lay in the shade
of this lop-sided wardrobe –
that looks like a caramelized ungainly antelope
with nothing between its head and the constellations
except the occasional stiff-winged aeroplane –

and sent my long gold clitoris to sea
between my legs, streamlined and sweet
like a barge
laden with sweetmeats and monkeys
bound for some distant land;
and this is the bed I saw the chickens from,
running across the yard without their heads,
and smelt the farmers
leaning on their cows that had cars' names –
a smell of blood and milking and desire
I was suddenly part of, and sunk in,
like necks in Startena.

BERNARD O'DONOGHUE

A Nun Takes the Veil

That morning early I ran through briars
To catch the calves that were bound for market.
I stopped the once, to watch the sun
Rising over Doolin across the water.

The calves were tethered outside the house
While I had my breakfast: the last one at home
For forty years. I had what I wanted (they said
I could), so we'd loaf bread and Marie biscuits.

We strung the calves behind the boat,
Me keeping clear to protect my style: ·
Confirmation suit and my patent sandals.
But I trailed my fingers in the cool green water,

Watching the puffins driving homeward
To their nests on Aran. On the Galway mainland
I tiptoed clear of the cow-dunged slipway
And watched my brothers heaving the calves

As they lost their footing. We went in a trap,
Myself and my mother, and I said goodbye
To my father then. The last I saw of him
Was a hat and jacket and a salley stick,

Driving cattle to Ballyvaughan.
He died (they told me) in the county home,
Asking to see me. But that was later:
As we trotted on through the morning mist,

I saw a car for the first time ever,
Hardly seeing it before it vanished.
I couldn't believe it, and I stood up looking
To where I could hear its noise departing

But it was only a glimpse. That night in the convent
The sisters spoilt me, but I couldn't forget
The morning's vision, and I fell asleep
With the engine humming through the open window.

Kindertotenlieder

Because we cannot see into the future,
It follows that what we anticipate
Can't happen. And so I've set myself
Imagining the worst that can be feared:
The child beneath her bike, the wheel still spinning;
Another deathbed, not in a curtain-cooled
Summer afternoon with farm-voices outside,
But foetid in a northern city
In December. I've watched my children's classmates
Wearing ties, lined up by hissing teachers.

But I find the point is passing where I can
Switch from this Hyde life and smiling watch them pore
Over the *Beano*. The mind too is a country
Like Somalia. The fly that a slow hand
Pushes from a lip again, again,
Will hold its ground and crawl towards an eyelid
That fails at last to keep up appearances
By opening to resume its death's stare.

The Nuthatch

I couldn't fathom why, one leafless
Cloudcast morning he appeared to me,
Taking time off from his rind-research
To spread his chestnut throat and sing
Outside my window. His woodwind
Stammering exalted every work-day
For weeks after. Only once more
I saw him, quite by chance, among
The crowding leaves. He didn't lift
His head as he pored over his wood-text.
Ashamed of the binocular intrusion,
Like breath on eggs or love pressed too far,
I'm trying to pretend I never saw him.

The Weakness

It was the frosty early hours when finally
The cow's despairing groans rolled him from bed
And into his boots, hardly awake yet.
He called 'Dan! come on, Dan!
She's calving', and stumbled without his coat
Down the icy path to the haggard.

Castor and Pollux were fixed in line
Over his head but he didn't see them,
This night any more than another.
He crossed to the stall, past the corner
Of the fairy-fort he'd levelled last May.
But this that stopped him, like the mind's step

Backward: what was that, more insistent
Than the calf's birth-pangs? 'Hold on, Dan.
I think I'm having a weakness.
I never had a weakness, Dan, before.'
And down he slid, groping for the lapels
Of the shocked boy's twenty-year-old jacket.

DUNCAN BUSH

The Hook

1

I named it sickle. But he
uses it, the old man, and he called it:
the hook.

No longer new; a flatter curve
of blade than the gold on red: crescent
of an ellipse;

and implement, not emblem:
dull, rust oiled with usage; nicked, the
harshened silver edge.

But a tool perfects, almost
like nature, more stringent than art: millenia
winnowed to this

shape since Egypt was
the world's grainhouse, longer:
a moon-edge

cutting finer than a straight:
grass, not flesh: only the point would embed,
opening an enemy

like a full sack, or the edge hack
a limb, the swung first past its mark;
but savage enough

a symbol of agronomy
for rising serfs. The crossed hammer beat
this out blue once

in a man's fist; but mass
produced now for a dwindling few, this tool,
this weapon:

the steel flattened, arched, made
keen, even the white ash turned smooth, and
ferruled, by machine.

But finely weighted, this one:
light, as if I hefted only a handle, even
to the left hand,

even as it learns the backsweep.
I stooped and swung; the wristy, ambidextral hook
slew grass,

forestroke and back. I think
no eye bought this, but wrist: by balanced weight,
like grain;

and that it is beautiful only
now, for the coarse use that refined it,
like the sea-stone.

   2

Beautiful too is the word:
swathe. I laid low all afternoon tall, green,
slender seeded grasses

of more elegance than poplars.
Their stems fell sheaved after the stroke
like armfuls of bluebells,

the blade was wet with sap.
Doubled I stooped, climbing the field
all the hot afternoon

for these red stigmata,
skinned blisters on the mounts of
both white palms.

Pig Farmer

Like boys who throw stones off the roadside
down on his stone-weighted tin roofs and pedal,
                              something in me flinches
at an uncouthness in this pig farmer
guarding his triangle of black-tramped
mud between 2 ragged hedges and a stapled wire fence.

18 months ago or so he pulled into this
freehold, waste-ground
landscape like a lay-by. Now he lives in
a scrapyard compound
2 alsatians prowl on slip chains.
They're half-trained, and look half-starved – like the
    silence they dog, perhaps,
            sullen
            ingratiating
            vicious –
in 3 moves.

Beleaguered, padlocked by misanthropy, he's here
to stay –
even the yellow-and-white, second-hand caravan trailer's
now on 4 breeze-block piles
like a Portakabin classroom...

                              In it he must learn
infancy's difficulties every night over again, blunted
digits listed, totted, in the red
Silvine exercise-book with the moiré cover
and multiplication-tables on the back and metric measures:
11 eggs;
a refill blue steel Calor-gas bottle;
the dusty, hard hundredweight Portland cement-bags shouldered in
        still owed for...

Is this the sum
of all his sojourn, his
existence? –
            barely numerate
accountancy, bleak
monomania

among feed and dung, feed and dung
where only your own
labour comes free and unreckoned, you
buy always more than you can
find or sell, and you can't
get eggs from straw...

He put 2 youths, trespassers, in the hospital last week.

Even the silence is harsh
and suffocated in him.

Outside, the bedraggled donkey, the look
of life-long suffering on its greying
face, stands and outwaits
in its own breath
the patience of February drizzle
and a winter when every stick of timber –
the yard's sodden, inedible driftwood, the fence-posts,
          the slimy cobbled hen-house –
has turned green.

The midden of trodden mud
will never green under the trotters of his pink and filthy pigs...

24 hours they stink windward from their corrugated Nissen domes,
once daily jostling to waste
and tepid bran-mash –
                              vomit
rolled in sawdust.
Their new metal trough
is star-blue, frost patterned from the galvanising.

But pigs, they say, find and eat
                              anything –
weeds; truffles of broken pottery grubbed
from the dirt; the dirt...
They'll crunch a corpse down past the signet-ring, the severed
finger that denied them it –
                              then snuff their shit
for more...

There is a moment for his whole, partial
subsistence here to be imagined brutal, bare
and barbarous as that.

Then he straightens
his back –
his scarecrow coat knotted about the waist with coarse,
          white hairy string –
and watched you stip looking at him and
go past.

Pneumoconiosis

This is The Dust:

black diamond dust.

I had thirty years in it, boy,
a laughing red mouth
coming up to spit smuts black
into a handkerchief.

But it's had forty years
in me now:
so fine
you could inhale it
through a gag.
I'll die with it now.
It's in me,
like my blued scars.

But I try not to think about it.

          I take things pretty easy, these days;
one step at a time.
Especially the stairs.
I try not to think about it.

I saw my own brother: rising,
dying in panic, gasping
worse than a hooked
carp drowning in air.
Every breath was his last.

I try not to think about it.

                         But
know me by my slow step,

the occasional little cough, involuntary
and delicate as a consumptive's,

and my lung full of budgerigars.

August. Sunday. Gravesend.

1

Leeward
        of the cement-factory's fallout
the hawthorns are dust-
choked, whiter
                than blown willows, than
with may.
Quarry, yard, the corrugated
metal sheds are
white
like bakeries.
                Silence. A coupling
clinks. Lime
gags the suburb's throat. Heat
                                settles
everywhere
through haze.

In time, a mix
of summer rains, the
hawthorn
petrifies.

2

The damp-drab concrete council houses whiten
like a bone
in sun. A back
lawn, worn
            to tufted dirt, rotating
litter.

Tyres. A toppled tricycle. A football of
black hexagons
            rolled, flaccid, to a halt.

It is like the moment after an explosion.

                                        Shards
of orange polypropylene –

a shattered toy
aeroplane
              are laid down
in the lettuce-bed's dry clods.
They will outlast the Pyramids:

the archaeology

of childhood, its lifelong
amnesia.

3

The river
glitters beyond
a horizon
of cranes. In Essex a car
window flashes.
                Each moment
glitters
like a dying mullet
for the boy –
              workless, too old
for school, kicking his toes thin
against a wall...

The day is timed by
                    brutal gum
turned in his mouth.
It is chewed grey, whorled
like a brain.
He will carry it
              all through a youth and stick
it every day beneath a table.

For him each day is
like a Sunday.

He has shaved
his head
blue as an armpit, and
wears badges.

TONY CURTIS

Thoughts from the Holiday Inn
(for John Tripp)

'When you're dead, you're bloody dead.'
We both liked the punch of that one, John, said
Ten or more years ago by an author breaking
Through his fiction, kicking the rules, risking
All our willing disbelief to shock through
To the truth. B.S. Johnson, that sad and tortured man, knew
The whole thing to be by turns a joke, by turns the need
To love each other into something close to sense. We bleed,
John, we bleed, and time bleeds from our wrists.
Your death was shocking, and tidies up another lovely, angry
            (when pissed),
Poet of a man, who would not, for anyone, be tidied into
            respectability
Longer than an evening, or his allotment in some anthology.
There's too much to be said, by too many, too soon.
But from this lunchtime watering place, this unlikeliest of rooms,
Spare me the modest time and space – by Christ, you've enough
Of both in death old mate – to work things out, sound off –
About the months you've missed, the months that we've missed you.
You'd have seen this place go up, the skyline that you knew
Transformed, jagged, blocked as urban planners brought rationality
To what the coal century had grown and shaped to the Taff's
            estuary.
We've needed you here, John, thrusting out your neck and stroking
            the chin
From a classy, fraying shirt to show the disdain we hold these
            people in,
These late-comers to a country and a nation in a mess.
They've given us the bum's rush today, John, I must confess.
We checked out the place for next year's Literature Festival
And sponsorship. As far as we could tell
It was a waste of time, for any management
Who'd given Sickle-Cell Research the thumbs down were clearly bent
On profit, and to hell with charity, never mind cultural P.R.
Well fed and disappointed, we returned to the bar.
Still, they'd named the two big function rooms, the 'Dylan Suite'

And 'Gwyn Jones Room'. 'Don't know him,' said the manageress,
      with complete
Honesty. 'He's one of our Academy's most distinguished senior
      members,'
I said, and thought, We do no more than blow upon the embers,
We scribblers who'd want to claim
That everything in Wales for praise or blame
Is brought to life and fact and mythical creation
By that writerly mix of ego and the grasp of a tradition.
What use we prove, the weight the world gives us, if any,
Is likely to be cheap and grudging, no more than a blunt penny
Flung to shut our mannered, metred whining.
Then, later, taken up again shining
From the rubbing our tongues and lives impart.
I hear you answer, John, 'It's a start, boy, some sort of bloody start.'
John, further down the Hayes, now I think of you, haunting those
      benches
And passing a coffee or the length of a fag below the rich stenches
From Brains's brewery snugged in behind the Royal Arcade.
As the big internationals move in and build and build the shade
And sunlight shift position down the city's roads.
In spruced-up Bute (re-named, as Tiger Bay encodes
A docklands past we'd best forget or sanitise
In tarted-up pubs or tree-lined low-rise
Flats – *The Jolly Tar* or *Laskar's Close*)
The men who clinch the deals, the gaffers, the boss
With the tax-free Daimler, the Series Seven,
Square out the mazy city into real estate concepts, proven
Returns for their money. They are gilt-edged applicants
For Euro-funds, Welsh Development grants.
This hotel is for the likes of them. It stretches eye to eye
With the brewery's silver funnel, two hundred bedrooms in the sky
Starting at fifty quid the night. 'Fat cats,' I hear you say,
'And that's before your breakfast. Stuff the fucking pool, O.K.'
Tax payer's rage? John, even you, an occasional connoisseur
Of hotel fitments and glimpses of the soft life, would incur
A gullet-sticking at this pricey junk, mock-Grecian style
Arches, columns, thick marble-facings done in tiles,
Plush, deep divans around an open fire beneath a metal canopy,
Surrogate logs you'd hardly warm your hands upon. You'd see
Beyond, the indoor pool, functional, gaunt,
More marble, sharp angles with, each end, broken columns to flaunt

The facile version of classic decor money'll buy
And set down in a city anywhere, across a sky
Or ocean. Continent to continent there must be travellers
Who need the reassurance of such nondescript pools and bars,
To step off the plane or train, taxi down concrete tracks
To what the Telex reservation guarantees predictable: stacks
Of credit-cards accepted, pool-side temperature just O.K.
An in-house movie they choose and relay
To each room in American or English – God forbid
The native patois – *(These people down here, the Welsh – did*
You say – a language all their own – an ancient tongue?
– King Arthur – well, I saw a movie when I was a kid, sung
The songs all that summer – Danny Kaye – got it!)
John, what kind of progress is all this shit?
They took the coal-miners and put 'em in a coal museum:
And the people drove down, coughed up three quid ten just to
          see 'em.
Tourists one-nighting en route the Beacons, Bath or Ireland:
'Cardiff – what's that?' 'The airport…it's halfways there. I planned
To break the trudge from Heathrow.' And what of the locals?
Lunchtimes bring yuppies of both sexes, the gals
Waft in like *Cosmo* covers, the men have knife-
Creased casuals, hook their index fingers through the keyrings of life.
And there's the midday nibblers, women past their prime
But dressed to the nines and painted, passing the time
Between Howells' upholstery and Hones and Jones with a small gin
And sandwich triangles of horseradish and smoked salmon,
Piquant, hardly fattening. Their cigarette smoke curls
Away with the suggestion of rope, these former good-lookers, girls
Who, thirty years before, bagged a man of promise or means
And moved up, to Cyncoed, out to Lisvane, a pool, lawns
Done by a man who brings his own machine and strips
His shirt in the long afternoons. They tip
Him with the last cut of September.
Their husbands are on the board and successfully bored. 'Remember,'
They'd say, 'when we had that little detached in Newport,
And we'd spend Sundays, you mowing and me trimming.' 'I've fought
Hard to get this far, and Christ, there's times I wonder,
What for? What have we got? Where's it gone? Just blunder
On to the next rung, dinner party, contract, barbecue,'
'Love, you're working too hard. Is the company proving too much
          for you?'

John, excuse this indulgence, that clumsy fiction, it's no digression,
I'm still concerned to understand progression.
When working-class is all you've known
These rich fish cruise by bright-coloured (if overblown)
Distracting – but these too are tenants of the pool
You plunged your wit and pen into. Fool
No one was your aim, and at last came the anger of *Life Under
        Thatcher*.
But winos in the Hayes betray a watcher
Who'd sum up the whole state of things in verses.
It's too easy to shoot off steam in curses
That pepper the mark but fail to penetrate.
Guys with real assets, clever portfolios, are immune to street hate;
They justify themselves in terms of respectability, vision, advancement.
The world's an oyster if you lift your nose off the pavement.
They've bought themselves out of the firing line.
Windows purr close, revs slipping the motor into fifth gear, it feels
        fine
To loosen out along the motorway – weekends in Pembs.
Or, turning right, over the Bridge, a trim two hours to dine by the
        Thames.
No one's rooted anymore, John, as you must have known –
'The old man' coming to smith in Taffs Well in the 30s where you'd
        grown
Up Welsh, not Cornish like him, in all but the language.
(The wounding of that loss, it seems, no achievements can assuage.)
And, because of that, confused, determined and concerned
As the rest of us, excluded from the *Gorsedd* but feeling you'd earned
The right to sound off for this Wales – Taffs and Gwerin,
To voice the peculiar place of the eighty per cent. The din
Of justified protest settled after '79 – Welsh cheque books, Channel
        Four.
The nationalist drummings the Sixties saw you working for
You realised later were too easy, too raw. Like R.S.
You loved the country with a passion, an anger, but the less
Misty, period-costume work will surely prove the best,
The more enduring; real poetry 'welcoming the rough-weather guest'.
John, I would rather have seen your ashes ebb from Barafundle
Bay. That grey day at Thornhill we watched your coffin trundle
Behind the curtains to the kind of anonymity
You'd rail against for other 'botched angels', losers we
Turn away from, society's mistakes, the hard-done-to,

Underdogs you wanted to feel close to.
The glow of a cupped-hand fag was light enough to draw
You to some alley, a derelict huddled there against a door,
One of the Hollow Men, a voter with no vote
Wrapped in old woollens, *Echoes* stuffed inside an overcoat.
'Cold enough, butt, eh? on the street. Here, have yourself a cuppa.
Take care, old fella, and watch out for the copper.
Those bastards aren't for the likes of us,
They don't give a tinker's cuss
As long as things stay down and quiet, and everything's neat.
You and me'll keep to the shadows, butt, and stay light on our feet.'
I've a feeling poetry's not the thing most apt
To dissect society, or politicise an audience one imagines trapped
In wilful ignorance, lobotomised by the trashy press,
Disenfranchised by the soapy box, seduced by the caress
Of the goodish life in the second half of this softening century.
You, fellow sprinter, took your chance through readings – could be
Five or fifty listeners, in club, gallery, college, school.
But articles in the London nationals, plays on the TV as a rule
Work most action, albeit short-lived. We
Poets light shower-burning fuses or rockets you see
Flash and quickly fade as the moment's charged
And spent. John, you saw the first decade of this city enlarged,
Pulled into the dream-shape someone thought we needed.
At fifty-nine who's to say you'd not changed things, not succeeded
In stirring up whatever stuff this corner of the pool had in
            suspension?
Talk of booze, too little care taken of yourself, prevention
Of the heart's explosion that took you in the early hours
With McGuigan's fight won and the tele drizzling showers
Of grey flakes down its mute screen,
Won't bring you back. You slid away. The barely-tuned machine
Packed up. Unlike Dylan, no insult to the brain, John. Often we'd talk
Of going to the States, whistle-stopping, the Chelsea in New York,
Our tour for the Yanks, I could have rigged.
Yes, if I'd pushed it, we two in tandem could have gigged
Over there. Like a lot of the others, I chickened out, I suppose.
Pembrokeshire a couple of nights – you with no change of clothes,
Just a battered attaché, poems, toothbrush, fags –
Was the limit of my stamina for your ways. Memory drags
Such petty guilts to the fore.
Though I treasure and feed off that reading we did on the man o'war,

Reluctant sailors pouring export ale down us
To forestall the poetry (they did) drown us
With hospitality in the middle of Fishguard harbour
Until we staggered past the missiles in her belly's store
Up to the frigate's redundant forward gun-turret, officers dressed
In cummerbunds, and elegant women. The talk was veiled, but
       impressed
Words like 'Responsibility', 'Capability' and 'Global role'. 'Yes, but
What do you do with all this training? All the missiles, shit-hot
Fire-power?' I remember, he answered you with, 'We can blow
       Fishguard
Away with each one, you know. We are, I suppose, a "hard
Fist gloved by our democratic masters".' John, before the evening
       ended –
You topped that with a poem scribbled on a cigarette pack. We
       descended
A precarious ladder to the launch with those lines of his and yours
       sinking
Into the night. And now, a decade later, the story has a ring
Any writer could tune. Perhaps that's what your Sandeman Port
       inquisitor
Pointed to – after the jaunts and applause, the writer's for
Filling the void, putting structure into space, a kind of race
Against apathy and oblivion. Too grand, you say, too heroic? Let's
       face
It, John, we've both indulged in our 'intervals of heat'
On the page and off. Both been chilled by the thought one couldn't
       beat
The odds, stuck in Wales, chiselling verse, weak in the flesh.
We're out on the edge of the world's concern, no Wall St, no Long
       Kesh.
Unless the challenge here is also to connect – radar dishes at
       Brawdy,
Hinkley over the water, Trawsfynydd, the poison brought in on our
       sea.
An *Anglo*, dipped in England's sewer should still produce the goods.
Albeit in 'invisible ink / on dissolving paper...' one loads
The futile quarto, pushes it out to travel or sink.
Standing here before the Holiday Inn, and its shiny 0-3-0, I think
How my grandfather, before the Great War, shunted down to Wales
       on the G.W.R.
How arbitrary one's identity is: with voice and gesture we are

Challenged to make sense of where and what we find ourselves. No
Border guards patrol the Dyke, no frontier seals us in at Chepstow.
Did you really ever want that, John, seriously?
From here I have to question that stance. Were you quite as you
    appeared to be?
This locomotive worked the sidings in Cardiff and the junction,
Was scrapped at Barry and now is made to function
As an image of our hard-bitten history. *9629*, freshly painted green
    and black,
Her valves de-gutted, holds to her half-dozen yards of track:
No driver on the footplate, no steam, no destination,
This featureless hotel her final station,
Under the flags of Canada, Commerce and the Dragon.
I turn around. On the island in the Hayes a wino tilts his flagon
And light flashes from the moment.

Gorsedd: the eminent bards of the Welsh National Eisteddfod; *gwerin:* Welsh
term for 'the people'; *Brawdy:* British and American airbase in Pembrokeshire.

PETER DIDSBURY

That Old-Time Religion

God and His angels stroll in the garden
before turning in for the night.
They've adopted the style
of rich and gifted young Englishmen this evening
and also, bizarrely even for them, decided that they'll speak
in nothing but Sumerian to each other
which all are agreed was a truly heavenly language.

It isn't long before God starts boasting,
in Sumerian of course, that He's the only Being He knows
Who knows by heart *The Bothie of Tober-na-Vuolich*,
and is about to prove it when Lucifer intercedes
to make the points that

> a) they've all agreed to speak Sumerian, which was never the
> tongue of that estimable poem, and that unless He wants to
> pay the usual forfeit, which wouldn't really be consonant
> with His divinity, He'd better give up the idea;

> b) should He decide to do it into
> instantaneous and perfect Sumerian metres,
> a feat of which they're all aware He's capable,
> He wouldn't be proving His grasp of the original
> and would run the risk of them thinking Him a show-off;

> & c) since He, God, and not Arthur Hugh Clough must be regarded
> as the only true author of *The Bothie*, as of all things,
> he, Satan, doesn't see what the point of it would be anyway.

In the silence which follows the Creator is keenly aware
of the voice of the nightingale, then murmurs of consensus,
then much delighted laughter from the angels.

Lucifer bows.

The nightingale stops singing.

God sighs. He could really do without these bitches sometimes
but *then* where would He be?

As if to answer this question to Himself
He withdraws to the farthest reaches of the garden
and leans on the parapet, smoking in fitful gloom,
for what seems like an eternity.
He lights each gasper from the butt of His last
then flicks the glowing end far into the dark,
displeased at His foreknowledge of where it will fall.
To KNOW what His more intelligent creatures have thought
of these lights that appear in August out of Perseus
and not to have disabused them of it, as He's always meant to,
is unforgivable. He gazes in their direction in the dark
and gives them His Word that soon He will change all that,
silent at first, then whispered, then *shouted* in Sumerian.

Eikon Basilike
(for the soul of William Cowper)

During the late and long continuing cold
I went for a walk in the empty heart of the city.
I stuffed the sun and moon in a deep string bag
and let them hang from my shoulder as I marched.
I noted the resemblance that my home now suddenly bore
to a level Baltic town, its frozen gardens, and its
bright green civic domes. The new white lawns
had frosted to such a depth that they'd lost
the visual texture of grass and begun to make pastiche
of a pavement, a complement to some old and
disgruntled buildings. I cast around for a route,
and chose to follow three hares in winter coats
who hopped across my path. They tempted me away
from that novel plaza which the ice revealed
and I found myself on a track beside a canal,
or rather a drain, which is different,
for it empties into the turbulent German Ocean.
There was dereliction on one side of the stream
and an Arctic kind of Xanadu on the other.

I shivered. My hip-flask was out of action.
I hadn't actually invented it yet
but knew I wouldn't be leaving it very much longer.
If this was what linguistic exercise meant
then I didn't think much of it. The deep structures
I could cope with, but the surface ones
were coming at me in Esperanto, and fragments of horrible Volapük.
I was walking through the urban fields that surrounded
the Stalag or temple or star-ship of the Power Station.
Yellow electricity vans kept cornering on the road
that crossed the bricky and entrenched landscape.
I recognised the faces of the drivers, and later spotted
most of the leading Romantic poets, all of whom were eating
substantial packing-up, in tents pegged out by the kerb.
It was a case of etcetera etcetera. Tiney, Puss and Bess
were proving considerate guides. I found I had plenty of time
to inspect the ceramic formers on their poles.
I noticed many ordinary things, several of which were lying
on the ice, between the high and weedy banks of the drain.
I began to think of the slicks of grey lawn that must exist
between runways on the edge of international airports.
Hot moonlit nights in Athens or Cairo, powdery channels of grass
that might just as well be anywhere, all of them rising in Hades.
The fat and impersonal transports were lifting on either side
and threatening my creatures with their cruel and silvery wings.
I could see the black pylons here and there but the power lines
were all of them lost in the low-level brume. I only heard them hum,
thrupping the atmospheric fridge with over and over again
a Vulgar Latin sentence which my guts were scarcely screwed to.
'It is all up with thee, thou hast already utterly perished.'
The hares bounded on, and finally halted outside the gate
on the bridge that carried the road across the stream
and into the precincts of the Generating Board.
I stood next to them, making the fourth in their row,
and I looked where they looked: below the rusty barbed wire
was an old white notice bearing the four bold letters
that denoted which mesmeric authority
we laboured under the caring aegis of.
Something – Something – G – B.
Like a name of God. But the letters were all wrong.
The three hares looked at me like animals in anthropomorphic films
when they've just led the hero to the scene of his triumph.

I thought I might begin to weep and yet I scarcely knew why.
The enamel plate was now announcing that this was *Eikon Basilike*,
a place whose sub-title I had no problem supplying
from my sad and emotional erudition, justified at last
by a portraicture of his sacred majestie, in his solitude and sufferings.

The Guitar

> *And what if all of animated nature*
> *Be but organic Harps diversely framed,*
> *That tremble into thought...*
>   COLERIDGE

Aerial songs, estuarial poetry.
An electric guitar is being played.
Its neck is five miles long,
and forms a margin of the River Humber,
where the thin soils are.
Aeolus swoops down, and begins to bounce on it.
He has serpents in his eyes.
He plucks the strings
with his Nebuchadnezzar toenails.
He's composing a piece called Early Memorials.
A train comes. His pinions take him
half a mile high in a lift.
The train courses over
the frets of the guitar,
but it is going backwards,
towards the hole in the middle.
Coleridge is sitting at a window
with his back towards the engine.
He must have been lunching in Goole,
but now he's fallen asleep.
'Dutch River,' he murmurs, 'Dutch River.'
He's dreaming of the advent of the railways
but will not remember, because I intend to
keep it from him.
It's a mercy that is available to me.
The train steams through fields of bright chives,
then it reverses and comes back as a diesel.
A madman steps out of a cabin and salutes it.

He stands by the flagpole outside his summer *kraal*.
The engine-driver waves.
The engine-driver and the madman
both went to the same school as me.
They sport the red blazer and the nose.
They chat for a bit while the engine grazes
on the chives that spring up through the ballast.
'Nice bit of road,' one says. 'Aye, nice road,' says the other.
The sky is like an entry in The Oxford English Dictionary.
The earliest reference for it is 1764,
in Randall's *Semi-Virgilian Husbandry*.
The loco swings its head from side to side
with the movements of an old-fashioned camera,
or a caterpillar. The mythic god of the winds, however,
who is still aloft, is getting tired of attending.
He flies up the line and starts twisting on the pegs.
Lunatic, driver, and diesel all look up.
Their faces assume an almost communal rictus.
They all jump in the carriage with Coleridge,
as the mighty lexicon twangs. They wish they were asleep.
The god puts his face right up to the window
and shakes his horrid locks at them.
They stare at the cattle grazing in his fields.
They note the herbaceous stubble
which makes frightful his visage of mud.

Back of the House

Sick of England, but happy in your garden
this hot afternoon, your English garden,
where everything looks like something else
and Language, fat and prone beneath her fountain,
idly dispenses curling parchment notes,
her coveted, worthless, licences to imitate.
There is too much to photograph here,
so put your camera down. Relax.
A fan of green depends from twigs like vines
but the punkah wallah has gone to stand
in the shade, where you cannot pick him out,

and grins at the print he left behind,
which moves its arm in air, and grins at *him*.
So pull the rope on the broken swing, to make us cool.
Impersonate a dancer from Bali or Siam,
or somewhere they posture with sticks and bits of string.
Look around you. That large bird was running away
from a poem by Keats, and it failed.
A pile of brushwood makes flagrant promises
to Andrew Marvell, and the boulevards are ringed by bombs.
Light, and shade, are the lustrations of *trompe l'œil*,
itself the name of a garden in France,
and the three bleached poles that limit the brassica
make a hitching rail for goblin cavalry
in the childhood garden that continued to grow,
commensurate with our stature. 'How far we used
to travel in only three paces,' you say
as we take an unhurried dozen to the gate.
When I walk off down the hot brick lane
I know I leave myself behind
in the coloured window, in the Byzantine
back of the house. I watch us still examining
the blasted elm, that rocks to your fingers
and threatens to fall. It would lie across
half the garden. I estimate its height
and step that far away, before I go.

A Winter's Fancy

> *To write a* Tristram Shandy *or a* Sentimental Journey *there is no way
> but to be Sterne; and Sternes are not turned out in bakers' batches.*

A winter's fancy.
I look out of my window
and perceive I am Laurence Sterne.
I am sitting in Shandy Hall.
It is raining.
I am inventing a Bag,
which will accommodate everything.
I'd weave it out of air if I could
but the rain slants down like a page of Greek

and the afternoon is a dish of mud,
far removed from gentle opinion.
I am heavy with God.
The weather used
to cloak itself in sentiment
but today it imitates the tongues of men
and wags in curtains at me, along a yard.
I am also John, an elderly bibliophile.
Once, long after I died, I returned to Coxwold
on a literary pilgrimage.
A red-faced lout leaned over my gate
and instructed me curtly to Sodding Sod Off.
He was full of choler.
I sometimes feel I can understand
what's been eluding me ever since Christmas.
I'm exhausting my karma of country parson
in a dozen lives of wit and kidneys,
caritas, the pox, and marbled endpapers.
Looking out from here, this afternoon,
I can just discern the porch of my church
where Nick and Numps are sheltering from
Thucydides, Books Six and Seven.
By the look of that cloud looming up like a skull
there will soon be nothing left to do
but to take to my bed.
The cattle squelch past beneath a sodden sky,
below my windows and before the eyes
of Peter Didsbury, in his 35th year.
I consider other inventions of mine,
which rise before me in the darkening pane.
Light me that candle, oh my clever hand,
for it is late, and I am admirably tired.

The Drainage

When he got out of bed the world had changed.
It was very cold. His breath whitened the room.
Chill December clanked at the panes.
There was freezing fog.

He stepped outside.
Not into his street but a flat wet landscape.
Sluices. Ditches. Drains. Frozen mud and leafcake. Dykes.
He found he knew the names of them all.
Barber's Cut. Cold Track. Lament. Meridian Stream.
He found himself walking.
It was broad cold day but the sky was black.
Instead of the sun it was Orion there.
Seeming to pulse his meaning down.
He was naked. He had to clothe himself.
The heifers stood like statues in the fields.
They didn't moan when he sliced the hides from them.
He looked at the penknife in his hand.
The needle, the thread, the clammy strips.
Now his face mooned out through a white hole.
The cape dripped. He knew he had
the bounds of a large parish to go.
His feet refused to falter.
Birds sat still in the trees.
Fast with cold glue. Passing their clumps
he watched them rise in their species.
The individuals. Sparrow. Starling. Wren.
He brought them down with his finger.
Knife needle and thread again.
It happened with the streams.
Pike barbel roach minnow gudgeon.
Perch dace eel. Grayling lamprey bream.
His feet cracked puddles and were cut on mud. They bled.
There was movement. He pointed. He stitched.
His coat hung reeking on him.
He made cut after cut in the cold.
Coldness and the colours of blood.
Red blue and green. He glistened.
He stitched through white fat.
Weight of pelts and heads. Nodding at the hem.
Feathers. Scales. Beaks and strips of skin.
He had the bounds of a large parish to go.
Oh Christ, he moaned. Sweet Christ.
The Hunter hung stretched in the Sky.
He looked at the creatures of the bankside.
He glistened. He pointed. He stitched.

PETER READING

FROM *Evagatory*

Came to an island whereon the natives make
caps (worn by prankster drolls) on the peaks of which,
   gleaming, repose the simulacra,
      sculpted in plastic, of great big dog turds.
Thus are they designated: **Shitheads**.

FROM *Stet*

     Pyrex, a pie-dish, deep-lined with apple lumps,
     deft in the left hand; with the right, flopping on
        pall of white-dusted droopy pastry,
           slicing off overlaps, jabbing steam-vents...

'52: Mummy paused, wiped a floured hand and tuned in the wireless –
   sad Elgar, crackling, then *death of our King, George the Sixth*.

               *   *   *

     Somewhere in *Far East* there was a *Narmistice*
     (I wasn't sure where either of these things were);
        wirelesses fizzled, grown-ups seemed to
           value *it* more than they did my birthday! –

I was just 7 (July 27th, '53) and the
   news there would be no more war made me feel comfy inside.

               *   *   *

'54: old Miss Clio was teaching us
[genuine name, 'Miss Clio' is, by the way]
   'There is no reason, is there, children,
       why you can't live with other little

children from other countries in happiness?
You are the ones whom we are depending on...'
   We have betrayed her, poor old Dodo –
       cleaving of crania, burnt-out Pandas...

                * * *

   '54: old Miss Clio was teaching us
   all about *Frontiers* (Asia and everywhere);
      my mate's big brother, so he told me,
         'died in Career for one of those things'...

when he was in the bath, you could see scars on both of Dad's
                                 shoulders
   (carrying rails for Japan) – I hated flipping Frontiers.

                * * *

   '55: comics (*better* class) offered us
   Decent Types it was hoped we would emulate –
      Shaftesbury, Gandhi, Dickens, Florence
         Nightingale, Faraday, Curie, Elgar...

'85: some of us clearly have been more moved by the *worse* ones –
   Bloody-Nosed Basher, The Yobbs, Sheik Fist The Middle East
                            Nit...

                * * *

'56: going home from the Juniors,
I read the headlines **Suez** and **Crisis Point** –
crikey! I thought, there must be something
terribly wrong with the nation's toilets;

soon if the Government didn't act there'd be all kinds of nasties
gushing up out of the drains, Britain would be [is] engulfed.

FROM *Ukulele Music*

'Life is too black as he paints it' and 'Reading's nastiness sometimes
seems a bit over the top' thinks a review – so does *he*.

Too black and over the top, though, is what the Actual often
happens to be, I'm afraid. He don't *invent* it, you know.

Take, for example, some snippets from last week's dailies before they're
screwed up to light the Parkray: Birmingham, March '83,

on her allotment in King's Heath, picking daffodils, Dr
Dorris McCutcheon (retired) pauses to look at her veg.

Dr McCutcheon (aged 81) does not know that behind her,
Dennis (aged 36) lurks, clutching an old iron bar.

Unemployed labourer Dennis Bowering sneaks up behind her,
bashes her over the head – jaw, nose and cheek are smashed-in.

Dennis then drags her until he has got her into the tool-shed,
strikes her again and again, there is a sexual assault,

also a watch and some money worth less than ten pounds are stolen.
'Is an appalling offence...' Bowering is told by the Judge.

Amateur frogmen discover a pair of human legs buried
Mafia-style in cement, deep in an Austrian lake.

Smugly, Americans rail over KA 007;
angrily, Moscow retorts. Hokkaido fishermen find

five human bits of meat, one faceless limbless female Caucasian,
shirts, empty briefcases, shoes, fragments of little child's coat,

pieces of movable section of wing of a 747,
one piece of human back flesh (in salmon-fishermen's nets),

one headless human too mangled to ascertain what the sex is.
USA/USSR butcher a Boeing like chess

(probably civil jumbos *are* used for Intelligence business;
pity the poor sods on board don't have the chance to opt out).

Sexual outrage on woman of 88 robbed of her savings.
Finger found stuck on barbed wire. Too black and over the top.

Clearly we no longer hold *H. sapiens* in great reverence
(which situation, alas, no elegiacs can fix).

What do they think they're playing at, then, these Poetry Wallahs?
Grub St reviewing its own lame valedictory bunk.

Fiction

Donald is a fictitious character
arrived at an age and bodily state
rendering suicide superfluous,
would rather sip Grands Crus than throw his leg.
He is a writer of fiction. He says
'Even one's self is wholly fictitious.'
Hatred once drew him to satiric verse
but he could think of nothing to rhyme with
'Manageress of the Angel Hotel',
or 'I call my doctor "Killer" Coldwill'
(a fictitious name, 'Coldwill', by the way),
or 'Headmaster of the Secondary Mod.'

Donald has created a character
called 'Donald' or 'Don' who keeps a notebook
dubbed 'Donald's Spleneticisms', e.g.:
'Complacent as a Country Town G.P.',
'Contemptible as County Council Clerks',
'A hateful little Welshman shared my train
with no lobes to his ears and yellow socks',
'Seedy as Salesmen of Secondhand Cars'.

In Donald's novel, 'Don' writes poetry –
titles such as 'It's a Small World', 'Fiction',
'Y – X', 'Remaindered', which he sends
to literary periodicals
under the nom de plume *Peter Reading*
(the present writer is seeking advice
from his attorney, Donald & Donald).
This fictitious bard has a doctor called
'Coldwill' who sleeps with the manageress
of the Angel (and sues 'Don' for libel).

In Donald's novel, 'Don' (whose nom de plume
is *Peter Reading*) sues a man whose *real*
name is 'Peter Reading' for having once
written a fiction about a poet
who wrote verse concerning a novelist
called 'Donald' whose book 'Fiction' deals with 'Don'
(a poet who writes satirical verse
and is sued by an incompetent quack,
the manageress of a pub, a Celt
with lobeless ears and yellow socks, acned
Council clerks and a Range Rover salesman).

In 'Reading's' fiction, the poet who writes
verse concerning the novelist 'Donald'
is sued by the latter who takes offence
at the lines '...an age and bodily state
rendering suicide superfluous,
would rather sip Grands Crus than throw his leg'.
For the Defence, 'Donald, Q.C.' says that
'Even one's self is wholly fictitious'.

FROM *Perduta Gente*

Newspaper, wrapped round the torso between the
        fourth and fifth jerseys
(night attire proper for doing a skipper in
        icy December
    under the Festival Hall),
carries a note to the Editor, from 'Ex-
        Soldier' of Telford,
    outlining plans to withdraw
    DHSS cash from those
    no-fixed-abode parasites.

Wound round a varicose indigo swollen
        leg, between second
    and third pair of trousers (which stink –
    urine and faeces and sick),
Property Pages delineate *bijou*
        River-View Flatlets
    £600,000 each.

FROM *Stet*

['Contented of Telford, Mrs' submits her poem *Faith* to the Editor.]

All this terrible rape and murder
        And mugging and violence galore
And poor little children beaten
        Oh! my heart can stand no more.
There is always someone on strike
        For better pay and terms,
Is there no end of this misery?
        No one ever learns.
But before despair descends
        Upon my sad head
A name crops up in the paper
        And I no longer wish I was dead!

I'm filled with fresh, new hope,
   I'm certain that Billy Graham,
With words of Truth and Love,
   Will bring an end to this horrid mayhem.

FROM *Going On*

This is unclean: to eat turbots on Tuesdays,
tying the turban unclockwise at cockcrow,
cutting the beard in a south-facing mirror,
wearing the mitre whilst sipping the Bovril,
chawing the pig and the hen and the ox-tail,
kissing of crosses with peckers erected,
pinching of bottoms (except in a yashmak),
flapping of cocks at the star-spangled-banner,
snatching the claret-pot off of the vicar,
munching the wafer without genuflexion,
facing the East with the arse pointing backwards,
thinking of something a little bit risqué,
raising the cassock to show off the Y-fronts,
holding a Homburg without proper licence,
chewing the cud with another man's cattle,
groping the ladies – or gentry – o'Sundays,
leaving the tip on the old-plum-tree-shaker,
speaking in physics instead of the Claptrap,
failing to pay due obeisance to monkeys,
loving the platypus more than the True Duck,
death without Afterlife, smirking in Mecca,
laughing at funny hats, holding the tenet
how that the Word be but fucking baloney,
failing to laud the Accipiter which Our Lord saith is Wisdom.

Started by *Australopithecus*, these are
time-honoured Creeds (and all unHoly doubters
shall be enlightened by Pious Devices:
mayhems of tinytots, low-flying hardwares,
kneecappings, letterbombs, deaths of the firstborns,
total extinctions of infidel unclean wrong-godded others).

FROM C

Verse is for healthy
arty-farties. The dying
and surgeons use prose.

*   *   *

What were bronzed on Margate sands,
flopped about by trembling hands,
malleable, conical,
have become ironical.
What was cupped in palm and thumb.
seres now under radium.
What was kneaded like warm dough
is where, now, malign cells grow.
What was fondled in a car
through white silk-smooth slippery bra
(Marks & Spencer, 38)
was plump cancer inchoate.

Truncation (catalexis): 'frequent in trochaic verse, where the line
of complete trochaic feet tends to create monotony. The following
trochaic lines exhibit t.: "Simple maiden, void of art,/ Babbling out
the very heart"...' – *Princeton Encyclopedia of Poetry and Poetics* (ed.
Preminger).

Song of the Bed-Sit Girl

I'm frozen in amber by street-light,
        pine-wallpaper planks box me in,
the phial on the faded mat opens
        an alternative to the Bin.

I shouldn't have left my husband
        if the *other man* hadn't occurred –
told me he loved me more than his wife,
        the turd.

At first I just wanted to screw him
        that night in the Tudor Rose.
Now I'm helpless and hollow and rue him
        when, after coming, he goes.

Now the sheets are brown-stained and arctic,
        oh! love's a perfidious fink,
and I snuffle the bed like a truffle-pig
        desperate to retrace his stink.

Now my head is filling with feathers,
        my thumb gnawed down to the quick,
all for true love of a man him*self*
        (not just a prick).

    CHORUS:
Don't fall for charisma or intellect,
        your motives were better venereal –
your men in the Arts are bastards and farts
        to whom love is mere raw material.

    CHORUS:
Ariadne deserted by Theseus
        had heartaches enough when you tally 'em,
but at least Dionysus helped her through her crisis –
        our victim has only Valium.

& the thumb bones crunch & the knot-holes howl
        & my head is filling with amber
& a truffle-pig in a feather wig
        plays a stone viola da gamba

& the tune is He Loves Me/He Loves Me Not
        & the empty phial rasps on the mat
& the stained sheets are cold & the tears are hot
        oh! My Darling/My Fucking Rat!

Soirée

One funny thing about loving someone
is how much you'll put up with – her parents'
conversazione for example,
or being sweet to these fools she works with
who smoke inferior cigars and think
it's savoir vivre, and drag me back to drink
inadequately and long past my bedtime,
and put on records (God!) stuff like Ray Conniff.
And all their damn fool questions 'tell me Peter,
what do you write *about*?' (cunts like you mate).
'Peter, you interested in history?'
(Mate, I ain't even interested in
the present.) Still I'm here because I love her.

FROM *C*

My fistulae ooze blood and stink,
I vomit puce spawn in the sink,
diarrhoea is exuded.
Do not be deluded:
mortality's worse than you think.

You find the Limerick inapposite? Try the pretty Choriamb?

Bed-sores without; swarm-cells within.
Rancified puke speckles my sheets.
Faeces spurt out quite uncontrolled
into my bed, foetid and warm.
Vomit of blood tasting of brass,
streaked with green veins, splatters my face.

In vomiting, the glottis closes, the soft palate rises and the abdominal muscles contract, expelling the stomach contents. In nausea, the stomach relaxes and there is reverse peristalsis in the duodenum.

FROM *Evagatory*

Snow-haired, an elder, dulled eyes gum-filled,
tuning a sweet-toned curious instrument,
    gulps from a goblet of local merlot,
  sings on a theme whose fame was fabled,
  that of a sad realm farctate with feculence
    (patois and translationese alternately):

Gobschighte damapetty,
  gobby Fer-dama,
  getspeeke baggsy,
  getspeeke parly
  comma cul, comma
  malbicker-bicker,
porky getspeeke?, porky?

Wonderful little Madam,
self-mocking Iron Lady,
who some said was a windbag,
some said talked
like an arsehole, like
a termagant – why,
why did some say that?

Pascoz vots clobberjoli,
  vots chevvy-dur dur,
  vots baggsymain chic,
  vots collier-prick,
  cuntyvach twitnit,
  iscst pukkerjoli –
illos jalouz dats porky!

Because your pretty frocks,
your permed-stiff hair,
your smart handbag, your
tight-sharp necklace,
satrapess so marvellous,
were so beautiful –
they were envious, that's it!

Ni iscst vots marrypappa
  grignaleto, ne.
  Mas vots pollytiq
  saggio sauvay
  vots salinsula,
  insulapetty,
et fair tutts egal mit-nochts.

Nor was your spouse
a pipsqueak – far from it!
But your many wise policies
were saving your islet,
your filthy isle, and
made all equal with nil.

LIZ LOCHHEAD

After the War
(for Susanne Ehrhardt)

After the war
was the dull country I was born in.
The night of Stafford Cripps's budget
My dad inhaled the blue haze of one last Capstan
then packed it in.
'You were just months old...'
The Berlin airlift.
ATS and REME badges
rattled in our button box.

Were they surprised that everything was different now?
Did it cheese them off that it was just the same
stuck in one room upstairs at my grandma's
jammed against the bars of my cot
with one mended featherstitch jumper drying
among the nappies on the winterdykes,
the puffed and married maroon counterpane
reflected in the swinging mirror of the wardrobe.
Radio plays. Them loving one another
biting pillows
in the dark while I was sleeping.
All the unmarried uncles were restless,
champing at the bit for New Zealand, The Black Country, Corby.
My aunties saved up for the New Look.

By International Refugee Year
we had a square green lawn and a twelve-inch tele.

Song of Solomon

You
smell nice he said
what is it?

Honey? He nuzzled a soap-trace
in the hollow of her collarbone.
The herbs of her hair?
Salt? He licked
a river-bed between her breasts.

(He'd seemed
not unconvinced by the chemical
attar of roses at her armpit. She tried
to relax have absolute faith in
the expensive secretions of teased civet to
trust the musk at her pulse spots
never think of the whiff of
sourmilk from her navel
the curds of cheese between the toes
the dried blood smell of many small wounds
the stink of fish at her crotch.)

No there he was above her apparently
as happy as a hog rooting for truffles.
She caressed him behind the ear
with the garlic of her cooking-thumb.

She banged shut her eyes
and hoped he would not smell her fear.

The Carnival Horses

All along Hudson they are sanding down
the carnival horses.
Outside antique shops, so many, so
slender young men bend attentively
at the curlicued flanks, their
eyes and noses almost closed to dust,
the noxious effects of chemical paintstripper.

That mercenary bitch next door
brasso-ing the handles on a hope-chest
is nothing to them.

Like grooms with curry-combs
plying their wire-brushes
around the tossed head and
always wild eyes, whisking
the ears clean of paint-layers,
the gummed-up old notes of the hurdygurdy,
exposing the perfect quotemarks of the nostrils.
What is it
(Falada, Falada)
we wish that he would say?

Later when he's
skewered in a loft
somewhere in NoHo
silhouetted with his flung hooves and tassel-tail
re-gilded against prettily exposed brick
he'll make each
new owner who paid through the nose for him imagine
he feels the long slide down the sticky pole,
that he could ride again
the perfect carousel at the fair he never
ever went to
on his favourite chosen beast
he never even for a dime possessed.

Bagpipe Muzak, Glasgow 1990

When A. and R. men hit the street
To sign up every second band they meet
Then marketing men will spill out spiel
About how us Glesca folk are really *real*
(Where once they used to fear and pity
These days they glamorise and patronise our city –
Accentwise once they could hear bugger all
That was not low, glottal or guttural,
Now we've 'kudos' incident'ly
And the Patter's street-smart, strictly state-of-the-art,
And our oaths are user-friendly).

It's all go the sandblaster, it's all go Tutti Frutti,
All we want is a wally close with Rennie Mackintosh putti.

Malkie Machismo invented a gismo for making whisky oot o'girders
He tasted it, came back for mair, and soon he was on to his thirdoro.
Rabbie Duins turned in his grave and dunted Hugh MacDiarmid,
Said: It's oor National Thorn, John Barleycorn, but I doot we'll
          ever learn it...

It's all go the Rotary Club, its ail go 'The Toast Tae The Lassies',
It's all go Holy Willie's Prayer and plunging your dirk in the haggis.

Robbie Coltrane flew Caledonian MacBrayne
To Lewis...on a Sunday!
Protesting Wee Frees fed him antifreeze
(Why God knows) till he was comatose
And didnae wake up till the Monday.

Aye it's Retro Time for Northern Soul and the whoop and the skirl
          o' the saxes.
All they'll score's more groundglass heroin and venison filofaxes.
The rent-boys preen on Buchanan Street, their boas are made of
          vulture,
It's all go the January sales in the Metropolis of Culture.

It's all go the PR campaign and a radical change of image –
Write Saatchi and Saatchi a blank cheque to pay them for the damage.

Tam o'Shanter fell asleep
To the sound of fairy laughter
Woke up on the cold-heather hillside
To find it was ten years after
And it's all go (again) the Devolution Debate and pro...pro...
          proportional representation.
Over pasta and pesto in a Byres Road bistro, Scotland declares
          hersel' a nation.

Margo McDonald spruced up her spouse for thon Govan By-
          Election
The voters they selectit him in a sideyways *left* defection,
The Labour man was awfy hurt, he'd dependit on the X-fillers
And the so-and-sos had betrayed him for thirty pieces of Sillars!

Once it was no go the SNP, they were sneered at as 'Tory' and
        tartan
And thought to be very little to do with the price of Spam in
        Dumbarton.
Now it's all go the Nationalists, the toast of the folk and the famous
– Of Billy Connolly, Muriel Gray and the Auchtermuchty
        Proclaimers.

It's all go L.A. lager, it's all go the Campaign for an Assembly,
It's all go Suas Alba and winning ten-nil at Wembley.
Are there separatist dreams in the glens and the schemes?
Well...it doesny take Taggart to detect it!
Or to jalouse we hate the Government
And we patently didnae elect it.
So – watch out Margaret Thatcher, and tak' tent Neil Kinnock
Or we'll tak' the United Kingdom and brekk it like a bannock.

JOHN ASH

The Hotel Brown Poems

1

Above every seaward-facing window
of the Hotel Brown is a canopy. At night
the perfumes of the garden will delight you...

It is a good place to fall in love
and a good place to write, though neither
is obligatory. You must, however,

praise the light, the changing colours
of the sea at dawn and dusk: these are
the divinities of the place. Amen.

2

Once in the cool, blue restaurant
of the Hotel Brown a friend said to me, –
'You don't realise how much your openness
frightens people: it hits them like a wave,'

and I smiled, not because his words
amused me, but because the scent of peppers
grilling in the kitchen overwhelmed me.
I could not think of ideas or people then –

only of the place, the scent, the way
long white curtains moved back and forth
across the boundaries of light and air.

3

The windows were open on to the small terrace.
The sea was motionless. Not a wave. I would not,
for the world, compare it to anything.

I pointed down the half-deserted quay
drowsy with a heat that seemed personal
like a memory, and said, 'That man, hunched

as if he were struggling against
a cold wind, is a poet, a friend of mine.
let's make ourselves known.'

4

Think of yourself as a wave. Hard.
Think of yourself as open. Equally hard.
Usually your gestures seem to take place
behind a glass partition, fogged with steam

and there is often the sense that things are closing in, –
have closed over you like the waters of a lamentation,
and the absence of obvious locks or bars only confirms
that depressingly, the fault lies in your soul as much

as hostile circumstances, the invisible clouds
of general despondency that hang off even the most
blissful shore, waiting to blow in, dulling
the water, the boats, your deepest words with dust.

5

As we walked towards the temple
the poet said to us: 'This may seem
a small island to you but once it was
an independent state with its own fierce navy.

The Athenians destroyed it utterly.'
The old ramparts were massive, finely jointed
but the area of jumbled stones and bushes they enclosed
seemed no bigger than a modest public park.

6

We saw him to the evening boat. A man
who walked like a dancer followed him aboard
carrying a single bicycle wheel, and the ship
departed, illuminated, unreasonably festive.

We walked back past the bars. The night
was already richly dark, full of murmured conversation
Light poured down the steps of the Hotel Brown,
traversed by a cold, rising breeze, as if to say –

'You are welcome, for the moment. This
is an interval in your life. Soon you must look to
the plots and masks and backdrops of your next act.
Here all moments are intervals. It is like music and like loss.'

Visigothic

It had been raining all day,
and I found myself trying to imagine
the life of the Visigothic kingdom.

We know which cities were destroyed
or abandoned in the years
of confusion, but others survived,

if somewhat reduced in size,
and the building of churches and palaces
continued. Laws were propounded,

and the kings wore crowns of particular
magnificence. Nor were they indifferent
to learning, since it was during this period

that the *Etymologies* of Isidore
were composed. Life was not without
its pleasures: we know, for example,

that King Sisebut reprimanded
Bishop Eusebius of Tarraco concerning
his excessive devotion to circus shows.

I concluded that it made no sense
for us to call them 'barbarians'. Theirs
was not an age of unrelieved darkness.

And the rain was still falling in the airshaft,
and sirens howled, and clouds obscured the towers.
Try as I might there was little I could see

in the pages of my books except
an elegant line of narrow arches
abandoned on a hillside somewhere,

its original purpose unknown,
and a list of names I could barely
pronounce: Leovigild, Recared...

Cigarettes

Problems of translation are, perhaps, not so great
between languages as between different versions
of the same language. Why, for example, does
'fag' mean homosexual in America, when,
in England, it means cigarette? Does this imply
that those who first observed the phenomenon
of smoking in the New World were homosexual?
This would cause some consternation on Columbus Day,
and, in all likelihood, the assumption is unjustified,
since Columbus and his crew were not English-speakers.
Yet, if we dismiss the idea of happy crowds of
homosexual Spanish or Italian mariners
returning to Europe with cigarettes in hand,
eager to introduce this new pleasure to their lovers,
we should perhaps concede that there is some connection
between the two ideas. It was Oscar Wilde, after all,
who described smoking as 'the perfect pleasure, because' –

he opined – 'it always leaves one unsatisfied.'
It is clear from this that he was thinking of sexual pleasure,
of the working class youths with whom he so recklessly dined
in fashionable restaurants of the eighteen-nineties.
A cigarette is like a passion in that it is inhaled deeply
and seems to fill all the empty spaces of the body,
until, of course, it burns down, and is put out amid
the shells of pistachio nuts, or whatever trash
may be at hand, and the passion may leave traces
that in time will grow malignant: he who has taken pleasure
may die many years after in the room of an anonymous
hotel or hospital, under the blank gaze of a washstand,
a bad painting or an empty vase, having forgotten entirely
the moment that announced the commencement
of his dying. And perhaps he will not understand:
it is another false translation, like someone stumbling over
the word for cigarette in a new and intolerable language.

The Wonderful Tangerines

1

Taking one's head off
is an odd way of showing
appreciation of the symphony,
but this is what she has done, –
the woman with the pastoral,
Marie Antoinette air
holding her smiling head
on a level with her hips,
and the guests murmur: 'Charming.
So clever. I suppose it is done
with mirrors.' But of course
it isn't. Strange to look
down on one's hat while
it is still on one's head.
The symphony is one of those
with picturesque titles, you know, –
The Claw-Hammer, The Flight-Bag,
The Spaniel, and so on...

2

'My dear I must tell you
about the cutlery.
None of it would match
and believing that music,
in propitious circumstances,
can alter the shape of
material objects, he placed it
in a transparent plastic
container next to the piano.
The concerto was a wild success
but still the supper was a shambles.'

3

For the rhapsodies
we arranged the grapes
in violin cases
under the German busts.
The members of the quartet concealed themselves
behind black curtains, only their hands
protruding through the narrow apertures provided.
The string emerged slowing from their cuffs.

They began with a lyrical andante
(composed by the principal string-master)
– slender, variously tinted threads
gently attenuated amid the eight, gesturing
hands. The effect was most poignant,
and they ended with the awesome counterpoint
of a Grosse Fugue, a mesh
so dense it might be mistaken
for topiary. When a volunteer
finally mounted the platform
to pull a single, trailing strand
and the entire, immense structure
collapsed before our eyes
the applause was tumultuous.

4

It is November.
Cloud-shadows scud across
the shallow lake water,
and the Duke moves sadly
towards the bathing huts.
It is too late in the season to swim
but this is not his intention.
He approaches a pale, once royal-blue,
much-weathered bathing hut
and enters. He kneels down
at the centre of the little room
and raises his eyes towards the far wall.
Nailed to it are six complete
and luxurious sets of women's lingerie,
a honeyed beige in colour.
There is a space on the right
for a seventh set. He reaches
in his pocket and brings out
the long, gleaming nails. A tear
forms in his eye.

Ferns and the Night

Und wir hörten sie noch von ferne
Trotzig singen im Wald.

This is the sort of place you might arrive at after a long journey
involving the deaths of several famous monsters,
only to be disappointed almost to the point of grief.

Heavy clouds hang in a clump above a wide, perfectly level plain
which is the image of a blank mind. Night is falling.
There is a wooden house, a lighted porch: it is a scene of
            'marvellous simplicity'. –
too marvellous perhaps: the very grain of the wood offers itself
for our admiration, and the light has such 'warmth'
it is hard to restrain tears. The clouds are now distinctly purple,
agitated, – a kind of frantically stirred borsch, suitable backdrop

for some new opera's Prelude of Foreboding, but not for this
          ambiguous scene
of severity tempered by domestic tenderness, in which we find
the 'young mother' looking for her child...He has run off
into deep woods nearby, leaving his blue train crashed on the lawn.
She calls his name, but after the third call it becomes difficult or
          exotic music,
a series in retrograde inversion, an entry in the catalogue of
          unknown birds:
she is already elsewhere, her torch illuminating the pure,
chlorophyll-green ferns of a forest, and the torch itself, a flame....

She finds that her bare feet are wet and that she is looking into a
          puddle,
Seeing the clouds reflected and her face (the moon also). She calls
          again
but has forgotten where she is, or whose name she is calling. Her
          own perhaps?
The wooden house, the lighted porch seem unreachable, –
artfully lit, a glassed-in exhibit in some future museum of the human.
Ferns and the night conceal the child whose laughter distantly
          reaches her.

Funeral Waltz

You know it too!...The charm of funerals in the rain,
the special effects men with their hoses well aimed,
huge drops exploding on
classically beautiful
black umbrellas.

You know them, –
the houses like fat vegetables
stuffed with old lace, ceramics, silverware, dust –
secure as bank vaults.
                    Who will inherit?
Vittorio is dining with
that Chinese actress again...
Will the kingdom be divided?

Who will keep
the chandeliers in good repair
and tend the lists of public enemies?

And who is being buried? (What
is being concealed?...) Is it
the young wife stabbed sixteen times with a flick-knife
or the industrialist's handsome son
garrotted when
his kidnappers tired
of waiting for his father's money?
Or is it the old woman who died laughing
after winning at cards? No these
are only nightmares, fairy-tales,
– reported in the newspapers:

it must be the Duke, the King, the Boss, the Father.

You know...
the feline grace of death bed politics,
calm distances of private investigations,
mosaics of espionage,
stylish impersonations of grief
wreaths gasping O, O, O, O...
the bells dropping into place exactly,
their commas and deaths-head semi-colons,
and corpses suave as angels!

And finally you know
the exquisite pleasures of anti-climax,
when it turns out that nothing of any value is left.
The sewing-machine doesn't work
the spokes of the umbrella are broken,
the clock is spilling its intestines,
the TV's burnt out,
the art collection contains nothing
but fake masterpieces and authentic trash
and the old bedstead (where he died)
is only good for a garden ornament,
– convolvulus contriving art-nouveau effects.

Why was nothing said? Why was the court kept in ignorance
of the loss of the colonies,
the liberation of the piano factories and the epidemic
of spontaneous sex-changes in the army?
Why was the baying of a triumphant mob
only a murmur?
                    Worse than the firing-squad
or guillotine they have been ignored.
Vermin and insects desert their wigs!
Everyone writes the word NOTHING in their diaries.

CIARAN CARSON

Calvin Klein's *Obsession*

I raised my glass, and – solid, pungent, like the soot-encrusted
    brickwork
Of the Ulster Brewery – a smell of yeast and hops and malt swam up:
I sniff and sniff again, and try to think of what it is I am remembering:
I think that's how it goes, like Andy Warhol's calendar of perfumes,
Dribs and drabs left over to remind him of that season's smell.
Very personal, of course, as *Blue Grass* is for me the texture of a fur
Worn by this certain girl I haven't seen in years. Every time that
    Blue Grass
Hits me, it is 1968. I'm walking with her through the smoggy early
    dusk
Of West Belfast: coal-smoke, hops, fur, the smell of stout and whiskey
Breathing out from somewhere. So it all comes back, or nearly all,
A long-forgotten kiss.

Never quite. Horses' dung is smoking on the cobbles. Cobblestones?
I must have gone back further than I thought, to brewers' drays
    and milk-carts,
Brylcreem, *Phoenix* beer. Or candy apples – rich hard dark-brown
    glaze
Impossible to bite at first, until you licked and licked and sucked a
    way
Into the soft core. A dark interior, where I'd also buy a twist of snuff
For my grandma. She'd put two pinches on a freckled fist, and sniff.
Then a sip of whiskey, and, as always, *I'm not long for this world.*
My father would make a face: *a whingeing gate,* he'd say, *hangs*
    longest –
Hoping it was true, perhaps – a phrase he'd said so often, he'd
    forgotten
When he said it last. That *Gold Label* whiskey – nearly like a
    perfume:
I go crazy because I want to smell them all so much,

Warhol's high-pitched New York whine comes on again, with
All those exhalations of the thirties and the forties: Guerlain's
Sous le Vent, Saravel's *White Christmas*, Corday's *Voyage à Paris*, or
Kathleen Mary Quinlan's *Rhythm*: bottles of bottle-green, bruise-
    blues

Darker than the pansies at the cemetery gate-lodge, bottles of
        frosted glass
And palest lilac – *l'odeur de ton sein chaleureux* – a rush of musk
And incense, camphor, beckons from the back of the wardrobe; I'd slipped
Through the mirror in a dream. *Opium* by Yves St Laurent? More
        than likely,
What my mother used to call a guilty conscience, or something
        that I ate:
Cheese and chopped dill pickle on wheaten farls, looking, if I
        thought of it,
Like Boots' *Buttermilk and Clover* soap –

Slipping and slipping from my grasp, clunking softly downwards
        through
The greying water; I have drowsed off into something else. The
        ornate fish
And frog and water-lily motif on the bathroom wallpaper reminds
        me
How in fact I'd stripped it off some months ago. It was April, a
        time
Of fits and starts; fresh leaves blustered at the window, strips and
        fronds
Of fish and water-lilies sloughed off round my feet. A Frank Ifield
        song
From 1963, I think, kept coming back to me: *I remember you –
        you're the one*
Who made my dreams come true – just a few – kisses ago. I'm taking
One step forward, two steps back, trying to establish what it was
        about her
That made me fall in love with her, if that's what it was; *infatuation*
Was a vogue word then –

It meant it wasn't all quite real. Like looking at my derelict back
        garden,
Its scraggy ranks of docks and nettles, thistles, but thinking
There was something else, flicking idly through the pages of a
        catalogue:
Flowered violets and whites, or grey and silver foliage, suggesting
Thunderclouds and snowstorms, rivers, fountains; artemesias and
        lilies,
Phlox, gentians, scillas, snowdrops, crocuses; and thymes and
        camomiles

Erupted from the paving-cracks, billowing from half-forgotten
        corners;
An avalanche of jasmine and wisteria broke through. Or, the
        perfume
Of *Blue Grass*, bittersweet, which is, just at this moment, just a
        memory.
How often did she wear it, anyway? I must look her up again some
        day.
And can it still be bought?

For there are memories that have no name; you don't know what
        to ask for.
The merest touch of sunshine, a sudden breeze, might summon up
A corner of your life you'd thought, till then, you'd never occupied.
Her mother, for example, owned this second-hand shop, which is
        where
The fur coat came from, anonymous with shades of someone else.
        Rummaging
Through piles of coats and dresses, I'd come across a thing that
        until then
I'd never wanted: a white linen fifties jacket with no back vent,
Just that bit out of fashion, it was fashionable, or maybe, as they say,
It was just the thing I had been looking for. So, a box of worn shoes
Might bring me back to 1952, teetering across the kitchen floor
In my mother's high heels –

Not that I wanted to be her; easing off the lid of her powder
        compact,
Breathing in the flesh-coloured dust, was just a way of feeling her
        presence.
And so I have this image of an assignation, where it all comes back,
Or nearly all, a long-forgotten kiss: subdued lighting, musak – no,
        a live
Piano – tinkling in its endless loop; there is candlelight and
        Cointreau,
Whispered nothings, as Kathleen Mary Quinlan's *Rhythm* meets,
        across
A discreet table, Calvin Klein's *Obsession*. He has prospered since
He saw her last. There is talk of all the years that separated them,
        whatever
Separated them at first. There is talk of money, phrased as talk of
Something else, of how there are some things that can't be bought.
Or maybe it's the name you buy, and not the thing itself.

Belfast Confetti

Suddenly as the riot squad moved in, it was raining exclamation marks,
Nuts, bolts, nails, car-keys. A fount of broken type. And the
    explosion
Itself – an asterisk on the map. This hyphenated line, a burst of
    rapid fire...
I was trying to complete a sentence in my head, but it kept
    stuttering,
All the alleyways and side-streets blocked with stops and colons.

I know this labyrinth so well – Balaclava, Raglan, Inkerman,
    Odessa Street –
Why can't I escape? Every move is punctuated. Crimea Street.
    Dead end again.
A Saracen, Kremlin-2 mesh. Makrolon face-shields. Walkie-talkies.
    What is
My name? Where am I coming from? Where am I going? A fusillade
    of question-marks.

33333

I was trying to explain to the invisible man behind the wire-grilled
One-way mirror and squawk-box exactly where it was I wanted to
    go, except
I didn't know myself- a number in the Holy Land, Damascus
    Street or Cairo?
At any rate in about x amount of minutes, where x is a small number,
I found myself in the synthetic leopard-skin bucket-seat of a Ford
    Zephyr

Gunning through a mesh of ramps, diversions, one-way systems.
    We shoot out
Under the glare of the sodium lights along the blank brick wall of
    the Gasworks
And I start to ease back: I know this place like the back of my
    hand, except
My hand is cut off at the wrist. We stop at an open door I never
    knew existed.

Clearance

The Royal Avenue Hotel collapses under the breaker's pendulum:
Zig-zag stairwells, chimney-flues, and a thirties mural
Of an elegantly-dressed couple doing what seems to be the Tango,
     in Wedgwood
Blue and white – happy days! Suddenly more sky
Than there used to be. A breeze springs up from nowhere –

There, through a gap in the rubble, a greengrocer's shop
I'd never noticed until now. Or had I passed it yesterday?
     Everything –
Yellow, green and purple – is fresh as paint. Rain glistens on the
     aubergines
And peppers; even from this distance, the potatoes smell of earth.

Night Patrol

Jerking his head spasmodically as he is penetrated by invisible
     gunfire,
The private wakes to a frieze of pull-outs from *Contact* and *Men
     Only*.
Sellotape and Blu-Tack. The antiquated plumbing is stuttering
     that he
Is not in Balkan Street or Hooker Street, but in a bunk bed
In the Grand Central Hotel: a room that is a room knocked into
     other rooms.

But the whole Victorian creamy facade has been tossed off
To show the inner-city tubing: cables, sewers, a snarl of Portakabins,
Soft-porn shops and carry-outs. A Telstar Taxis depot that is a
     hole
In a breeze-block wall, a wire grille and a voice-box uttering
     gobbledygook.

The Irish for No

Was it a vision, or a waking dream? I heard her voice before I saw
What looked like the balcony scene in *Romeo and Juliet*, except
        Romeo
Seemed to have shinned up a pipe and was inside arguing with her.
        The casements
Were wide open and I could see some Japanese-style wall-hangings
        the dangling
Quotation marks of a yin-yang mobile. *It's got nothing*, she was
        snarling, *nothing*
To do with politics, and, before the bamboo curtain came down,
That goes for you too!

It was time to turn into the dog's-leg short-cut from Chlorine
        Gardens
Into Cloreen Park, where you might see an *Ulster Says No*
        scrawled on the side
Of the power-block – which immediately reminds me of the
        Eglantine Inn
Just on the corner: on the missing *h* of Cloreen, you might say.
        We were debating,
Bacchus and the pards and me, how to render *The Ulster Bank –*
        the Bank
That Likes to Say Yes into Irish, and whether eglantine was alien
        to Ireland.
I cannot see what flowers are at my feet, when yes is the verb repeated,
Not exactly yes, but phatic nods and whispers. *The Bank That*
        Answers All
Your Questions, maybe? That Greek portico of Mourne granite,
        dazzling
With promises and feldspar, mirrors you in the Delphic black of
        its windows.

And the bruised pansies of the funeral parlour are dying in reversed
        gold letters,
The long sigh of the afternoon is not yet complete on the
        promontory where the victim,
A corporal in the UDR from Lisbellaw, was last seen having driven
        over half
Of Ulster, a legally-held gun was found and the incidence of
        stress came up

On the headland which shadows Larne Harbour and the black
  pitch of warehouses.
There is a melancholy blast of diesel, a puff of smoke which might
  be black or white.
So the harbour slips away to perilous seas as things remain
  unsolved; we listen
To the *ex cathedra* of the fog-horn, and *drink and leave the world*
  unseen –

What's all this to the Belfast businessman who drilled
Thirteen holes in his head with a Black & Decker? It was just a
  normal morning
When they came. The tennis-court shone with dew or frost, a
  little before dawn.
The border, it seemed, was not yet crossed: the Milky Way trailed
  snowy brambles,
The stars clustered thick as blackberries. They opened the door
  into the dark:
The murmurous haunt of flies on summer eves. Empty jamjars.
Mish-mash. Hotch-potch. And now you rub your eyes and get
  acquainted with the light
A dust of something reminiscent drowses over the garage smell of
  creosote,
The concrete: blue clouds in porcelain, a paint-brush steeped in a
  chipped cup;
Staples hyphenate a wet cardboard box as the upturned can of oil
  still spills
And the unfed cat toys with the yin-yang of a tennis-ball,
  debating whether *yes* is *no*.

GEORGE SZIRTES

FROM **Porch**

2. *The Japanese Hive*

But move beyond the porch, into the house
Where memory is paper thin, a series
Of partitions and bricked-up fireplaces.
Where are the dead men, gazing, pondering theories
Of lives beyond theirs, of our lives and spaces?
What have they left? The skeleton of a mouse,

the wasps' Japanese hive, fragile fontanelles
in the roof's skull, a piece of greaseproof paper
stretched across a blank pane, each one a taut
eardrum, listening. From these you must shape a
resonance that fits your head, a box of caught
echoes or photographs of names that ring bells.

Doors may be shut but a head lies open to
the sky which rains down crumpled streets and faces.
There are wheel tracks running all along the room.
Crowds are pressing down the hall. They leave traces
then they disappear, swept clear by the vast broom
that must be tidying, letting the wind through.

The Courtyards

1

As if a mind subsumed its intellect,
an ear tuned in to noise within the skull,
a mouth spoke words of greeting to a dull
audience of teeth, or an eye observed
the rigging of its fibres and the curved
elastic walls where images collect;

as if a street had turned its stately back
on public matters, and had found a way
of contemplating its own poverty,
had rattled up its years of emptiness
and counted them out on an abacus
of winding stairs, or on a curtain track;

the small lift shuts and forces itself up
a narrow throated shaft with groans of chains
and pulleys, and the whole building complains;
but as you rise through slices of pale light
the brown intensifies to cream, and white,
a trancelike ring of silence at the top.

2

Think of a glove turned neatly inside out;
think of your hand running along a rail
as children run down galleries grown stale
with refuse; think of hands reversed; of keys
and locks; think of these blocks as hollow trees
still echoing to something inchoate;

think of fear, precise as a clean hand
searching in dark corners, with the skill
that years of practice manage to instil;
think of locks where keys will never turn;
of rooms where it takes experts to discern
a movement that the eye can't understand:

The inchoate is what gets lost. You hear
a crazy woman singing,...*Tannenbaum,*
O tannenbaum...but then her words become
confused with curses, shouts of *God* and *Fate*,
and this is not exactly inchoate
but in such imprecision there is fear.

3

Outside, a rusticated, vermiform
ebullience; outside, a cluttering
of pediments, pilasters, pargeting,
embroidery; outside, the balconies
expand in their baroque epiphanies,
their splendid Biedermeyer uniforms;

outside, the casement windows under rolls
of stonework, rough or smooth or both; façades
with manners courtly as old playing cards;
outside, the straining figures stiffly bent
to hold up yet another pediment
disfigured by a web of bullet-holes;

outside, the falling masonry, the hard
emphatic counter-patterns of collapse,
the shattered panes and almost hingeless flaps
that bang like toy guns to disturb the dust.
Inside, the iron-work, the lines of rust;
inside, the piles of rubble in the yard.

4

Inside, the caretaker; his wife; his cat;
a cage for small bikes; rows of potted plants
reaching for light; stuff that no one wants
left in the stairwell; little dingy signs
for manicurists, tailors; heavy lines
of washing stretched out tight from flat to flat;

inside, a sort of life. At one o'clock
the ringing feet of children up the stair,
the scrape of chalk where someone scrawls a bare
diagrammatic girl with breasts like bells
and leaves a message in rough capitals;
inside, the noisy opening of locks.

Inside, I think of someone else, a blind
and aged woman treading the fourth floor
as if it were a jetty from a shore
suspended in a band of warming light.
She feels her way to the door opposite.
The hollow building trembles in her hand.

5

Think of an empty room with broken chairs,
a woman praying, someone looking out
and listening for someone else's shout
of vigilance; then think of a white face
covered with fine powder, bright as glass,
intently looking up the blinding stairs.

There's someone moving on a balcony;
there's someone running down a corridor;
there's someone falling, falling through a door,
and someone firmly tugging at the blinds.
Now think of a small child whom no one minds
intent on his own piece of anarchy:

Think of a bottle lobbing through the air
describing a tight arc – one curious puff –
then someone running, but not fast enough.
There's always someone to consider, one
you have not thought of, one who lies alone,
or hangs, debagged, in one more public square.

6

As if the light had quietly withdrawn
into a state of grace; as if the sun
had moved out to the country, or had gone
abroad; as if the shadows had grown old
and grey, or found their recesses too cold
and spread themselves across a civic lawn.

Then what is left? I see the woman grip
the handrail as she feels her way along.
She clutches fervently a ball of string,
an old steel key. She turns the corner, calls
to someone downstairs; and the steel key falls,
suspended like an odd metallic drip.

As if the past could ever lose its teeth:
As if the eye could swallow everything
and leave the world in darkness, blundering
about the courtyards! As if all the words
not spoken here could congregate like birds
and block out the faint noises from beneath!

7

Uncertainly she calls out from the top
of the thin stairs. The key won't fit the lock.
The key won't turn. The key is firmly stuck
inside the door. Then how to get up there
but run up every storey by the stair,
and hope she'll still be there when the stairs stop,

and hope she'll still be there when the stairs stop.

The Big Sleep

A perfect bubble of space floated above him.
A pool opened
At his feet and he dived in.
Eyes of glazed terracotta swam in dim
Wreaths in a building like a church. What had happened
To Marlowe? Some Mickey Finn

Been shot into his veins. The stillness froze
To further stillness,
The cold grew jaws.
A library like Michelangelo's
Stretched its long neck before him. A stewardess
Showed him through doors

Into a courtyard where the statues talked
In stern-sweet voices,
An orange tree
Fountained at the centre and a baby milked
Its mother's breast with gentle and precise
Movements while she

Glanced sadly up at him with the sea in her eyes.
You're doing fine
Marlowe. Now do
The difficult thing. Get up and walk. To his surprise
The ground stood firm, longing to be defined
By his feet, so he walked through

Into his own heart's aching and felt strong,
A youthful Marlowe
Full of clarity and hope
But something in his head was still wrong.
A woman's voice was crying through a window:
Europe! Europe!

MICHÈLE ROBERTS

The Return

This cathedral is God's
great whorled ear. Under
a roof of giant cockleshells
sung prayers stream
up, shoals of bright fish
flicking through water
over pebbles of stained glass.

This is my father's country
I've entered. This
is my father's house
– the Anglican one – I scorned:
its prim hats
and habits, its
grenadier parsons, its
teapot God.

I'm back, Dad! Your
prodigal daughter
in a shiny black mac
with my battered
heart, my suitcase of poems.

Sssh. There is a wedding
going on here
in a swarm of red
deaconesses
a roar of choirs.

My father leaps up
in the high space
and the mother I thought was lost
ricochets
round him. Strong
arches and vaults of flesh
enclose them. These
two make the sculptured air.
They are the architects. This
design is their dance.

I believe in the big ribbed boat
of the upturned church.
I believe in the body:
the house
the man and woman build
with the sweat of love.

New Year's Eve at Lavarone

The world is reversed. Gone into negative.
Pale monochrome of peaks, a white lid
on the lake, the valley newly scooped out
of white blocks then specked with brown
grains. Pines bristle thinly
on the mountain's flank. Each black branch
is lined exactly with white like cut plush.
White fur paws of spruce trees.

We push up into steep woods. Our toecaps
cut steps in the blank ramp ahead. Walls
of snow plot the curve of the vanished
track. What were meadows are now full
wedges of white we plough across, knee-deep.
Behind us, our scribbles on winter's diagram.
Under our boots, the creak of snow's broken
crust; below that, the rustle of layers of manuscript.

The forest's a palimpsest, a folk-tale.
Some of its actors' names we recover from
fragile prints: hare, squirrel, fox, goat.
Others we guess at: this white blot might be
a badger's sett. Here is a magic tree
ribbed solid with icicles, dripping
candles of water. Here are white logs
laid out like dead brides.

Our narrator, the man in the red woollen cap
leads us to the myth's heart. He scrapes with his
stick in a white dip, exposes a perfect circle
of glazed grey ice. He uncovers the mirror

of the mother, she who goes away
comes back, goes away. Her cold eye blinks
unblinks. Our kiss on her round mouth is chalk,
inscribes us on her body's blackboard: want, want.

Next March, he tells us, all
the whiteness of these hills
will loosen, will slide off
like a nightdress, like a shroud.

Lacrimae rerum

Another leak
in the lavatory roof
drip drip down the lightbulb.
I pissed in the dark, raindrops
smacking my shoulder-blades.

This morning I woke
to fresh wet birdsong
under a cloud of quilt
last night's hot sweetness
still fizzing between my legs.

I was fooled into swallowing spring
jumping up to make tea
and rinse dishes, whistle
a liquid kitchen oratorio.

It's your birthday next week.
This time next year
I think you'll be gone
quietly as this water
slipping over my hands.

After your funeral
we'll return
to your parched house.
We'll try to hold our mother up
like this exhausted roof.

I carry your dying
inside me
as real as milk

as I'll carry on
getting the roof fixed
making love
weeping into the washing-up.

GRACE NICHOLS

Abra-Cadabra

My mother had more magic
in her thumb
than the length and breadth
of any magician

Weaving incredible stories
around the dark-green senna brew
just to make us slake
the ritual Sunday purgative

Knowing how to place a cochineal poultice
on a fevered forehead
Knowing how to measure a belly's symmetry
kneading the narah pains away

Once my baby sister stuffed
a split-pea up her nostril
my mother got a crochet needle
and gently tried to pry it out

We stood around her
like inquisitive gauldings

Suddenly, in surgeon's tone she ordered,
'Pass the black pepper,'
and patted a little
under the dozing nose

My baby sister sneezed.
The rest was history.

Those Women

Cut and contriving women
hauling fresh shrimps
up in their seines

standing waist deep
in the brown voluptuous
water of their own element

how I remember those women
sweeping in the childish rivers
of my eyes

and the fish slipping
like eels
through their laughing thighs

Tropical Death

The fat black woman want
a brilliant tropical death
not a cold sojourn
in some North Europe far/forlorn

The fat black woman want
some heat/hibiscus at her feet
blue sea dress
to wrap her neat

The fat black woman want
some bawl
no quiet jerk tear wiping
a polite hearse withdrawal

The fat black woman want
all her dead rights
first night

third night
nine night
all the sleepless droning
red-eyed wake nights

In the heart
of her mother's sweetbreast
In the shade
of the sun leaf's cool bless
In the bloom
of her people's bloodrest

the fat black woman want
a brilliant tropical death yes

Walking with My Brother in Georgetown
(August 1984)

Dih city dying
dih trenches seem smaller
dih streets
dih houses
an everyting an everybody
look suh rundown
an stamp wid dih dry ah hunger

You been away too long girl
smile mih brudder

Dih city dying
we need a purging
new fires burning
some incense
dih sun too indifferent

You been away too long girl
smile mih brudder

An ah hearing dub-music blaring
An ah seeing dih man-youths rocking
Hypnosis on dih streets
Rocking to dih rhythm of dere own deaths
Locked in a shop-front beat

You been away too long girl
smile mih brudder

Dih city dying
we need new blooding
an boning
too many deaths unmourning
Jonestown, Walter
time like it ground still

Hibiscus blooming
People grooving
Girl, why yuh sehing dih city dying
Seh me brudder sighing

Maybe I lying
Maybe I dying.

My Northern-Sister

*(for the Finland-Swedish poet, Edith Södergran, 1892-1923,
who kept faith in her words despite the critics)*

Refusing the crown that would wreathe her as dumb,
my Northern-Sister comes, saying, 'It does not
become me to make myself less than I am.'

And she moves into forest
and she brings me out handfuls of snow,
a rugged fir,
a taste of wild-thyme,
which is only a taste of her own joyousness –
the fearless gates she keeps open,
including the one for death.

And she gives me heather and pine,
a taste of blue air,
the talking-memory of my own childhood trees,

Weaving a tender chemistry with her red
red heart.

And what have I got to give her?
Only the little thing she says
she always wanted –
a small letter, to be read on a garden bench
(near my hibiscus hedge)
with a cat in the sun.

Edith, my sister, come and sit down.

FRANK KUPPNER

FROM *A Bad Day for the Sung Dynasty*

69. *A Faded Inscription*
'Arriving very early I knocked vigorously on your door,
But an old lady from a window opposite told me
You were probably gone up the mountain to find a cool place
       to jerk off in;
Somewhat alarmed by her smile, I hurried away without waiting.'

* * *

242.
Delegated to decide which old poems should be kept,
And which destroyed, to lessen the excess baggage of time,
In a bad mood, hungover, he burns scroll after scroll,
Hugging his own works to his heart and crooning.

243.
Morosely he gazes at the old text in front of him;
What on earth is he to make of all those absurd squiggly lines?
Something sunlight something something laughter;
Happiness something something something she.

244.
Stolidly he ponders the old text in front of him;
Delight something buttocks pliant something;
Sunburst something buttocks something balcony;
He frowns at the girl noisily pouring out wine.

245.
In the open-air conclave of scholars he inspects his antique text:
Joy something wine something light something;
Something dancing something eyes something follow;
What is that idiot over there laughing about?

246.
Something something something hands something;
Something perhaps reaches something pineapple;
Better death something love her;
Something something something something giggling.

247.

Something breasts something something bosom;
Something bust something bosom something;
Breast something something caterpillar something;
A look of doubt crosses the old scholar's face.

248.

Death something decrepitude something annihilation;
Something something something rotting putrefaction;
Groans something something shrieks groans;
The old scholar makes a signal to the wine-girl.

249.

Something something something something something;
Something something something smiling something;
Something smiling something something something;
The old scholar finds himself involuntarily smiling.

FROM *The Autobiography of a Non-Existent Person*

XXVIII

So, the beloved person walks over to a window,
and takes a look out at a normal scene, containing
people, roads, vehicles, parts of other houses,
windows, items abandoned in a garden,

including several trees; the occasional wall;
the occasional distant running figure – and thinks,
'How odd, that one of the strangest of all sea-worms
is an animal whose body has roughly the size and shape

of a walnut – of an ordinary walnut –
but which has a proboscis roughly a metre in length.
It lives only in the Mediterranean Sea –
that is to say, in a hole in a rock in that sea –

that is to say: it secretes its walnut-body
in such an aperture, while its lithe proboscis
projects out of the hole, and sniffs around,
searching for food in the immediate environment.

This description applies only to the female.
For many years, scientists were quite unable,
despite intensive research, to find the male.
They had a shrewd idea he must be somewhere –

and indeed, somewhere he was. And where was that?
It was discovered that, inside the female,
there floated tiny comma-shaped individuals.
It has been established that these, without much doubt,

are in fact the males. Bonellia viridis
is, I think, the scientific name for this organism.'
Thinking which, she shuts the window, and observes
the scene continue through glass. Inside her body

numberless societies of living transients
are born, flourish, and die. That subtle smile
has some influence there, but not too much.
In fact, to be honest, practically none.

Anyway, forty years pass, and she is walking
at 23 minutes to eleven in the morning,
past a building scheduled to be demolished,
though as yet she does not know that. Shall she ever?

Or look at this same building from a different view.
From here we cannot see her. And, needless to say,
we do not miss her. All the which time, swarms
of bacteria – or organisms which I

in my ignorance call bacteria – live, die,
split up, live, die, inside the various
divisions of her substance. At the moment,
she is on the way to visit an outlying daughter.

I do not say that this is the woman I love.
I do not say that that is the woman I love.
I do not even claim that anybody loves them.
But I ask you to tell me what else love might be.

                              *   *   *

XXXIV

A pleasant morning. The trees rustle as usual.
If I were alive, is this where I would choose
to be? There is space enough; there is laughter enough.
Even the rooms which are unoccupied
seem, somehow, to be occupied. But, if the chance
had not been missed, what would I have grown into?

Into a fish, perhaps, too stupid to know
it needs to come to the surface of the water
to breathe – which, when it felt the need of air,
drifts towards warmth; and, since the warmer water ·
lies at the surface, manages to survive
until it strays within the power of beings
intelligent enough to provide it with
a tank, artificially heated at
the base! In which case, it sinks to the bottom,
finds its required warmth, and asphyxiates.

Perhaps we are all such fishes anyway.
And could our warm air be love? Finding it,
we sink to the bottom and asphyxiate.
But would the asphyxiation then teach us
how overrated was breathing? What does it matter.

I climbed out of bed, with the strange self-confidence
so typical of the merely potential; took up
the unremarkable, dark blue, ill-used book
from its place on the floor, where I had dropped it, on
the previous evening, and continued reading
a list of the marvels of the animal kingdom,
including, of course, plants. 'Nature' it opined
'is stranger than fiction.'
                              Previously, I had
– on preceding days – always agreed with this;
but by now I had frankly lost interest. Who cares
about these prodigies? Only the utterly boring
exist here. A mug casually abandoned
on a table (which ought to have been cleared away,
but wasn't) seems to me in my present mood
far more remarkable than the fact that fish

do not drink water – or, at the very least,
pretend not to. An unhappy, weeping woman,
in the middle of another long grey featureless night,
intermittently masturbating to relieve
the emotional pressure being put upon her,
is far more lovely than the three-toed sloth
hanging upside down from branches, with its fur
a greenish tint thanks to the operation
of symbiotic algae. Even when she stops,
lets her green-coloured nightie slip back down
below her navel, turns over on her stomach,
and begs to be abused with a few branches
which lie scattered about the bedroom, the fact
that a snail is at the partition wall, bending
round the corner its eyes on their long stalks,
and chuckling to itself at our stupidity,
does not impress me as much as her sudden anecdote
about her father. Let the starfish wave
an eye at the end of each of its arms, in seas
which have no conception of dry land; let the ants
enslave 600 other different species
and convince them they are on this earth to benefit
ants; and let her mother – yes, even that
incredible form of life, try to convince her
that she is a fool to put up with the sort of treatment
that I *inflict* on her – what do we care
for the occasional blind passer-by,
we who gather stars each night, exploding, cooling,
condensing, forming, blaring out with incredible
light, plundering the starlit sky, until it
is almost as dark, almost as mysterious,
almost as deep, almost as promising,
and almost as impossible as that there.
Oh, you do not see it; but I see it.
I see it. I see it. I see it. I see it. I see it.

CHARLES BOYLE

The Chess Player

I'm thinking of a famous grandmaster
on the sixteenth floor of a hotel in Bucharest,
kept awake by the gypsy music
of a wedding party downstairs.

I'm seeing him watch from his window
some cleaning women emerge
in the sodium-lit small hours
from the national exhibition centre,
and the rails from the station stretching
towards the vanishing point of asylum.

When at last he falls asleep
to the strains of the last violin,
he dreams fitfully
of a lady with a parasol
stepping out on the first marble square
of a black and white chequered piazza.

His task is to guide her across
to the shade of the colonnade
before history takes over,
before the city lies in ruins.

The light is hot and even
and, like the Pyramids when they were built,
the stones are so perfectly cut
a knife blade couldn't slip between them.

[1988]

A Tour of the Holy Land

In this city, the taxi drivers have a grim sense of humour
and drive too fast. They look at you, not the road,
in the rear-view mirror. They tell you their woes
in lurid, neon tones, sparing nobody, and expect yours
to be at least as bad. They wind down the window
to spit out phlegm and cigar butts and to shout at girls,
but you are already two blocks away before you can put a name
to the face of the one who, waiting to cross, has tied your heart
in a knot.
          Amanda. Miranda. Their names are the names of streets
that lead unerringly to an angle of shadow
on the Indian bedspread, or a small bottle containing bluish liquid
rolling along the dresser top until only the moment
keeps it from falling. Like a sultry, pouting mouth
that is about to ask for the loo but just might,
just because it is so unexpected, be about to reveal
some notorious truth – how else explain the countenance
of one who, simply by entering your field of vision,
excites your interest? But you cannot just barge across
and ask for the meaning of life on a plate, because the big words
are timid, are terrified of zoos, they have gone into hiding
somewhere between the library books and the worry about supper
and feeding the plants... 'Have you ever,' one asks,
'been here before?' And so the game of hunt-the-thimble begins
without benefit even of names, for the host is not formal.

No wonder the tourists have to check their map
at every corner. A sullen wind almost tears it from them
but they have high hopes of the alleyways tucked in behind,
the markets you could stroll in on weekday afternoons
when there's nothing on TV, when the weather is better
than it has been these past years... The Gateway to Adventure
is not a ruined inn where Columbus slept but a cracked
gutter or a pool of oily rainwater or the sight
of a restaurant fascia that sets your memory reeling backwards
from the shock of recognition: and no time is allowed
to adjust the focus and snap the shutter, for the city
is in the throes of major reconstruction.

                                                  The farmlands
are receding, the milk-churn a pinprick of light
that continues to glow, faintly, after the current
has been switched off. It seems only yesterday you phoned
from that kiosk, yet children have grown to adults
in the night between. Even the cathedral is sinking
by so many inches a year into the mire, terminal mites
are eating its heart out – and when the pumping
machines have stopped and the last phalanx of scaffolding
has been dismantled, what will greet us, then, in the proverbial
light of dawn? Or when, years later, the taxi drops you
at the block where she lived? Not, surely, the object of faith,
though the stained glass windows may retain at least some
of the original blue... The driver says something
you don't catch, or something so extraordinary you must
have misheard. It's too early to say. You count the change
and enter the lobby. The lift is a tiny cage – almost you forget
which button to press, see hers with another's initials
scratched on the panelling, begin to wonder
whether it's all been a terrible mistake. Other versions
have the bottle empty and not rolling but thrown; it broke
and you cut your hands, but that too may be a childhood incident
you have been told of so often you have come to believe in.

Frog Prince

Am I good or bad, clever or stupid?
Stendhal asks himself
in the summer of 1832.

A life of falling in love and off horses...
Carriage wheels on cobbles, a rattle
of distant muskets: it's half past one

in the morning and already too hot to think
or sleep, yet eleven hundred pretty women a year –
he has seen the official statistics –

leaving the ballrooms of Paris at dawn
are catching colds from which they die.
Meanwhile the Duke of Frioul

at the age of thirty-eight – 'the age when,'
as Stendhal himself remarks, 'if one is disillusioned,
boredom begins to appear on the horizon' –

is strolling about, alone and slightly drunk,
in the gloom of the Palais Royal gardens,
where a boy is catching frogs

for the knife of Dr Edwards, an Englishman,
who seeks a cure for the women's complaint
and to discover how we breathe.

Cairo's Poor

Older than stone, older than any politics
and still with us, the parched Nile's flood
squatting fifteen to a room in Cairo's slums.

There are streets the sun won't touch,
I'm foreign as the sun. Stoned out of mind
in this crazy town, breathing jasmine

with the fumes, you move into the dark:
these hard and gentle faces, their daughters'
brief allure... At the Café Riche

they come at you, selling beads and flowers
and plastic belts – where I am talking
with Mr Mohammed Ebrahim Abdel Hamin, M.Sc.,

a kind of English: 'The poor – how you say it? –
they are old hat. All Egypt is excited
by her bright commercial future.'

NUALA NÍ DHOMHNAILL

An Crann

Do tháinig bean an leasa
le *Black & Decker*,
do ghearr sí anuas mo chrann.
D'fhanas im óinseach ag féachaint uirthi
faid a bhearraigh sí na brainsí
ceann ar cheann.

Tháinig m'fhear céile abhaile tráthnóna.
Chonaic sé an crann.
Bhí an gomh dearg air,
ní nach ionadh. Dúirt sé
'Canathaobh nár stopais í?
Nó cad is dóigh léi?
Cad a cheapfadh sí
dá bhfaighinnse *Black & Decker*
is dul chun a tí
agus crann ansúd a bhaineas léi,
a ghearradh anuas sa ghairdín?'

Tháinig bean an leasa thar n-ais ar maidin.
Bhíos fós ag ithe mo bhricfeasta.
D'iarr sí orm cad dúirt m'fhear céile.
Dúrtsa léi cad dúirt sé,
is cad a cheap fadh sí
dá bhfaigheadh sé siúd *Black & Decker*
is dul chun a tí
is crann ansúd a bhaineas léi
a ghearradh anuas sa ghairdín.

'Ó,' ar sise, '*that's very interesting.*'
Bhí béim ar an *very*.
Bhí cling leis an -*ing*.
Do labhair sí ana-chiúin.

Bhuel, b'shin mo lá-sa,
pé ar bith sa tsaol é,
iontaithe bunoscionn.

As for the Quince

There came this bright young thing
with a Black & Decker
and cut down my quince tree.
I stood with my mouth hanging open
while one by one
she trimmed off the branches.

When my husband got home that evening
and saw what had happened
he lost the rag,
as you might imagine.
'Why didn't you stop her?
What would she think
if I took the Black & Decker
round to her place
and cut down a quince tree
belonging to her?
What would she make of that?'

Her ladyship came back next morning
while I was at breakfast.
She enquired about his reaction.
I told her straight
that he was wondering how she'd feel
if he took a Black & Decker
round to her house
and cut down a quince tree of hers,
et cetera et cetera.

'O,' says she, 'that's very interesting.'
There was a stress on the 'very'.
She lingered over the 'ing'.
She was remarkably calm and collected.

These are the times that are in it, so,
all a bit topsy-turvy.
The bottom falling out of my belly

Thit an tóin as mo bholg
is faoi mar a gheobhainn lascadh cic
nó leacadar sna baotháin
líon taom anbhainne isteach orm
a dhein chomh lag san mé
gurb ar éigin a bhí ardú na méire ionam
as san go ceann trí lá.

Murab ionann is an crann
a dh'fhan ann, slán.

Ceist na Teangan

Cuirim mo dhóchas ar snámh
i mbáidín teangan
faoi mar a leagfá naíonán
i gcliabhán
a bheadh fite fuaite
de dhuilleoga feileastraim
is bitiúman agus pic
bheith cuimilte lena thóin

ansan é leagadh síos
i measc na ngiolcach
is coigeal na mban sí
le taobh na habhann,
féachaint n'fheadaraís
cá dtabharfaidh an sruth é,
féachaint, dála Mhaoise,
an bhfóirfidh iníon Fharoinn?

as if I had got a kick up the arse
or a punch in the kidneys.
A fainting-fit coming over me
that took the legs from under me
and left me so zonked
I could barely lift a finger
till Wednesday.

As for the quince, it was safe and sound
and still somehow holding its ground.

[translated from the Irish by Paul Muldoon]

The Language Issue

I place my hope on the water
in this little boat
of the language, the way a body might put
an infant

in a basket of intertwined
iris leaves,
its underside proofed
with bitumen and pitch,

then set the whole thing down amidst
the sedge
and bulrushes by the edge
of a river

only to have it borne hither and thither,
not knowing where it might end up;
in the lap, perhaps,
of some Pharaoh's daughter.

[translated from the Irish by Paul Muldoon]

Féar Suaithinseach

Nuair a bhís i do shagart naofa
i lár an Aifrinn, faoi do róbaí corcra
t'fhallaing lín, do stól, do chasal,
do chonnaicis m'aghaidhse ins an slua
a bhí ag teacht chun comaoineach chughat
is thit uait an abhlainn bheannaithe.
Mise, ní dúrt aon ní ina thaobh.
Bhí náire orm.
Bhí glas ar mo bhéal.
Ach fós do luigh sé ar mo chroí
mar dhealg láibe, gur dhein sé slí
dó fhéin istigh im ae is im lár
gur dhóbair go bhfaighinn bás dá bharr.

Ní fada nó gur thiteas 'on leabaidh;
oideasaí leighis do triaileadh ina gcéadtaibh,
do tháinig chugham dochtúirí, sagairt is bráithre
is n'fhéadadar mé a thabhairt chun sláinte
ach thugadar suas i seilbh bháis mé.

Is téigí amach, a fheara,
tugaíg libh rámhainn is speala
corráin, grafáin is sluaiste.
Réabaíg an seanafhothrach,
bearraíg na sceacha, glanaíg an luifearnach,
an slámas fáis, an brus, an ainnise
a fhás ar thalamh bán mo thubaiste.

Is ins an ionad inar thit
an chomaoine naofa féach go mbeidh
i lár an bhiorlamais istigh
toirtín d'fhéar suaithinseach.

Tagadh an sagart is lena mhéireanna
beireadh sé go haiclí ar an gcomaoine naofa
is tugtar chugham í, ar mo theanga
leáfaidh sí, is éireod aniar sa leaba
chomh slán folláin is a bhíos is mé mo leanbh.

Miraculous Grass

There you were in your purple vestments
half-way through the Mass, an ordained priest
under your linen alb and chasuble and stole:
and when you saw my face in the crowd
for Holy Communion
the consecrated host fell from your fingers.

I felt shame, I never
mentioned it once,
my lips were sealed.
But still it lurked in my heart
like a thorn under mud, and it
worked itself in so deep and sheer
it nearly killed me.

Next thing then, I was laid up in bed.
Consultants came in their hundreds,
doctors and brothers and priests,
but I baffled them all: I was
incurable, they left me for dead.

So out you go, men,
out with the spades and scythes,
the hooks and shovels and hoes.
Tackle the rubble,
cut back the bushes, clear off the rubbish,
the sappy growth, the whole straggle and mess
that infests my green unfortunate field.

And there where the sacred wafer fell
you will discover
in the middle of the shooting weeds
a clump of miraculous grass.

The priest will have to come then
with his delicate fingers, and lift the host
and bring it to me and put it on my tongue.
Where it will melt, and I will rise in the bed
as fit and well as the youngster I used to be.

[translated from the Irish by Seamus Heaney]

HARRY CLIFTON

Office of the Salt Merchant

Once in a while,
I have wished to see more than the head
Of that girl who smiles,
Disembodied, behind blood-red

Service hatches...
I wanted her hands,
From which a visiting merchant detaches
Yellow and white invoices, to extend,

As if in kindness to myself,
Pale salt in graded rows
Of crucibles along the empty shelf
Of the sales window,

Where I might see the atmosphere change
Her anaemic samples
As I did before, and stay once more in the range
Of a common example.

Monsoon Girl

In the airconditioned drone
Of a room we rent by the hour,
You go to the telephone,
Lovely and naked, to put through a call
For drinks, or hire a car
To take us home.

Your nudity dapples the walls
With shadows, and splashes the mirrors
Like a vision, in the blue light
That bathes you, a pleasure-girl
On a lost planet, sincere
But only at night.

Outside, it will rain
For weeks, months on end...
We'll come here again
As we did before, where Chinese women,
Blank and inscrutable, attend
Nightly to our linen.

We'll come again
In drunkenness, for the child's play
Of lovemaking, or to part the rain
Like curtains of jet beads,
And dream the rainy months away
On pampered beds

Where forgetfulness lies down
With executive power
After hours, in a tangle of legs
And juices, a world turned upside down,
And I feed on the lotus-flower
Of your delicate sex.

At three, we'll be driven back
Through depths of Bangkok
Already tomorrow. There will be roads
Closed, and a dope squad
Flashing its query through windowglass,
Letting us pass...

There will be lights
In Chinatown, sampans on the river —
The poor starting early. Elsewhere the night
Will separate us, having seeded within you
Miscarriage of justice forever,
And the rain will continue.

The Desert Route

Exempted from living, abandoned
To some infinite fascination he has
With a gentle goat by a wall,
Here where the trade routes start

The idiot sits, clad in the cast-offs
Of a town full of tailors,
Unembarrassed
By any such thing as self.

Around him in chaos, preparations
For the desert... camels genuflecting
To necessity, loaded with iron bedsteads,
Struggling to rise; and donkeys

With lank, hopeless penises,
Jesuit eyes,
Marking time.
                    In time they all set out,
Like free beings, across a desert

He will never go through again, relieved
Of space and time
To be lost in. Doesn't even notice
How everything still moves outwards

To the same end...the camel trains,
The slow asphalting-gangs
On the superhighway, laying down
Lines of purpose, almost merging

At times, almost parallel,
Except at the border, where a soldier
With three stripes, wishing himself elsewhere
Is waving the landrovers on...

HELEN DUNMORE

Sisters leaving before the dance

Sisters leaving before the dance,
before the caller gets drunk
or the yellow streamers unreel
looping like ribbons
here and there on the hair of the dancers,

sisters at the turn of the stairs
as the sound system
one-twos, as the squeezebox
mewed in its case

is slapped into breath, and that scrape
of the tables shoved back for the dance
burns like the strike of a match
in the cup of two hands.
Ripe melons and meat

mix in the binbags with cake
puddled in cherry-slime, wind
heavy with tar
blows back the yard door, and I'm

caught with three drinks in my hands
on the stairs looking up
at the sisters leaving before the dance,
not wishing to push past them
in their white broderie anglaise and hemmed

skirts civilly drawn
to their sides to make room
for the big men in suits,
and the girls in cerise

dance-slippers and cross-backed dresses
who lead the way up
and take charge of the tickets, and yet
from their lips canteloupe
fans as they speak

in bright quick murmurs between
a violin ghosting a tune
and the kids in the bar downstairs
begging for Coke, peaky but certain.

The sisters say their *good nights*
and all the while people stay bunched
on the stairs going up, showing respect
for the small words of the ones leaving,
the ones who don't stay for the dancing.

One sister twists a white candle
waxed in a nest of hydrangeas –
brick-red and uncommon, flowers
she really can't want – she bruises the limp

warm petals with crisp fingers
and then poises her sandal
over the next non-slip stair
so the dance streams at her heels
in the light of a half-shut door.

The sea skater

A skater comes to this blue pond,
his worn Canadian skates
held by the straps.

He sits on the grass
lacing stiff boots
into a wreath of effort and breath.

He tugs at the straps and they sound
as ice does when weight troubles it
and cracks bloom around stones

creaking in quiet mid-winter
mid-afternoons: a fine time for a skater.
He knows it and gauges the sun
to see how long it will be safe to skate.

Now he hisses and spins in jumps
while powder ice clings to the air
but by trade he's a long-haul skater.

Little villages, stick-like in the cold,
offer a child or a farm-worker
going his round. These watch him
go beating onward between iced alders
seawards, and so they picture him
always smoothly facing forward, foodless and waterless,
mounting the crusted waves on his skates.

Dancing man

That lake lies along the shore
like a finger down my cheek,

its waters lull and collapse
dark as pomegranates,

the baby crawls on the straw
in the shadow-map of his father's chair

while the priest talks things over
and light dodges across his hair.

There's a lamp lit in the shed
and a fire on, and a man drinking

spiritus fortis he's made for himself.
But on the floor of the barn

the dancing man is beginning to dance.
First a beat from the arch of his foot

as he stands upright, a neat
understatement of all that's in him

and he lowers his eyes to her
as if it's nothing, nothing –

but she has always wanted him.
Her baby crawls out from the chairs

and rolls in his striped vest laughing
under the feet of the dancers

so she must dance over him
toe to his cheek, heel to his hair,

as she melts to the man dancing.
They are talking and talking over there –

the priest sits with his back to her
for there's no malice in him

and her husband glistens like the sun
through the cypress-flame of the man dancing.

In the shed a blackbird
has left three eggs which might be kumquats –

they are so warm. One of them's stirring –
who said she had deserted them?

In the orchard by the barn
there are three girls wading,

glossy, laughing at something,
they spin a bucket between them,

glowing, they are forgotten –
something else is about to happen.

DAVID HARTNETT

The Fleece

We went to the hovel of the midnight shearer
And lay together, naked, on a wooden board.
Swiftly his sharp-toothed comb skimmed and whirred
Peeling back the fleece our love had grown
Until it dropped away, limp in the straw,
Still warm from us, a loosened milky gown,
Though brambles snagged and blood-spots dabbed the wool.
I saw him knead its softness to a roll.
Then through wicket gates to a dark field
Weightless, we ran and lay together, numb.
Prickling stars of sweat our skins bristled
Until, wherever limb brushed against limb,
A luminous froth uncurled, shivered into flame.
By dawn what fleece had clothed us, new or old?

Two Winters

I was watching as my father shovelled snow
Outside the house we lived in years ago
And, mourning the furrowed white, had started calling
Stop through the glass when he vanished. Snow was still falling

As we went, my son (this palm a small hand's sheath),
On your first winter walk. Our mouths smoked breath
And coiled it in wreaths for a statue of boy Pan
Peeping from his cloak of flakes, his caked pipes frozen.

A boy (I said) *once dreamed snow fell for years*
Till houses and gardens were gone and the rays of stars
*Like birds' feet flecked the white...*then stroked stone curls:
You had slipped my grasp. Your firm prints faded miles.

Then, as the teeming air milled on the land,
I felt a shovel's weight ghosting my hand –
From the house my father was mouthing as if to shout,
The shovel grew feathersoft, hollow as a flute.

House of Moon

In the house of moon he is still eating breakfast
In vest and braces, bent above the steam
From his porridge's whorled andromeda of sugar –
And, for the child who laughs, stroking white bristles
I've never seen anything like it in all my puff.

In the house of moon she is still lighting the fire
Knelt at its pyre of wood and crumpled paper,
Her fingers splaying the flames like orange velvet –
And, for the child who gasps, fingering plaits
That flick her waist: *It doesn't hurt anymore.*

House of moon you begin where the landing ends
Or up in the attic or underneath the stairs –
Your doors are always open and never lead me
To the whispering blind man shrunk in his last ward
Or the crematorium drapes drawn on her coffin.

LINTON KWESI JOHNSON

Mekkin Histri

now tell mi someting
mistah govahment man
tell mi someting

how lang yu really feel
yu coulda keep wi andah heel
wen di trute done reveal
bout how yu grab an steal
bout how yu mek yu crooked deal
mek yu crooked deal?

well doun in Soutall
where Peach did get fall
di Asians dem faam-up a human wall
gense di fashist an dem police sheil
an dem show dat di Asians gat plenty zeal
                              gat plenty zeal
                              gat plenty zeal

it is noh mistri
wi mekkin histri
it is noh mistri
wi winnin victri

now tell mi someting
mistah police spokesman
tell mi someting

how lang yu really tink
wi woulda tek yu batn lick
yu jackboot kick
yu dutty bag a tricks
an yu racist pallyticks
yu racist pallyticks?

well doun in Bristal
dey ad noh pistal
but dem chaste di babylan away
man yu shoulda si yu babylan
how dem really run away
yu shoulda si yu babylan dem dig-up dat day
                             dig-up dat day
                             dig-up dat day

it is noh mistri
wi mekkin histri
it is noh mistri
wi winnin victri

now tell mi someting
mistah ritewing man
tell mi someting

how lang yu really feel
wi woulda grovel an squeal
wen soh much murdah canceal
wen wi woun cyaan heal
wen wi feel di way wi feel
feel di way wi feel?

well dere woz Toxteth
an dere woz Moss Side
an a lat a addah places
whey di police ad to hide
well dare woz Brixtan
an dere woz Chapeltoun
an a lat a addah place dat woz burnt to di groun
                             burnt to di groun
                             burnt to di groun

it is noh mistri
wi mekkin histri
it is noh mistri
wi winnin victri

Bass Culture
(for Big Yout)

1

muzik of blood
black reared
pain rooted
heart geared

all tensed up
in di bubble an di bounce
an di leap an di weight-drop

it is di beat of di heart
this pulsing of blood
that is a bubblin bass
a bad bad beat
pushin gainst di wall
whey bar black blood

an is a whole heappa
passion a gather
like a frightful form
like a righteous harm
giving off wild like is madness

2

BAD OUT DEY

3

hotta dan di hites of fire
livin heat doun volcano core
is di cultural wave a dread people deal

spirits riled
an rise an rail thunda-wise
latent powa
in a form resemblin madness
like violence is di show
burstin outta slave shackle
look ya! boun fi harm di wicked

man feel
him hurt confirm
man site
destruction all aroun
man turn
love still confirm
him destiny a shine lite-wise
soh life tek the form whey shiff from calm
an hold di way of a deadly storm

5

culture pulsin
high temperature blood
swingin anger
shattering di tightened hold
the false fold
round flesh whey wail freedom
bitta cause a blues
cause a maggot suffering
cause a blood klaat pressure
yet still breedin love
far more mellow
than di soun of shapes
chanting loudly

6

SCATTA-MATTA-SHATTA-SHACK!
what a beat!

7

for di time is nigh
when passion gather high
when di beat jus lash
when di wall mus smash
an di beat will shiff
as di culture alltah
when oppression scatta

Inglan Is a Bitch

w'en mi jus' come to Landan toun
mi use to work pan di andahgroun
but workin' pan di andahgroun
y'u don't get fi know your way aroun'

Inglan is a bitch
dere's no escapin' it
Inglan is a bitch
dere's no runnin' whey fram it

mi get a lickle jab in a big 'otell
an' awftah a while, mi woz doin' quite well
dem staat mi aaf as a dish-washah
but w'en mi tek a stack, mi noh tun clack-watchah!

Inglan is a bitch
dere's no escapin it
Inglan is a bitch
noh baddah try fi hide fram it

w'en dem gi' yu di lickle wage packit
fus dem rab it wid dem big tax racket
y'u haffi struggle fi mek en's meet
an' w'en y'u goh a y'u bed y'u jus' cant sleep

Inglan is a bitch
dere's no escapin' it
Inglan is a bitch fi true
a noh lie mi a tell, a true

mi use to work dig ditch w'en it cowl noh bitch
mi did strang like a mule, but, bwoy, mi did fool
den awftah a while mi jus' stap dhu ovahtime
den awftah a while mi jus' phu dung mi tool

Inglan is a bitch
dere's no escapin' it
Inglan is a bitch
y'u haffi know how fi suvvive in it

well mi dhu day wok an' mi dhu nite wok
mi dhu clean wok an' mi dhu dutty wok
dem seh dat black man is very lazy
but if y'u si how mi wok y'u woulda seh mi crazy

Inglan is a bitch
dere's no escapin' it
Inglan is a bitch
y'u bettah face up to it

dem have a lickle facktri up inna Brackly
inna disya facktri all dem dhu is pack crackry
fi di laas fifteen years dem get mi laybah
now awftah fifteen years mi fall out a fayvah

Inglan is a bitch
dere's no escapin' it
Inglan is a bitch
dere's no runnin' whey fram it

mi know dem have work, work in abundant
yet still, dem mek mi redundant
now, at fifty-five mi gettin' quite ol'
yet still, dem sen' mi fi goh draw dole

Inglan is a bitch
dere's no escapin' it
Inglan is a bitch fi true
is whey wi a goh dhu 'bout it?

Reality Poem

dis is di age af reality
but some a wi a deal wid mitalagy
dis is di age of science an' teknalagy
but some a wi a check fi antiquity

w'en wi cyaan face reality
whey wi dhu?

wi leggo wi clarity
some latch aan to vanity
some hole insanity
some get vizshan
start preach relijan
but dem cyaan mek decishan
w'en it come to wi fite
dem cyaan mek decishan
w'en it come to wi rites

man,
dis is di age af reality
but some a wi a deal wid mitalagy
dis is di age af science an' teknalagy
but some a wi a check fi antiquity

dem one deh gaan outta line
dem naw live in fi wi time
far dem seh dem get sine
an' dem bline dem eye
to di lite a di worl'
an' gaan search widin
di dark a dem doom
an' a shout 'bout sin
instead a fite fi win

man,
dis is di age af reality
but some a wi a deal wid mitalagy
dis is di age af science an' teknalagy
but some a wi a check fi antiquity

dis is di age af decishan
soh mek wi leggo relijan
dis is di age af decishan
soh mek wi leggo divishan
dis is di age af reality
soh mek wi leggo mitalagy
dis is di age af science an' teknalagy
soh mek wi hol' di clarity
mek wi hol' di clarity
mek wi hol' di clarity

SEAN O'BRIEN

After Laforgue
(in memory of Martin Bell)

I have put a blockade on high-mindedness.
All night, through dawn and dead mid-morning,
Rain is playing rimshots on a bucket in the yard.
The weatherman tells me that winter comes on
As if he'd invented it. Fuck him.

Fuck sunshine and airports and pleasure.
Wind is deadheading the lilacs inland.
You know what this means. I could sing.
The weekend sailors deal the cards and swear.
The Channel is closed. This is good.

In the sopping, padlocked, broad-leaved shade of money
Desperate lunches are cooking
In time for the afternoon furies and sudden
Divorces of debt from the means of production.
Good also. These counties are closed.

Myself, I imagine the north in its drizzle,
Its vanished smoke, exploded chimneys: home
In bad weather to hills of long hospitals, home
To the regional problems of number, home
To sectarian strife in the precincts of Sheffield and Hartlepool,

Home from a world of late-liberal distraction
To rain and tenfoots clogged with leaves,
To the life's work of boredom and waiting,
The bus-station's just-closing teabar,
The icy, unpromising platforms of regional termini,

Home to dead docks and the vandalised showhouse.
Home for Mischief Night and Hallowe'en, their little tales,
When the benches (the sodden repose of old bastards in dog-smelling
        overcoats)
Vanish, when council employees dragged from the pub
Will be dragging the lake in the park,

Watching their footprints fill up
And hating those whose bastard lives
Are bastard lived indoors. Home,
As Sunday extends towards winter, a shivery kiss
In a doorway, *Songs of Praise*, last orders. Home.

Rain, with an angel's patience, remind me.
This is not the world of Miss Selfridge and Sock Shop,
Disposable income and lycra, illiterate hearsay
And just-scraping-in-after-Clearing to Business in Farnham.
This world is not Eastbourne. It has no opinions.

In this world it rains and the winter
Is always arriving – rebirth of TB
And *The Sporting Green* sunk to the drainbed.
Here is the stuff that gets left in the gaps
Between houses – ambitious settees in black frogskin

And minibars missing their castors, the catalogues
Turning to mush, the unnameable objects
That used to be something with knobs on,
And now they live here, by the siding, the fishhouse,
The building whose function is no longer known.

It is Londesborough Street with the roof gone –
That smell as the wallpaper goes, as it rains
On the landing, on pot dogs and photos
And ancient assumptions of upright servility.
Nothing is dry. The pillow-tick shivers

And water comes up through the scullery tiles
And as steam from the grate. There are funerals
Backed up the street for a mile
As the gravediggers wrestle with pumps and the vicar
Attempts to hang on to his accent.

Rain, with an angel's patience, teach me
The lesson of where I came in once again,
With icy vestibules and rubber pillows,
The dick-nurse, the wet-smelling ash in the yard
And the bleary top deck like a chest-ward.

Teach me the weather will always be worsening,
With the arctic fleet behind it –
The subject of talk in the shop, at the corner,
Or thought of when stepping out into the yard
To the sirens of factories and pilot-boats,

There like a promise, the minute at nightfall
When rain turns to snow and is winter.

A Corridor
(for Henry Katz)

The shoulder-high tiles in municipal green,
The brown walls, the bare lavatorial floor
Which is always about to be damp,
The heavy swing doors we shall not
Be exploring today; the long view
We are taking this late afternoon –
Whose end is obscure
With November indoors, it would seem –
In the fifties, when we were much smaller
And quickly impressed by the minor displays
Of the State which would aim us
From cradle to grave, you remember:
All this we inherit, a corridor
Built by the Irish for God and the Queen.

We trap our germs in handkerchiefs.
We do not spit when on the bus.
Out where the city once turned into fields
Are prefabs growing permanent:
To each its patch of grass, from each a vote.
And here where the corridor turns in a fury of echoes
My father is leaving the party for nowhere,
The intimate cell where the struggle is waged
Over doughnuts in Lyons, the afternoons hung
With sheets of Players, the talk of betrayal.
It's what lies before us when we are too old
To be sure – which was never his problem.
The problems he had were the world

And his terrible spelling, I'm told.
They have rolled up the speeches, the grass from the park
After Mayday and stored them in here.

Behind the baize door a committee
Is handing the scholarships out –
A régime of deaf butchers and bandit accountants
Rewarded for lifetimes of ignorance,
Waiting to get our names wrong.
In the clinic a sinister lady
Will study my feet and insist
I can reach the trapeze.
My grandfather wheels a dead man
To the morgue for a pittance
And votes the wrong way as a duty
To something the next war was meant to disprove.
We vanish to Mafeking, Simla,
The moth-eaten middle of Ireland
Where Marx is a nightmare
That God isn't having
And people like us are a gleam of prolepsis
In somebody's eye – the well-meaning
Impotent heirs to the corridor,
Pacing it out past the dinner-money's chink,
Cries from the dentist and telephones nobody answers,
Incompetent dreaming, corrupt and forgetful,
The cellars of pamphlets for futures
That nobody lived. This is ours. Keep walking.

Fiction and the Reading Public

You read, and then you go to sleep:
That's work's permission to be dead.
And while you sleep you watch them pulp
Whole libraries you have not read.

They make you read what money writes,
A thing left in a carriage,
Spine unbroken, loud with secrets,
Five Ways to Wreck Your Marriage...

Dexter had to give up reading –
Lulu said it wasted time
When he could give himself to money.
Dexter planned the perfect crime.

Dexter stunned her with a bundle
Of old *Partisan Reviews*.
The arm discovered in Death Valley
Livened up the evening news.

If Lulu stands for capital
And Dexter stands for wit,
If Lulu's in the mortuary
And Dexter's deep in shit,

Then what's required is a book –
Psychosis in a Trailer!
Someone put the money up
And sent for Norman Mailer.

Mailer worked on it for hours.
The plans he made were vast,
And though in fact no text appeared
He spent the money fast.

When Dex said, Norm, I'd love to read
My life before I vanish,
Mailer shrugged, I'm sorry, Dex,
I just can't seem to finish:

My novel need not terminate
Because its hero fries.
Remember, fiction's *fictional*,
And therefore never dies.

When Dexter hung his head and cried,
But Norman, wait a minute:
What kind of story stays alive
Without the hero in it?

Mailer punched the grille and said,
You've got me beaten, Jack.
Go shoot the Pope. Read Wittgenstein.
But just get off my back.

Of that of which I cannot speak
I am condemned to silence,
Plus *you're* condemned, let's not forget,
For readership with violence.

As Mailer left, he did not mourn
The book he had not made:
He only muttered to a guard
That art had been betrayed.

They came to Dexter on Death Row
And asked his final need,
And Dexter said, I don't suppose
There's anything to read?

They brought him *Fonda's Workout Book*
And *How to be a Sucker.*
Here Dex, these ought to shut you up,
Pretentious little fucker.

Somebody Else

In fact you are secretly somebody else.
You live here on the city's edge
Among back lanes and stable-blocks
From which you glimpse the allegations
Of the gardening bourgeoisie that all is well.
And who's to argue? Lilac's beaten to the punch
By cherry blossom and the spire disappears
Among the leaves. Merely to think of
The ground-cover detail this outline implies,
The seeds and saplings and their names,
The little wayside trestles where they're bought,
The just-so cafés, the innumerable
And unnumbered high-hedged roads
For coming home down sleepily,
For instance – that would blind you
With a migraine, were one possible
In this redemptive climate. Sit.

It is somewhere you thought you had seen
From a train. You were not coming here.
It is something you thought was a striking vignette
By an as-yet-uncredited hand. It is somewhere
In moments of weakness at Worcester Shrub Hill
Or in Redditch or Selby you wished
You could enter. You already had. This is it,
The good place, unencumbered by meaning.
For hours no one comes or goes:
The birds, the light, the knowledge
That this place is endlessly repeated –
Is the known world and the elsewheres too –
Will do the living for you. Were you moved
To halve a gravestone you might find
That *England, 2pm* was written through it.

Long before now you've imagined
A woman at work in an attic,
Applying the back of her elegant wrist
To a strand of loose hair. She was sorting
A life, in a shaft of pale dust
Where a slate had come loose, but now
She is quite frankly reading. Kneeling
By a doll's house full of Guardsmen
She's stunned by what she thought she thought.
In the kitchen three storeys below
Are an unopened newspaper next to the hob
And a cat coming in, going out,
Like a trouper, addressing its bowl
In the permanent meantime through which
You come walking so fluently
People would think you belong.
As to the man in her life,
If you lived at a different hour
You'd see him performing his vanishing act
On the bridge by the station.
The train doesn't come, only noises.
A stiff breeze unsettles the fireweed,
Leading the eye to the drop where the stream,
Which is almost as real as the Boat Race,
Goes quietly down to the bend where it vanishes too.
As to sex, you have gained the impression

That somehow it's meant to encourage the others
Who might overrate or not do it at all,
Either way missing the point, although no one
As far as you know has yet clarified that.
The tree-shadows washing the ceiling,
The damp patch in bed, and her manner,
Both brisk and erotic, of pausing
To put up her hair before dressing,
All these suggest you are here.
What, then, of scholarship?
In the 'history room' whose fake stained glass
Is viewed with that tolerant humour
(What isn't?) are somebody's books
In a version of English you half understand.
You search the catalogue
Of the Festival of Britain
Repeatedly for evidence of you
And think it must have been mislaid.
When will you learn? What could it mean,
Conspiracy, when everyone conspires
Against themselves and does not know it?

Le Départ

You've been leaving for years and now no one's surprised
When you knock to come in from the weather.
The crew is past embarrassment:
They can live with their nautical names, and with yours.
So sit, take down your glass, and talk
Of all that is not you, that keeps you here
Among the sentimental stevedores
In the drinking clubs in the dank afternoons
Of your twenty-ninth year. There may be news.

Indeed. Somebody drowned last night, walked sideways
Off a Polish fishmeal hulk. A rabid Paraguayan bear
Was seen among the kindly hookers eating fruit.
A hand-carved coelacanth was found
When the cells were dug out to lay drains...

How can you not be struck by these arrivals?
The perfect boat is sailing Tuesday week.
It's heading southwards, way beyond the ice –
Starsailing seems quite plausible by night.
Until then there is querulous Ninepin
(The loss of his ticket for thieving)
And Madeleine's never-secret grief
(Be kind, and ask politely what)
And someone selling crocodiles
And hash from the sump of a jungle...
Now even the Juvaro have secret accounts –
Sell them your Service Forty-Five
And get a tape-recorder back...
The Amazon's an answering service:
No one's ever really lost. A month ago
Rocheteau, stuck for credit, offered up
The pelvic bones of Mungo Park
In exchange for a fifth of *Jim Beam*...
We always thought that Scot was lying about Africa.

It is easily night: soft boom of lighter-boats
beyond the fogwall, swung on inauthentic tides
That left you here, that left you here
As the lovesongs go over the warehouse
among patrolling cats and a lost A.R.P.
With his bucket of sand and his halberd.

You are doped on the stairs on the way to the moon
With Yvonne, who has aged but not quite,
Who knows the words to every song
And places one flattering palm on your spine
Till you move, who keeps a special bottle
For you (but half gone, half gone) by the bed,
A black fire of sugar that says all there is
About travelling. You're halfway there.

And all shall sing until the awful morning
Reminds them of themselves,
Then sleep in early restaurants,
Boastful of such daft endurance,
And then inspect the shipping lists
Until the time is right.

'You talk in your sleep,' says Yvonne.
'So I woke you. All this travelling –
You leave the girls for what?
Are we not always, always travelling?
Let's drink to that, and one before you go.'

Cousin Coat

You are my secret coat. You're never dry.
You wear the weight and stink of black canals.
Malodorous companion, we know why
It's taken me so long to see we're pals,
To learn why my acquaintance never sniff
Or send me notes to say I stink of stiff.

But you don't talk, historical bespoke.
You must be worn, be intimate as skin,
And though I never lived what you invoke,
At birth I was already buttoned in.
Your clammy itch became my atmosphere,
An air made half of anger, half of fear.

And what you are is what I tried to shed
In libraries with Donne and Henry James.
You're here to hear a message from the dead
Whose history's dishonoured with their names.
You mean the North, the poor, and troopers sent
To shoot down those who showed their discontent.

No comfort there for comfy meliorists
Grown weepy over Jarrow photographs.
No comfort when the poor the state enlists
Parade before their fathers' cenotaphs.
No comfort when the strikers all go back
To see which twenty thousand get the sack.

Be with me when they cauterise the facts
Be with me to the bottom of the page,
Insisting on what history exacts.
Be memory, be conscience, will and rage,
And keep me cold and honest, cousin coat,
So if I lie, I'll know you're at my throat.

MATTHEW SWEENEY

The Eagle

My father is writing in Irish.
The English language, with all its facts
will not do. It is too modern.
It is good for plane-crashes, for unemployment,
but not for the unexplained return
of the eagle to Donegal.

He describes the settled pair
in their eyrie on the not-so-high mountain.
He uses an archaic Irish
to describe what used to be, what is again,
though hunters are reluctant
to agree on what will be.

He's coined a new word
for vigilantes who keep a camera watch
on the foothills. He joins them
when he's not writing, and when he is.
He writes about giant eggs,
about a whole new strain.

He brings in folklore
and folk-prophecy. He brings in the date
when the last golden eagle
was glimpsed there. The research is new
and dodgy, but the praise
is as old as the eagle.

The Desert

He wanted *rim-bel-terfass* and nothing else.
He wanted a space-shot of the desert.
He wanted that Algerian woman he'd known
years before, who'd fed him *couscous*,
with rosewater made by her own mother.

He'd had a male friend who taught there,
on an oasis – he wanted him back there,
arriving, in the small hours, once a year
with dates, and goat-cheese, and the strong
red wines that held their own in France.
He wanted to be able to visit him –
take the train from Algiers, a rucksack
with bacon and whiskey on his back,
no advance warning, no Arabic, no French –
and send a series of postcards to himself
till, one by one, they all arrived back.

rim-bel-terfass: a stew made of gazelle meat, with Saharan
truffles (Sahara dish). *Larousse Gastronomique.*

Monkey

Even when the monkey died
they never invited us round
to eat green banana curry
and play braille scrabble
in that room underground
where twin hammocks hung
near the dead monkey's cage
that held him still, stuffed
and gutted, body-shampooed,
face locked in a rage
that quick death provides.
And none of us knew
what went on at the end,
whether poison, or heart,
or if one of them blew
their monkey away,
then turned on the other
and aimed that Luger,
that well-oiled Luger
at the brain of a brother,
but flung the gun down.
And with their excuse gone

we expected invites,
one big wake, perhaps,
complete with champagne,
and Joe, the taxidermist,
waiving his bill –
his grief-contribution,
his goody for the party.
We're all waiting still.

A Couple Waiting

Leaving the door of the whitewashed house ajar
the man runs to the top of the hill
where he shields his eyes from the evening sun
and scans the sea. Behind him, a woman
holds a curtain back, but when he turns
and shakes his head, she lets the curtain fall.
She goes to the mirror beneath the flag
where she searches her face for signs of
the change her body tells her has begun.
The man shuts the door and sits at the table
where a chicken's bones are spread on two plates.
He thinks of his friends on the Atlantic,
coming up the western coast, laden
with well-wrapped bundles for his stable
that no horse uses. He thinks of his country,
and how his friends and he, with the help
of those bundles, would begin to set it right.
He calls the woman over and feels her stomach,
then asks why she thinks the boat is late.
Like him, she's harassed by an image –
the boat, searchlit, in French or Spanish waters,
guns pointed, a mouth at a megaphone.
Like him, she does not voice her mind,
instead sends him to the hill once more
in the dying light, to watch the red sun
sink in the water that's otherwise bare,
while she sits in the dark room, thinking
of the country their child will grow up in.

Ends

At my end of the earth the Atlantic began.
On good days trawlers were flecks far out,
at night the green waves were luminous.
Gulls were the birds that gobbled my crusts
and the air in my bedroom was salty.
For two weeks once a whale decayed
on the pale beach while no one swam.
It was gelignite that cleared the air.

The uses of village carpenters were many.
Mine made me a pine box with a door,
tarpaulin-roofed, a front of fine-meshed wire.
It suited my friend, the albino mouse
who came from Derry and ate newspaper
and laid black grains on the floor.
When he walked his tail slithered behind.
And when I holidayed once, he starved.

JO SHAPCOTT

Phrase Book

I'm standing here inside my skin,
which will do for a Human Remains Pouch
for the moment. Look down there (up here).
Quickly. Slowly. This is my own front room

where I'm lost in the action, live from a war,
on screen. I am an Englishwoman, I don't understand you.
What's the matter? You are right. You are wrong.
Things are going well (badly). Am I disturbing you?

TV is showing bliss as taught to pilots:
Blend, Low silhouette, Irregular shape, Small,
Secluded. (Please write it down. Please speak slowly.)
Bliss is how it was in this very room

when I raised my body to his mouth,
when he even balanced me in the air,
or at least I thought so and yes the pilots say
yes they have caught it through the Side-Looking

Airborne Radar, and through the J-Stars.
I am expecting a gentleman (a young gentleman,
two gentlemen, some gentlemen). Please send him
(them) up at once. This is really beautiful.

Yes they have seen us, the pilots, in the Kill Box
on their screens, and played the routine for
getting us Stealthed, that is, Cleansed, to you and me,
Taken Out. They know how to move into a single room

like that, to send in with Pinpoint Accuracy, a hundred Harms.
I have two cases and a cardboard box. There is another
bag there. I cannot open my case – look out,
the lock is broken. Have I done enough?

Bliss, the pilots say, is for evasion
and escape. What's love in all this debris?
Just one person pounding another into dust,
into dust. I do not know the word for it yet.

Where is the British Consulate? Please explain.
What does it mean? What must I do? Where
can I find? What have I done? I have done
nothing. Let me pass please. I am an Englishwoman.

The Surrealists' Summer Convention Came to Our City

We were as limp as the guidebooks
to the city. We had our ankle tendons
severed to combat the heat.
We dined on carp all summer:
the magazines were full of recipes.

The city fathers talked about a new guidebook
which would inform the tourists
in languages and dialects for all.
It was delightful in the streets
but there was outrage in the suburbs now that
it was no longer safe to stay in at night.

The carp was piquant but we were getting bored
picking out the lead shot. Some of the tourists
said it wasn't sporting. We got tired
of being barracked and decided to shock
by stringing violins with carp-gut.

The Philharmonia played especially sweetly that summer;
they made a recording of the Floral Dances
which is still controversial because of the sound
of chattering monkeys in the coda.
Weekends we shared dinner in our block, sitting
on the carpet and, by autumn, eating minced carp.

We ate carp with oranges and, retinas
stinging with zest, waited for the season to flop,
the mayor's lung complaint to become fatal,
the city's sheaf of stocks to falter.
But all that flopped that year were
the fishy moustaches on the breeding carp.

MICHAEL DONAGHY

City of God

When he failed the seminary he came back home
to the Bronx and sat in a back pew
of St Mary's every night reciting the Mass
from memory — quietly, continually —
into his deranged overcoat.
He knew the local phone book off by heart.
He had a system, he'd explain,
perfected by Dominicans in the Renaissance.

To every notion they assigned a saint
to every saint an altar in a transept of the church.
Glancing up, column by column, altar by altar,
they could remember any prayer they chose.
He'd used it for exams, but the room went wrong —
a strip-lit box exploding slowly as he fainted.
They found his closet papered floor to ceiling
with razored passages from St Augustine.

He needed a perfect cathedral in his head,
he'd whisper, so that by careful scrutiny
the mind inside the cathedral inside the mind
could find the secret order of the world
and remember every drop on every face
in every summer thunderstorm.
And that, he'd insist, looking beyond you,
is why he came home.

I walked him back one evening as the snow
hushed the precincts of his vast invisible temple.
Here was Bruno Street where Bernadette
collapsed, bleeding through her skirt
and died, he had heard, in a state of mortal sin;
here, the site of the bakery fire where Peter stood
screaming on the red hot fire escape,
his bare feet blistering before he jumped;
and here the storefront voodoo church beneath the el
where the Cuban *bruja* bought black candles,
its window strange with plaster saints and seashells.

Shibboleth

One didn't know the name of Tarzan's monkey.
Another couldn't strip the cellophane
From a GI's pack of cigarettes.
By such minutiae were the infiltrators detected.

By the second week of battle
We'd become obsessed with trivia.
At a sentry point, at midnight, in the rain,
An ignorance of baseball could be lethal.

The morning of the first snowfall, I was shaving,
Staring into a mirror nailed to a tree,
Intoning the Christian names of the Andrews Sisters.
'Maxine, Laverne, Patty.'

A Reprieve

> *Realising that few of the many tunes remembered from boyhood days...*
> *were known to the galaxy of Irish musicians domiciled in Chicago, the*
> *writer decided to have them preserved in musical notation. This was the*
> *initial step in a congenial work which has filled in the interludes of a*
> *busy and eventful life.*
>
>   − POLICE CHIEF FRANCIS O'NEIL:
>   *Irish Folk Music: A Fascinating Hobby, With some*
>   *Account of Related Subjects* (Chicago, 1910)

Here in Chicago it's almost dawn
and quiet in the cell in Deering Street stationhouse
apart from the first birds at the window and the milkwagon
and the soft slap of the club in Chief O'Neil's palm.
'Think it over,' he says, 'but don't take all day.'
Nolan's hands are brown with a Chinaman's blood.
But if he agrees to play three jigs
slowly, so O'Neil can take them down,
he can walk home, change clothes,
and disappear past the stockyards and across the tracks.

Indiana is waiting. O'Neil lowers his eyes,
knowing the Chinaman's face will heal, the Great Lakes
roll in their cold grey sheets and wake,
picket lines will be charged, girls raped
in the sweatshops, the clapboard tenements burn.
And he knows that Nolan will be gone by then,
the coppery stains wiped from the keys of the blackwood flute.

Five thousand miles away Connaught sleeps.
The coast lights dwindle out along the west.
But there's music here in this lamplit cell,
and O'Neil scratching in his manuscript like a monk
at his illuminations, and Nolan's sweet tone breaking
as he tries to phrase a jig the same way twice:
'The Limerick Rake' or 'Tell her I am' or 'My Darling Asleep'.

The Raindial

The sun goes in. The light goes out.
A million shadows fade away.
It could be any time of day.
Now dream that you don't dream about
The garden of this Hackney squat
Where dark drops stipple on the *Sun*,
The umbrella skeleton,
The sink, the broken flowerpot...

A cold rain slicks the garden path
That leads you down the overgrowth
Toward the monument to Thoth:
A drowned shark in a birdbath.

Above its fin the zodiac
Spins upon its sentinel.
The gnomon knows, but will not tell
the time nor give your future back.
The gnomon knows. And round it's writ
As these long (   ) pass swift away
So too the hope of man decays.
TippExed under pigeonshit,
The years, the months, the weeks, the days.

Machines

Dearest, note how these two are alike:
This harpsichord pavane by Purcell
And the racer's twelve-speed bike.

The machinery of grace is always simple.
This chrome trapezoid, one wheel connected
To another of concentric gears,
Which Ptolemy dreamt of and Schwinn perfected,
Is gone. The cyclist, not the cycle, steers.
And in the playing, Purcell's chords are played away.

So this talk, or touch if I were there,
Should work its effortless gadgetry of love,
Like Dante's heaven, and melt into the air.

If it doesn't, of course, I've fallen. So much is chance,
So much agility, desire, and feverish care,
As bicyclists and harpsichordists prove

Who only by moving can balance,
Only by balancing move.

IAN DUHIG

Nineteen Hundred and Nineteen

Dismissed from Tlaltizapa for changing sex
Manuel Palafox sulked in Arenista. At markets
he bought chimoyas, limes and ink from Oaxtepec.
Some days he wore his twenty-ounce sombrero,
deerskin pants and "charro" boots. On others
gold-embroidered blouses and red kerseymere skirts.

He wrote to Magonistas: 'Zapata is finished.
He takes orders from Obregon. Rally the Peones!
Death to Carranza! Tierra y Libertad!'
He wrote to Lenin: 'Trotsky is finished.
Seek concord with the Ukraine Makhnovshchina.
Brest-Litovsk's a cock-up. Regards to the Missus.'

He wrote to Freud: 'Were you coked when you dreamt up this?
No Mexican has even heard of the sexual revolution.
All Eros last year now it's Thanatos, bloody Thanatos.
Jung was right – grow a beard, you think you're Moses.
I hope your jaw drops off. Regards to the Missus.'
At last he wrote to Yeats: 'Dear Willie, how's the Vision?

Mine's double, ha-ha. Shit. Willie, I'm finished
in Mexico – it's full of bigots. Ireland can't be worse.
I'll work. Your brother paints – I'll hold his ladders.
You can have my poems. The one about this year –
change it round – it'll do for Ireland. What happened
to my lift with Casement? Willie, GET ME OUT OF HERE!'

Shopping in Cashel for pulque, Michael Robartes –
'Research Assistant to a popular writer' –
itched in his Connemara Cloth. Himself well-known
for a Special Devotion to the Virgin of Guadaloupe,
he frowned on local talk of a drunken madwoman
in red skirts, publicly disputing with the bishop.

Fundamentals

Brethren, I know that many of you have come here today
because your Chief has promised any non-attender
that he will stake him out, drive tent-pegs through his anus
and sell his wives and children to the Portuguese.
As far as possible, I want you to put that from your minds.
Today, I want to talk to you about the Christian God.

In many respects, our Christian God is not like your God.
His name, for example, is not also our word for rain.
Neither does it have for us the connotation 'sexual intercourse'.
And although I call Him 'holy' (we call Him 'Him', not 'It',
even though we know He is not a man and certainly not a woman)
I do not mean, as you do, that He is fat like a healthy cow.

Let me make this clear. When I say 'God is good, God is everywhere',
it is not because He is exceptionally fat. 'God loves you'
does not mean what warriors do to spear-carriers on campaign.
It means He feels for you like your mother or your father –
yes I know Chuma loved a son he bought like warriors
love spear-carriers on campaign – that's *Sin* and it comes later.

From today, I want you to remember just three simple things:
our God is different from your God, our God is better than your God
and my wife doesn't like it when you watch her go to the toilet.
Grasp them and you have grasped the fundamentals of salvation.
Baptisms start at sundown but before then, as arranged,
how to strip, clean and re-sight a bolt-action Martini-Henry.

Captain Dung Takes a Butcher's

Till you're dead, I'll be ghosting your word-processor screen.
Call me with a spellcheck. Call me Captain Iamb Dung,
the bluff but monomaniac detective
of telescopic vision, a guanoed alp of mac
and a Ph.D. in practical deconstruction.

Slip in Granzotto's disc of that Welsh adventurer
Dutch-auctioning the log from an ancient caravel,
in its Genoese master's best English hand:
an image of a glass book and a flogging angel
will fire your synapses at the precise centenary.

(Granzotto's unenlightening on Ap Meurig Hen –
that's Old MacMorris or Mr America himself.
The figleaf over no bibliography
refers us to Cervantes' satirical preface
and the untranslated testament of Bachelli*)

Tap up the boy from Mobi's school. His book of forecasts
includes an eastern civilisation called the Ind
and a vowel gone A.W.O.L. from his psalter.
I trace it rising like Nelson from O'Connell Street
and illuminating the capital of Ireland.

(When Columba first stole that psalter his fingers shone
like cucumbers, his ears like cauliflowers
picked up my flat feet: Q – sorry – cue the Buñuel shot,
for *El*'s spike through the keyhole, a pet crane's bill,
that pointedly pointed transcendental signifier).

Sulle ragioni per cui non scrissi una biografia di Cristoforo Colombo.

I'r Hen Iaith A'i Chaneuon

*'If the tongue only speak all that the mind knows
There wouldn't be any neighbours'* – THE RED BOOK OF HERGEST

When I go down to Wales for the long bank holiday
to visit my wife's grandfather who is teetotal,
who is a non-smoker, who does not approve
of anyone who is not teetotal and a non-smoker,
when I go down to Wales for the long, long bank holiday
with my second wife to visit her grandfather
who deserted Methodism for The Red Flag,
who won't hear a word against Stalin,

who despite my oft-professed socialism
secretly believes I am still with the Pope's legions,
receiving coded telegrams from the Vatican
specifying the dates, times and positions I should adopt
for political activity and sexual activity,
who in his ninetieth year took against boxing,
which was the only thing I could ever talk to him about,
when I visit my second wife's surviving grandfather,
and when he listens to the football results in Welsh
I will sometimes slip out to the pub.

I will sometimes slip out to the pub
and drink pint upon pint of that bilious whey
they serve there, where the muzak will invariably be
The Best of the Rhosllanerchrugog Male Voice Choir
and I will get trapped by some brain donor from up the valley
who will really talk about 'the language so strong and so beautiful
that has grown out of the ageless mountains,
that speech of wondrous beauty that our fathers wrought,'
who will chant to me in Welsh his epileptic verses
about Gruffudd ap Llywellyn and Daffydd ap Llywellyn,
and who will give me two solid hours of slaver
because I don't speak Irish and who will then bring up religion,
then I will tell him I know one Irish prayer about a Welsh king
on that very subject, and I will recite for him as follows:
'Na thracht ar an mhinisteir Ghallda
Na ar a chreideimh gan bheann gan bhrí,
Mar ni'l mar bhuan-chloch da theampuill
Ach magairle Annraoi Rí.' 'Beautiful,'
He will say, as they all do, 'It sounds quite beautiful.'

I'r Hen Iaith A'i Chaneuon: The title is Welsh and means 'To the Old
Tongue and Its Songs'. The Irish translates roughly as: 'Speak not to me
of the foreign prelate/ Nor of his creed with neither truth nor faith/ For the
foundation stone of his temple/ Is the bollocks of King Henry VIII.'

The Lady Who Loved Insects

Yatai Bayashi is the Festival of Drums:
men beat Taikos through the night;
KODŌ (Children of the Drum) KODŌ (Heartbeat);
but I danced Nishimonai to bones,
ground chalk for my breasts, gallstone
for my teeth, for I was twelve and marriageable.

For the Perfume Contest I chose
Grape-and-Cherry brocade over simple
cotton trousers; mixed aloes
with cinammon and tulip for wine-breath,
conch to mask the candlesmoke and sweet-pines
for memory. I won the Jijū and Genji, my Shining Prince.

His morning poem was a disappointment –
life in his shinden worse. He bored me with pillow-books,
gossamer diaries, his healthy attitude to sex.
He thought me too good at Chinese for a woman
and beat me when I capped his verses.
I murdered him by the cinder garden.

No one sees my face now. My maids gossip
or get drunk. They say I am possessed by foxes
because I won't take lovers. 'Ghosts and women,'
I whisper through the screens, 'are best invisible.'
My "novels" astonish the Fujiwara. They send me gifts
of paper, and cicadas with gilded wings.

SEBASTIAN BARRY

Hermaphroditus
atque in perpetuum, frater, ave atque vale

Surprised by night she plays young brother
in jacket and bow. Her brief hair confuses.

Tables are put where the oak grows,
between them she walks in the late air.

The Ball ends two years of polite distrust.
To mark it, a friend with his evening's wine

falls at our feet, and a girl that passes
smiles at the boy in her voice. She

wishes to sit, and I lift her up
where a branch of the oak droops down

till her legs hang warm from the black bark.
Our play is elaborate, we never kiss. But

does she think it a fabrication? The days
dwindle quietly. She returns to England.

Christ-in-the-Woods
(for Jack Gilbert)

You never bearded more than syllables
on the gray terrace of the cleric valley
imagining perhaps I was not impressed
by you being the thinned in your estate.
I was impressed in the lost extreme
by the remote newness slumming with your geometry,

the ten-league boots for the solo journey,
and the night-station, coffee idiom
walking like my confrère the Hampshire hare
whom white eyes in my eyes made hurry.
Monsieur, Signor, O Kirios, Mister,
my five-dollar jacket accosts your puddle,

the Italian squares supplementing it
busy with idleness under their plumage of signs.
About six the calendar begins to leak,
the sad calender of my dead writers
in the loo by the lake in the sad domain,
a wooden bird and a scatalogical recreation.

Most matters seem sad till I sort them so,
the dictionary becomes a kindred of cheering up
and what I name gets pretty lively under the lamp.
Ah, Jack, we are too polite to be the same.
You can't make out the well's blood drowned in dark
and I am blinded by its black litter at midday.

You say that when the bucket hardens
you sense a brief settling like a trout,
any mooned man's signal to drag up
the helpful language his face explains,
how all silent neighbours who gripped there
remember the temporary gesture in the rock.

With a burrow of guilt I know I have forgotten,
who was a neighbour reasonably open to revelation.
But I see the alphabetical dust you raised,
a fountain in a prospect without horizon,
and your syllables under the water-colours cooling
are soon divided and etymologised: Ho là.

Mary Donnelan, Seamstress of the Mad

Mary, the half-cocked shadow under the awning
of the locked butcher's is just a bin of rabbits gone bad
not the very incarnation of a novelette villain,
sweet tooth, sharp nail, deceptive smile and all.
So press on with your linen layers gripped by one paw
out of the mere appearances of the dawn street
in under the arch of the Sligo Lunatic Asylum,
leaving the moon to glister at the waking women
of the whole town, stirring in their caves to break
the fresh ice on the liquid slugging in the washing-jugs.

Here in the brown halls of a world apart, the moon's
own men are dreaming in one half of sugar and spice,

the moon's good women in the other of slugs and snails.
As you pick your way to the sewing-room, remember the similar
barracks in Athlone, where the red cloths of the uniforms
were plaques of middle-burning coals on the dark walls
and your father, Gibson's batman, was not your father,
your mother not your mother, and you made your own story
like any other orphan or farmed-out child, and the big bells
tolled every other story in symbol from the old cathedral
and, daughter of grace or disgrace, you learned to sew
so that sofas and armchairs even could have family
histories, decked as icons and pictorial panels on their backs.
Mary, in the hours coloured purple and blackly baked

of that previous country, walk in in your second-best bonnet
with a flourish of pheasant feather, and take your needle
off the work-desk grained with dawnlight from the grubby
lattices, and apparel Sligo's mad in astute designs
because they are the creatures in the keepers' dominion
who can't lift a hand outside their dreams, sleeping
or waking. Work in the dark to put them in a good light
of dresses, for instance, to make the captain's wife jealous
with sure pleating and ribbing and shoulders smeared with gold
or otherwise they'll wander in the cambered corridors and close
yards with their arms hitched like yard-arms. Mary,
with charity cloth beyond all redemption, redeem them.

Fanny Hawke Goes to the Mainland Forever

Ashblue porcelain, straw dolls, child's rocking-chair,
neat farms, boxwood beards, gilded sheaves for prayer,
Fanny Hawke of Sherkin Island, Quaker,
leaving her boundary stones to marry
a Catholic lithographer in Cork City,
no one on the new pier to wave her away,
neither an Easter visit or Market Day.
Only the hindview of a sleepy fox, its brush

shoving like a sheaf of sense through bushes.
Goodbye to the baskets in a judged heap
in an angle of the breakfast room,
the sun ignoring the Atlantic and leaping
alone into the midst of her family,
rustle, starch, and grave methods,
to that good hypocrisy, goodbye.
Goodbye little brother with your long face.

Small smooth shells on the great strands
come with her on her fingers as nails.
She smells the lobster the boatmen found
in the ghostly sea when she herself was asleep,
waiting while she dreamt for this morning,
something spangled and strewn on the lightly
grassed dunes, something tart in the air
while she walked, banging her skirts.

Come, little Fanny Hawke, into the bosom
of us hard Catholics, be an outlaw for us.
Bring what you own in a seabox on
a true voyage like anything worthwhile,
your linens with simplest stitchings,
your evening head-cloths, your confident
plainness. Be sure that you bring all fresh
despite that they have cast you completely

onto the desert and mainland of your love
Up the century, Fanny, with you, never mind.
Look at your elegant son, an improved Catholic
squaring up landscapes in his future
to paint them as they are like a Quaker.
There is your other son, a scholarship painter,
a captain in a war, asthmatic, dying young,
all happening even as you set out, oh Fanny.

JOHN BURNSIDE

Holyland

As childhood persists,
like Palestine:
wine-coloured maps,
pages of fish-scale and vellum,

or like an exercise
in mathematics:
the tossed stone
and spreading ripples,

there is something I must calculate
or parse,
a simple equation,
a sentence, constructed of time

and words that no longer
mean what they said,
like *species*, or *spirogyra*.

Septuagesima

> *Nombres.*
> *Están sobre la pátina*
> *de las cosas.*
> JORGE GUILLÉN

I dream of the silence
the day before Adam came
to name the animals,

the gold skins newly dropped
from God's bright fingers, still
implicit with the light.

A day like this, perhaps:
a winter whiteness
haunting the creation,

as we are sometimes
haunted by the space
we fill, or by the forms

we might have known
before the names,
beyond the gloss of things.

Language

The deep house; the other.
Names I have yet to find
on the borders of language,
words between *silt* and *swan*
denoting the fishpool and tree fern
household that stands for the self
in dreams: the mysterious,
perched on the tripwire of being
another's exact opposition,
arrived when the city is finally
still, the neighbourhood stopped,
the suburb's fastidious
gardens gift-wrapped in dew.

DAVID DABYDEEN

Catching Crabs

Ruby and me stalking savannah
Crab season with cutlass and sack like big folk.
Hiding behind stones or clumps of bush
Crabs locked knee-deep in mud mating
And Ruby seven years old feeling strange at the sex
And me horrified to pick them up
Plunge them into the darkness of bag,
So all day we scout to catch the lonesome ones
Who don't mind cooking because they got no prospect
Of family, and squelching through the mud,
Cutlass clearing bush at our feet,
We come home tired slow, weighed down with plenty
Which Ma throw live into boiling pot piece-piece.
Tonight we'll have one big happy curry feed,
We'll test out who teeth and jaw strongest
Who will grow up to be the biggest
Or who will make most terrible cannibal.

We leave behind a mess of bones and shell
And come to England and America
Where Ruby hustles in a New York tenement
And me writing poetry at Cambridge,
Death long catch Ma, the house boarded up
Breeding wasps, woodlice in its dark-sack belly:
I am afraid to walk through weed yard,
Reach the door, prise open, look,
In case the pot still bubbles magical
On the fireside, and I see Ma
Working a ladle, slow –
Limbed, crustacean-old, alone,
In case the woodsmoke and curry steam
Burn my child-eye and make it cry.

The Servants' Song

White hooman haad like hassa-bone stick in yu gum
Cassava pelt from she eye when she stare an scaan yu,
Dress-up in silk day time, prappa scunt in she silva slippa,
Everyday ting wraang wid she how she fuss
Is like bitch in heat how she yap an spit an scratch an cuss –
'Yu fine me gold ring yet wha me lass?'
'No Missie…yes Missie…yes Missie…no Missie' an yu bow till
            yu neck turn rubba
'Well fine am, fine am, fine am leh me see!
Else me go whip all ayuh nigga tief-man!
Gwan, gwan, gwan! Haak-tuh!'
So we run
An we saach
Wid cutlass
Wid taach
In bush
In backdam
In gyden
In yaad
Till we bruk-up
Till we maad.
Gaad-O-Laad!
We saach kitchen, hall-kana in de house
We saach we hair like we comb fo louse.
Trow way de curry an look in de pot
Trow way de baby an look in de cot
Bu no ring deh!
O me mama, how me friken wha Missie go seh!
Wha we go do? We wring we haan
Saary – saary we bin baan –
Till Peta, chupit in e ead since e bin young baai when e fall dung
            coconut tree –
Man chase am, hooman scaan am, call dem husband 'Peta' when
            dem a cuss –
Dis maad – rass, maga – baai seh,
'Leh we go look in duck-battie, me geh mind da ring deh-deh
All night me studyation dis ting an me know e deh-deh.'
He run fowl-pen, pick out waan by chance
Raise up e fedda, skin e leg an peep –

How aweh laugh!
Duck na know wha do am, duck halla, duck leggo waan shit –
An ring come out – if yu see leap!
If yu see dance!
All bady hug up a maad baai an shake e haan
Hooman squeeze up e lolo how dem so happy!
An all bady seh, 'Aweh use to mock yu Peta, now aweh go laan.'
Den we wash ring, tek am gi Missie
She put am on she finga
Bu we na tell she wheh we fine am.
An when she show aff an she kiss she ring she na know why all
    aweh laugh so loud
She beg we foh tell till she beat we, bribe we, but leh she kiss we
    rass first!

Nightmare

Bruk dung de door!
Waan gang sweat-stink nigga
Drag she aff she bed
Wuk pun she
Crack she head
Gi she jigga
Tween she leg!

Dem chase she backdam:
Waan gang cane-stiff cack
Buss she tail till she blue an black
Till she crawl tru de mud an she bawl an she beg.

Dem haul she canal-bank like bush-haag
Cut she troat over de dark surging wata
When dem dun suck dem raise dem red mout to de moon
An mek saang,

Deep in de night when crappau call an cush-cush
Crawl dung hole, lay dem egg in de earth
When camoudie curl rung calf dat just drap
An black bat flap-flap-flap tru de bush...

Wet she awake, cuss de daybreak!

The Canecutters' Song

*The slow throbbing of a drum at long intervals, growing
louder and quicker as the song proceeds, then breaking into
a wild uncontrolled beating at the last few lines of the song.
The men move slowly around the solitary canecutter with
slight dance gestures that also intensify gradually.*

CANECUTTER:

White hooman walk tru de field fo watch we canecutta,
Tall, straight, straang-limb,
Hair sprinkle in de wind like gold-duss,
Lang lace frack loose on she bady like bamboo-flag,
An flesh mo dan hibiscus early maan, white an saaf an wet
Flowering in she panty.
O Shanti! Shanti! Shanti!
Wash dis dutty-skin in yu dew
Wipe am clean on yu saaf white petal!
O Shanti! Shanti! Shanti! –
So me spirit call, so e halla foh yu
When me peep out at yu tween cane-stalk, strain me nose foh
          ketch yu scent
Bram-bram bram-bram beat me haat till me friken yu go hear –
Bu daylight separate me an yu, an dis mud on me haan
Dis sweat from me face, dis rag on me back...
Yu puss-mouth glow, mesh wid light, sun a seed an sprout deh
Me too black fo come deh –
Bu when night come how me dream...
Dat yu womb lie like starapple buss open in de mud
An how me hold yu dung, wine up yu waiss
Draw blood from yu patacake, daub am all over yu face
Till yu dutty like me an yu halla
Like when cutlass slip an slice me leg, an yu shake
Like when snake twist rung me foot, when we cut cane...
So me dream
When night come
An masquita wake up from de bush,
Malabunta move.

CHORUS:

Baai yu ever dream she drawsie-down!
Baai yu ever wuk she wid yu tongue!
Baai yu ever taste she pokey
Saaf an drippy like baigan-chokey!

Elegy

So yu lean over landing, early cole maaning
Old man, yu sick? Is wha do yu? Wha wraang?
An yu haan weak, tremble, an yu mout move
Bu word na deh, an yu eye stare out at de field, laang, laang,
Bu yu na see calf stir an struggle foh suck
An yu na hear high from jamoon tree bluesaki saang –
Is old yu old...is dah wha mek...

Snakeneck, Fisheye, Badman, Rich'ed,
Young yesterday, all a dem baais, Tiefman, Blackbattie, Goose,
Late late in de night ayuh drink rum ayuh beat drum,
Roast crab, curass, tell jumbie story till maaning come...
Is wheh dem deh? All lay up dem net, all put dung dem cutlass,
          all let dem sheep loose,
All dead!
An Jasmattie beating claat on de riverbank – tump! tump! tump!
          tump!
How she haan straang an she back straight an she bubby sweet
          sapadilla-brung!
Yu memba when yu fuss see she how yu troat lump?
How she young bady leap, leak blood, when yu roll she pun de
          grung?...

All dem slingshat buss, all dem fence bruk –
Dung, so jackass graze in dem vegetable gyaaden, bird a peck,
Fireside crack, an battamhouse, an puckni na blow, bellnay na wuk –
An is wha mek...?

CAROL ANN DUFFY

Psychopath

I run my metal comb through the D.A. and pose
my reflection between dummies in the window at Burton's.
Lamp light. Jimmy Dean. All over town, ducking and diving,
my shoes scud sparks against the night. She is in the canal.
Let me make myself crystal. With a good-looking girl crackling
in four petticoats, you feel like a king. She rode past me
on a wooden horse, laughing, and the air sang *Johnny,
Remember Me.* I turned the world faster, flash.

I don't talk much. I swing up beside them and do it
with my eyes. Brando. She was clean. I could smell her.
I thought, Here we go, old son. The fairground spun round us
and she blushed like candyfloss. You can woo them
with goldfish and coconuts, whispers in the Tunnel of Love.
When I zip up the leather, I'm in a new skin, I touch it
and love myself, sighing Some little lady's going to get lucky
tonight. My breath wipes me from the looking-glass.

We move from place to place. We leave on the last morning
with the scent of local girls on our fingers. They wear
our lovebites on their necks. I know what women want,
a handrail to Venus. She said *Please* and *Thank you*
to the toffee-apple, teddy-bear. I thought I was on, no error.
She squealed on the dodgems, clinging to my leather sleeve.
I took a swig of whisky from the flask and frenched it
down her throat. *No*, she said, *Don't*, like they always do.

Dirty Alice flicked my dick out when I was twelve.
She jeered. I nicked a quid and took her to the spinney.
I remember the wasps, the sun blazing as I pulled
her knickers down. I touched her and I went hard,
but she grabbed my hand and used that, moaning...
She told me her name on the towpath, holding the fish
in a small sack of water. We walked away from the lights.
She'd come too far with me now. She looked back, once.

A town like this would kill me. A gypsy read my palm.
She saw fame. I could be anything with my looks,
my luck, my brains. I bought a guitar and blew a smoke ring
at the moon. Elvis nothing. *I'm not that type*, she said.
Too late. I eased her down by the dull canal
and talked sexy. Useless. She stared at the goldfish, silent.
I grabbed the plastic bag. She cried as it gasped and wriggled
on the grass and here we are. A dog craps by a lamp post.

Mama, straight up, I hope you rot in hell. The old man
sloped off, sharpish. I saw her through the kitchen window.
The sky slammed down on my school cap, chicken licken.
Lady, Sweetheart, Princess I say now, but I never stay.
My sandwiches were near her thigh, then the Rent Man
lit her cigarette and I ran, ran...She is in the canal.
These streets are quiet, as if the town has held its breath
to watch the Wheel go round above the dreary homes.

No, don't. Imagine. One thump did it, then I was on her,
giving her everything I had. Jack the Lad, Ladies' Man.
Easier to say Yes. Easier to stay a child, wide-eyed;
at the top of the helter-skelter. You get one chance in this life
and if you screw it you're done for, uncle, no mistake.
She lost a tooth. I picked her up, dead slim, and slid her in.
A girl like that should have a paid-up solitaire and high hopes,
but she asked for it. A right-well knackered outragement.

My reflection sucks a sour Woodbine and buys me a drink. Here's
looking at you. Deep down I'm talented. She found out. Don't mess
with me, angel, I'm no nutter. Over in the corner, a dead ringer
for Ruth Ellis smears a farewell kiss on the lip of a gin-and-lime.
The barman calls Time. Bang in the centre of my skull,
there's a strange coolness. I could almost fly. Tomorrow
will find me elsewhere, with a loss of memory. Drink up son,
the world's your fucking oyster. Awopbopaloobop alopbimbam.

The Captain of the 1964 *Top of the Form* Team

Do Wah Diddy Diddy, Baby Love, Oh Pretty Woman
were in the Top Ten that month, October, and the Beatles
were everywhere else. I can give you the B-side
of the Supremes one. Hang on. *Come See About Me?*
I lived in a kind of fizzing hope. Gargling
with Vimto. The clever smell of my satchel. Convent girls.
I pulled my hair forward with a steel comb that I blew
like Mick, my lips numb as a two-hour snog.

No snags. The Nile rises in April. Blue and White.
The humming-bird's song is made by its wings, which beat
so fast that they blur in flight. I knew the capitals,
the Kings and Queens, the dates. In class, the white sleeve
of my shirt saluted again and again. *Sir!...Correct.*
Later, I whooped at the side of my bike, a cowboy,
mounted it running in one jump. I sped down Dyke Hill,
no hands, famous, learning, *dominus domine dominum.*

*Dave Dee Dozy...*Try me. Come on. My mother kept my mascot Gonk
on the TV set for a year. And the photograph. I look
so brainy you'd think I'd just had a bath. The blazer.
The badge. The tie. The first chord of *A Hard Day's Night*
loud in my head. I ran to the Spinney in my prize shoes,
up Churchill Way, up Nelson Drive, over pink pavements
that girls chalked on, in a blue evening; and I stamped
the pawprints of badgers and skunks in the mud. My country.

I want it back. The captain. The one with all the answers. Bzz.
My name was in red on Lucille Green's jotter. I smiled
as wide as a child who went missing on the way home
from school. The keeny. I say to my stale wife
Six hits by Dusty Springfield. I say to my Boss *A pint!*
How can we know the dancer from the dance? Nobody.
My thick kids wince. *Name the Prime Minister of Rhodesia.*
My country. *How many florins in a pound?*

Poet for Our Times

I write the headlines for a Daily Paper.
It's just a knack one's born with all-right-Squire.
You do not have to be an educator,
just bang the words down like they're screaming *Fire!*
CECIL-KEAYS ROW SHOCK TELLS EYETIE WAITER.
ENGLAND FAN CALLS WHINGEING FROG A LIAR.

Cheers. Thing is, you've got to grab attention
with just one phrase as punters rush on by.
I've made mistakes too numerous to mention,
so now we print the buggers inches high.
TOP MP PANTIE ROMP INCREASES TENSION.
RENT BOY: ROCK STAR PAID ME WELL TO LIE.

I like to think that I'm a sort of poet
for our times. My shout. Know what I mean?
I've got a special talent and I show it
in punchy haikus featuring the Queen.
DIPLOMAT IN BED WITH SERBO-CROAT.
EASTENDERS' BONKING SHOCK IS WELL-OBSCENE.

Of course, these days, there's not the sense of panic
you got a few years back. What with the box
et cet. I wish I'd been around when the Titanic
sank. To headline that, mate, would've been the tops.
SEE PAGE 3 TODAY GENTS THEY'RE GIGANTIC.
KINNOCK-BASHER MAGGIE PULLS OUT STOPS.

And, yes, I have a dream – make that a scotch, ta –
that kids will know my headlines off by heart.
IMMIGRANTS FLOOD IN CLAIMS HEATHROW WATCHER.
GREEN PARTY WOMAN IS A NIGHTCLUB TART.
The poems of the decade...*Stuff 'em! Gotcha!*
The instant tits and bottom line of art.

Adultery

Wear dark glasses in the rain.
Regard what was unhurt
as though through a bruise.
Guilt. A sick, green tint.

New gloves, money tucked in the palms,
the handshake crackles. Hands
can do many things. Phone.
Open the wine. Wash themselves. Now

you are naked under your clothes all day,
slim with deceit. Only the once
brings you alone to your knees,
miming, more, more; older and sadder,

creative. Suck a lie with a hole in it
on the way home from a lethal, thrilling night
up against a wall, faster. Language
unpeels to a lost cry. You're a bastard.

Do it do it do it. Sweet darkness
in the afternoon; a voice in your ear
telling you how you are wanted,
which way, now. A telltale clock

wiping the hours from its face, your face
on a white sheet, gasping, radiant, yes.
Pay for it in cash, fiction, cab-fares back
to the life which crumbles like a wedding-cake.

Paranoia for lunch; too much
to drink, as a hand on your thigh
tilts the restaurant. You know all about love,
don't you. Turn on your beautiful eyes

for a stranger who's dynamite in bed, again
and again; a slow replay in the kitchen
where the slicing of innocent onions
scalds you to tears. Then, selfish autobiographical sleep

in a marital bed, the tarnished spoon of your body
stirring betrayal, your heart over-ripe at the core.
You're an expert, darling; your flowers
dumb and explicit on nobody's birthday.

So write the script – illness and debt,
a ring thrown away in a garden
no moon can heal, your own words
commuting to bile in your mouth, terror –

and all for the same thing twice. And all
for the same thing twice. You did it.
What. Didn't you. Fuck. Fuck. No. That was
the wrong verb. This is only an abstract noun.

Stealing

The most unusual thing I ever stole? A snowman.
Midnight. He looked magnificent; a tall, white mute
beneath the winter moon. I wanted him, a mate
with a mind as cold as the slice of ice
within my own brain. I started with the head.

Better off dead than giving in, not taking
what you want. He weighed a ton; his torso,
frozen stiff, hugged to my chest, a fierce chill
piercing my gut. Part of the thrill was knowing
that children would cry in the morning. Life's tough.

Sometimes I steal things I don't need. I joy-ride cars
to nowhere, break into houses just to have a look.
I'm a mucky ghost, leave a mess, maybe pinch a camera.
I watch my gloved hand twisting the doorknob.
A stranger's bedroom. Mirrors. I sigh like this – *Aah*.

It took some time. Reassembled in the yard,
he didn't look the same. I took a run
and booted him. Again. Again. My breath ripped out
in rags. It seems daft now. Then I was standing
alone amongst lumps of snow, sick of the world.

Boredom. Mostly I'm so bored I could eat myself.
One time, I stole a guitar and thought I might
learn to play. I nicked a bust of Shakespeare once,
flogged it, but the snowman was strangest.
You don't understand a word I'm saying, do you?

Warming Her Pearls

Next to my own skin, her pearls. My mistress
bids me wear them, warm them, until evening
when I'll brush her hair. At six, I place them
round her cool, white throat. All day I think of her,

resting in the Yellow Room, contemplating silk
or taffeta, which gown tonight? She fans herself
whilst I work willingly, my slow heat entering
each pearl. Slack on my neck, her rope.

She's beautiful. I dream about her
in my attic bed; picture her dancing
with tall men, puzzled by my faint, persistent scent
beneath her French perfume, her milky stones.

I dust her shoulders with a rabbit's foot,
watch the soft blush seep through her skin
like an indolent sigh. In her looking-glass
my red lips part as though I want to speak.

Full moon. Her carriage brings her home. I see
her every movement in my head...Undressing,
taking off her jewels, her slim hand reaching
for the case, slipping naked into bed, the way

she always does...And I lie here awake,
knowing the pearls are cooling even now
in the room where my mistress sleeps. All night
I feel their absence and I burn.

PAULA MEEHAN

Two Buck Tim from Timbuctoo

I found it in the granary under rubble
where the back gable caved in,
a 78 miraculously whole in a nest of smashed records,
as if it had been hatched by a surreal hen,
a pullet with a taste for the exotic.

I took it in and swabbed it down,
put it on the turntable and filled the cottage
with its scratchy din. Ghosts of the long dead
flocked from their narrow grooves beneath foreign soils
to foxtrot round my kitchen in the dusk.

I'd say Leitrim in the forties was every bit as depressed
as Leitrim is today, the young were heading off
in droves, the same rain fell all winter long.
Eventually one old woman was left looking at her hands
while the Bell Boys of Broadway played 'Two Buck Tim from
            Timbuctoo',

and dreamt her daughters back about the place, the swing of a skirt,
a face caught in lamplight, with every revolution of the disc.
This winter I have grown unduly broody. As I go
about my daily work an otherworldly mantra turns
within my head: Two Buck Tim from Timbuctoo,

Two Buck Tim from Timbuctoo. It keeps me up at night.
I roam about the rooms. I hope to catch them at it.
I want to rend the veil, step out onto their plane,
spiral down a rain-washed road, let some ghostly partner
take the lead, become at last another migrant soul.

My Love about his Business in the Barn

You're fiddling with something in the barn,
a makeshift yoke for beans to climb,
held together like much in our lives
with blue baling twine, scraps of chicken wire.

Such a useless handyman: our world could collapse,
frequently *has* with a huff and a puff.
You'd hoke a length of string from your back pocket,
humming a Woody Guthrie song, you'd bind

the lintel to stone, the slate to rafter,
'It'll do for the minute if the wind stays down.'
And so I've learned to live with dodgy matter:
shelves that tumble to the floor if you glance

at them sideways; walls that were not built
for leaning against; a great chasm in the kitchen
crossable only by a rope bridge; a blow hole
by our bed where the Atlantic spouts.

On stormy nights it drenches the walls, the ceiling.
Days you come home reeking of *Brut* and brimstone
I suspect you've been philandering underground
and not breaking your back beyond on the bog.

So is it any wonder when I see you
mooching in the barn this fine May morning,
a charm of finches lending local colour,
that I rush for my holy water, my rabbit's foot?

That I shut my eyes tight and wait
for the explosion, then the silence,
then the sweet aftershock when the earth skids
under me, when stars and deep space usurp my day?

The Leaving

He had fallen so far down into himself
I couldn't reach him.
Though I had arranged our escape
he wouldn't budge. He sat
days in his room checking manuscripts

or fixing photos of his family
strictly in the order they were taken.
I begged him hurry for
the moonless nights were due;
it was two nights' walk through the forest.

The soldiers had recently entered our quarter.
I dreaded each knock on the door,
their heavy boots on the stairs.
Our friends advised haste;
many neighbours were already in prison.

His eyes were twin suns burning.
Silence was his answer to my pleas.
I packed a change of clothes, half
the remaining rations,
my mother's gold ring for barter.

The documents at a glance would pass.
It wasn't for myself I went but
for the new life I carried.
At the frontier I recalled him that last morning
by the window watching the sun

strut the length of the street, mirroring
the cloud's parade. He wore
the black shirt I'd embroidered with stars
and said nothing. Nothing.
Then the guide pushed me forward.

Between one sweep of the searchlight
and the next, I slipped into another state
gratefully, under cover of darkness.

MICHAEL HULSE

The Country of Pain and Revelation

The woman sitting on the glinting barrier
watching a stir of air relentlessly uplift
        the silver undersides of leaves
    is breathing very carefully, as if

afraid that she might be too tender for breathing.
Her hand is resting in the dusty hair of the
        man lying jack-knifed on the grass
    between the glittering strips of metal

that run down the centre reserve. She does not see
the slowed traffic, the flashing lights approaching. She
        is elsewhere. Again the country
    of pain and revelation has a guest.

Again the great light has ground the peaks to powder.
Again in the valleys the shadows have sheltered
        the traveller standing alert
    at the rail of the ferry, the trader

bargaining with the goatherd, and the trapper, still
and meticulous in his secretive sidelight.
        It is the discovered country
    from which, returning in wonder as if

from memories of the dreams we thought forgotten,
we sunder in awe, wanting. What is the meaning
        of graining in a rockface? What
    annunciation hides in a hut built

high on an outcrop overlooking the nowhere,
bared to the higher nowhere of the air? And why must
        we find that after our truest
    transmigrations, after our fertile hopes,

we still are left with smashed metal and glass, resting
fingers in the hair of a dying lover? She
        knows the name of the place. Leaning
    forward, she kisses the dusty lips and

cradles his head and places her cheek against his,
and he learns to say yes, say yes, and goes home to
    a lighted house, a dazzle of
  horror, security, darkness and love.

Fornicating and Reading the Papers

I

John Stubbs of Lincoln's Inn has written a pamphlet:
    The Discoverie of a Gaping Gulf
to swallow England by a French Marriage.
    The queen has seen the pamphlet, at least
the title page. She is burning with choler.
    She says this Stubbs is a seditious villain.

This is the stage set up in the market place
    at Westminster. This is seditious Stubbs.
This is the butcher's knife, keen against his wrist.
    This is the mallet that strikes against the knife.
The moment his right hand is off, seditious Stubbs
    doffs his hat with his left, crying *God save the queen!*

II

Wet from the shower
    towelling your breasts
you ask me if I've read
    Motley's *Rise of the Dutch Republic.*

My heart is in another question: *What*
    is the price of a virtuous woman?
Ads in the London Underground reply:
    Buy her a diamond before someone else does.

III

The Sudanese minister shrugs. *It is only a hand,*
    he declares, a small price to pay
for the preservation of law and order.
    The minister drums his fingers on the desk.

This is the guilty man, whose hand
    was found in another man's pocket.
He watches the amputation carefully.
    No noble words are waiting in his mouth,
no thoughts of God or saving in his head.

    His hand is preserved in a jar of surgical alcohol.

IV

A dusty lane
    in the polder
the flat
    loveliness
and the high
    cloud-shattered sky
caressed by alders
    the room where we lay
shuttered against the day
    breathing
the white smell
    of apples in the loft
the fragrance of grass
    the touch of it:
for days I was whistling
    those bars from the rondo
movement of Beethoven's first
    piano concerto.

V

He is a missionary. From Detroit.
    They, the Sendero Luminoso, know
that he is the CIA. America made flesh.
    Into that flesh they drive needles, beneath
the toenails. One of his eyes has been pulped
    by a rifle-butt. They have crushed his testicles.

They know what they know. They are the gods
    on the shining path of righteousness.
Now they hack off his fingers one by one.
    Unable to give the answers they require,
My God, why hast thou he breathes, and
    passes out again, till the pain revives him.

VI

Maria said to Yerma
Haven't you held
a living bird in your hand?
well that's what it's like,
having a child inside,
only more in the blood.

To Gottlob Fabian
died at Tarnast, 4 March 1844

In Vormärz Brandenburg
six iron generations back
across the blood and soil
you worked a windmill at Tarnast.

I know your stolid windmill,
gentle and firm, wooden and white,
set on the flats of Brandenburg,
tenderly taking the wind.

I know the stones, the stones that grind,
the principle of what is fine.
I know your watchfulness, your eye,
your patience, and your sky:

we are sails of the same windmill
stilled, tensed to a nameless, windstill
breathing culled from the very air,
again becoming air.

Gottlob Fabian was one of my German forefathers, the remotest I am aware
of. Since the poem deliberately moves upon sensitive territory, I should state
that my awareness of his existence comes from an *Ahnenpass* (Third Reich
documentation of "Aryan" ancestry) which until her death was in my mater-
nal grandmother's possession.

Getting a Tan

The white
ideal went
with a sense of ethics and of dress. But we've thrown
off the moral whalebone,
and like sand-lizards lie
flat, tanned and complacent.

How hard
now to think back
to times when only peasants were tanned (we don't think
in terms of fleshy pink):
you might as well have tried
to sunbathe in a sack.

We can't
imagine, say,
Elizabeth Bennet flinging aside her staid
virgin-brittle brocade
and stays, and getting tanned
topless at St Tropez.

SUJATA BHATT

White Asparagus

Who speaks of the strong currents
streaming through the legs, the breasts
of a pregnant woman
in her fourth month?

She's young, this is her first time,
she's slim and the nausea has gone.
Her belly's just starting to get rounder
her breasts itch all day,

and she's surprised that what she wants
is *him*
   inside her again.
Oh come like a horse, she wants to say,
move like a dog, a wolf,
       become a suckling lion-cub –

Come here, and here, and here –
but swim fast and don't stop.

Who speaks of the green coconut uterus
the muscles sliding, a deeper undertow
and the green coconut milk that seals
her well, yet flows so she is wet
from his softest touch?

Who understands the logic
behind this desire?
Who speaks of the rushing tide
      that awakens
her slowly increasing blood – ?
And the hunger
      raw obsessions beginning
with the shape of asparagus:
sun-deprived white and purple-shadow-veined,
she buys three kilos
of the fat ones, thicker than anyone's fingers,
she strokes the silky heads,
some are so jauntily capped...
      even the smell pulls her in –

Muliebrity

I have thought so much about the girl
who gathered cow-dung in a wide, round basket
along the main road passing by our house
and the Radhavallabh temple in Maninagar.
I have thought so much about the way she
moved her hands and her waist
and the smell of cow-dung and road-dust and wet canna lilies,
the smell of monkey breath and freshly washed clothes
and the dust from crows' wings which smells different –
and again the smell of cow-dung as the girl scoops
it up, all these smells surrounding me separately
and simultaneously – I have thought so much
but have been unwilling to use her for a metaphor,
for a nice image – but most of all unwilling
to forget her or to explain to anyone the greatness
and the power glistening through her cheekbones
each time she found a particularly promising
mound of dung –

Maninagar Days

They are always there
just as pigeons or flies
can be *always there*
and the children have to fight them off,
especially during those hot May afternoons
when they dare to jump down from the trees
into the cool shaded spots, the corners between
the canna flower beds
still moist from the morning's watering.

Monkeys in the garden –
I'm talking about rhesus monkeys
the colour of dirt roads and khaki
                and sometimes even of honey.
Rhesus monkeys that travel in small groups,

extended families; constantly feuding brothers, sisters,
uncles, aunts, cousins screaming through
the trees – while the grandmother sits farther away
sadly, holding on to the sleepy newborn.
Somehow they manage to make peace
before every meal.

Now and then a solitary langur:
the Hanuman-monkey, crossing the terrace
with the importance of someone going to the airport.
A lanky dancer's steps
with black hands, black feet
sharp as black leather gloves and black leather shoes
against the soft grey body.
Sharp
and yet delicate
as if they were brush-stroked in
with a Japanese flourish.
And black-faced too,
with thick tufts of silver grey eyebrows,
a bushy chin. So aloof
he couldn't be bothered
with anyone.

Some people live with rhesus monkeys
and langurs in their gardens.
To these children
the monkeys are as normal and common as dogs.
And yet, the monkeys remain magical.

The children feel closer
to the monkeys, although they never
really play together, although the monkeys
probably hate the children:
those three children, two girls and a boy
who are all a bit afraid
of the full-grown-to-their-prime males
that stretch themselves and stretch themselves
to the height of wisdom and fatherly wit.

The monkeys are not at all cuddly like toys.
No.

They are lean twirls, strong tails, fast shadows
abrupt with yellow teeth.
The monkeys are not so innocent
the elders warn,
not so content with their daily routine
for they are turning
into urban thieves, imitating
and even outdoing the crows:

One day a tall monkey leaped down on the clothesline
and stole a blinding white shirt.
Another day, a very muscular monkey
bounded out of the neighbour's house
with a huge rock of golden *gur*, solid raw sugar.
The boy was impressed. His mother
would have difficulty carrying such a load.

Still, the children treat the monkeys
as if they were children newly arrived from a foreign
country, unable to speak the language yet.

And the children's grandmother comes out
to the front door from time to time.
Just awakened from her afternoon nap, now
she readjusts her thin white sari
and squints against the sun
watching over them all –
And the faint May breeze that struggles
through the monkey crowded branches
is Hanuman's breath.
How could you know it, how could you miss it
unless you had lived
in such a garden.

Monkeys in the garden.
They are always there,
usually in the gulmuhore trees
chewing on the sour rubbery leaves
and the even more delicious bright
scarlet-orange flowers: petals
sparkling as sliced blood oranges,
water-plump green stems...

The monkeys have become everything
to the children, although
the children are not aware of it yet,
and one summer the children can't help
learning everything from them:
their noise, their shadows, their defiant stare,
the way they shake their heads,
the curve of their elbows
their weight on the trees...
In fact, without the monkeys
the trees begin to look a little barren
to the children.

Oh there are days when the monkeys refuse
to come down from the gulmuhore trees
and that makes the children jealous
and unhappy.
Oh there are days when the monkeys
never intrude, never interfere
with the children's favourite hide-outs.
Peaceful days, one would think
with the monkeys chatter-reclining and nibbling,
dozing and basking, jabbering and
lice-picking safe above in the gulmuhore trees
while the children run about exhausting
one game after another right below.
Peaceful hours one would think.
But the children are jealous
for they too love to eat
the gulmuhore flowers and leaves.

Invariably they try
to convince the monkeys to throw some flowers down
and then, that failing,
invariably they try to persuade the monkeys
to come down into their garden
(maybe with some flowers)
and then, that failing,
they are simply angry, so angry
at the monkeys, they terrify them off
into the neighbouring gardens.

Oh with monkeys like that
the children believe in Hanuman.
In their secret wishes the children reinvent
the perfect monkey: Hanuman,
wild and fierce and loyal and gentle...

One day the boy defended his sisters
single-handedly with a stick like a sword
he chased the whole band of monkeys
not up the trees but to the back of the house:
a complete disappearance.
Then there was such silence
the girls were afraid – where
had all the birds gone? And the neighbour's dog?
A few minutes later the boy returned
running, chased by the monkeys,
and the stick like a sword was in the hand
of the angry leader...

Monkeys in the garden.
Some people have monkeys
in their dreams, monkeys in their nightmares,
monkeys crossing their shadows
long after they have stopped being children
long after they have left such a garden.

Hanuman is the son of the wind god Maruti and Anjana, a goddess turned into
a monkey by a curse. Hanuman is the most powerful, most intelligent and most
learned of the monkeys. He is also considered to be the 'Ideal of the perfect
servant: A servant who finds full realisation of manhood, of faithfulness, of
obedience. The subject whose glory is in his own inferiority' (P. Thomas: *Epics,
Myths and Legends of India*). This ideal servant-master relationship is espe-
cially evident in Hanuman's devotion to Ramachandra in the epic *Ramayana*.

GEOFF HATTERSLEY

Minus Three Point Six

Suppose there are three doors:
Religion, Insanity, Suicide.
Suppose you're on TV,
the hostess asks which door you'll take.
Suppose ten million viewers

and a studio audience of enemies
are all shouting their preference
and in the din the hostess mishears:
you ask for Religion, get Insanity.
You're shoved through and the door closes.

You try to shout for help, you want
to explain there's been a mistake,
you can't, can't move, feel as if
you're held in place by chains
or a pair of huge hands.

It's so dark you can't see yourself,
so quiet you could hear a plant move
though there are none moving.
There are no words in your head, just numbers.
You try but can't stop thinking about them:

One and one is two plus seventeen is eighteen
minus three point six is fifteen point eight
multiplied by twenty-seven point seven is
four thousand three hundred and sixty-five point six
divided by five point five is

Slaughterhouse

At last, I was ready to say goodbye
to a tether made of fishnet stockings.
My friends told me not to, that I needed
a bandage for my head, needed a crutch for it.
I muttered Jolly Good like a jolly fellow,
caught the next bus. When I got where it was going
a man tried to sell me a Coke for five dollars.
I asked the next for the way to the slaughterhouse.
He told me to follow the smell of meat and bone.
The smell was powerful, at some distance even.

*

The first time I ate grilled octopus tentacles
– a strange moment, one I feel a need to mention.
An undercover cop had leeched onto me at a bar,
between mouthfuls of ouzo and tentacles
was pretending to be the greatest punk rock band ever.
He asked if I wanted to dance, the meathook
in my hand was reassuring. He loved every minute
of his pathetic life. Young men with sticks
surrounded our piled-high table
after he told the barman he should fuck his bill.

*

The morning after I ate grilled octopus tentacles
a man helped me buy powder in the pharmacy,
took me by the arm and found me a hotel room.
I was embarrassed among strangers the rest of the day
– they were passing round photos taken on the beach
that summer I weighed fifteen and a half stone.
At night I searched every room in the place,
sifting through bins stuffed with used tampons and shit-roll
for one small thing that would let me know where I was.
The landlady joined me about half-two.

*

I did press-ups and pull-ups and ran on the spot.
I brushed my teeth and shaved away three months
of enthusiastic cunnilingus.

I practised speaking without using shit and fuck
and held myself erect. Bumping into her on the stairs
I complimented her on her repertoire
but suggested she make more of a noise.
What do I most wish now, as I pick my teeth here
some years later? That she had understood a word I said
and that my nose hadn't been so obviously running.

*

The slaughterhouse started my head pounding
and there is a harsh sound, a hundred cows
screaming in unison. I went nuts there
and then. Years of treatment would have followed
if I hadn't escaped the building that minute.
I hitched a lift with a man who told me
I had good legs, sexy legs. He needed glasses
and a room at a hotel, I replied
– did he have his wallet? Yes he did. His head cracked
as he landed in the road, I didn't look back.

*

What I fell in love with was her singing,
not that it was what you'd call good singing.
It would reach me in my room as I lay naked
in the baked afternoons, talking aloud
to the insects on the ceiling and walls.
It was the happiness that surprised me,
and how it lingered a long time after.
I was never a music critic, no,
Not bad, I'd say, turning this way and that,
looking in the mirror at my pale face.

The Cigar

The cigar was huge. It was carried in
by three underfed slave-children in chains.

Everything halted: spoons on their paths to mouths,
hands and feet meeting knees beneath tables.

The American glanced deliberately about him,
the beginnings of an imbecilic grin...

Before the cartoon gapes of the paying customers,
he summoned a blow-torch and lit the thing.

Thick, acrid smoke began immediately to fill
the neat, symmetrical interior of the restaurant.

Chandeliers fell crashing; in the darkness,
bottles of wine hurried back to the cellar,

remarkable creatures leapt from their plates,
forked just in time by the sweating manager.

The cigar was by now expanding at an alarming
rate, taking on a new, strange form, developing

what seemed to be a head...One woman –
one woman abandoned her life's jewellery

and collapsed to the ground with her legs wide open
moaning 'Give it to *me*! Give it to *me*!'

One man, tears streaming down his drunken nose,
gobbled a photograph of his wife and children.

Waiters, their bow-ties on the verge of hysteria,
rushed to and fro with bowls of hot veal soup.

The American, completely overcome
with joy at this fine thing, celebrated loudly

by eating the whole five-pound lump
of garlic stilton with port-wine on the dessert trolley.

The room was small and becoming increasingly
smaller. There seemed no escape

Frank O'Hara Five, Geoffrey Chaucer Nil

I think on the whole I would rather read
Frank O'Hara than Geoffrey Chaucer, and
this fine, non-smoking morning could well be
the right time to try out a new (uh hum)

poetic form. It's the funniest thing:
I am *here*, thirty years of age, having
put booze and all sorts of, say, 'dubious
substances' behind me, now sweating it

all out in a small, constipated room
with a plump tomato of a woman,
conjugating Middle English verbs. I have
developed a line, a very brief line,

in gestures of friendliness, and in my
trousers an idea is taking shape...

Mucky

She puts down the magazine
and says she needs a bath,
looking at me as though
I do too or perhaps
only wanting me there with her

whether I'm mucky or not.
She's read 'The Platonic Blow'
(attributed to Auden)
just now and shows the face
that makes me grin and want

to hold her and startle her
with something of my own.
How mucky could I be? I
wonder, as the water
flows and the mirror steams.

Eccentric Hair

There was something grinning on the telly:
Everything's creative, it said, meaning
staring at a shadow on the ceiling.
I didn't switch off, just sort of grunted.
I wasn't good for much at the time
except worrying about the first post
coming ten minutes after the second,
the cop who parked outside my house reading
How The CIA Murdered Bob Marley
and the gangsters who tailed me when I went
to the bank, to the shops, to the dentist.
I was low, listening to the same song
over and over: *Don't Tell Me You Don't Believe It
        & Call Yourself A Friend*
and I'd no idea what I wanted,
other than to be able to relax
and see the funny side of things again,
maybe think back to being seventeen,
wishing I was Bob Dylan or someone
or at least had pretty eccentric hair.
I just needed to get out more, out of the house.

My suit was at the drycleaners so I wore jeans
and a denim jacket. I leaned against the bar
avoiding the eyes of the other customers:
the place was full of all the fools I'd ever been.
I heard them getting more and more maudlin.

IAN McMILLAN

Ted Hughes Is Elvis Presley

I didn't die
that hot August night.
I faked it,

stuffed a barrage balloon
into a jump suit.
Left it slumped
on the bathroom floor.

Hitched a ride on a rig
rolling to New York. Climbed
into the rig, the driver said
'Hey, you're...'
'Yeah, The Big Bopper. I faked it,
never died in that plane crash.
Keep it under your lid.'
I tapped his hat with my porky fingers.
He nodded. We shared a big secret.

Laid low a while in New York.
Saw my funeral on TV in a midtown bar.
A woman wept on the next stool but one.

'He was everything to me. Everything.
I have a hank of his hair in my bathroom
and one of his shoelaces
taped to my shoulderblade.'

'He was a slob' I said.
She looked at me like I was poison.
'He was too big, too big,' I said.
'He wanted to be small, like
a little fish you might find in a little pond.'

I needed a new identity.
People were looking at me.
A guy on the subway asked me
if I was Richie Valens.

So I jumped a tramp steamer
heading for England.
Worked my passage as a cook.
In storms the eggs
slid off the skillet.

Made my way to London.
Saw a guy, big guy, guy with a briefcase.
Followed him down the alley,
put my blade into his gut
and as the blood shot
I became him
like momma used to say
the loaf became Jesus.

I am Elvis Presley.
I am Ted Hughes.

At my poetry readings I sneer and rock my hips.
I stride the moors
in a white satin jump suit,
bloated as the full moon.

Bless my soul,
what's wrong with me?

At night I sit in my room
and I write, and the great bulbous me
slaps a huge shadow on the wall.

I am writing a poem
about the death of the Queen Mother
but it won't come right.

I look up. Outside a fox peers at me.
I sing softly to it,
strumming my guitar.

Soon, all the foxes
and the jaguars and the pigs
and the crows are gathering
outside my window, peering in.

I sing *Wooden Heart, Blue Hawaii.*
There is the small applause
of paws and feathers.

I am Ted Hughes. I am Elvis Presley.
I am down at the end of lonely street
and a jump suit rots in a southern coffin
as people pay their respects to a barrage balloon.

I sit here,
I can feel the evening shrinking me
smaller and smaller.
I have almost gone. Ted,
three inches long, perfect.
Elvis, Ted.

The Er Barnsley Seascapes

1. *Goldthorpe er Seascape*

Park the car. Wind
the window down. Listen.
Shanties echoing
up the tight street

as the pitmen sing
their way from work.
The YTS lamplighter
stands, and his matches

cough out in
the well-trained wind.
He was not a clever
boy at school

so all he can say is
shit, not like us
clever people, who wind
the window down to catch

the dying tradition
on our Japanese tape recorders.
Shanties, clinking like
cardboard money,

the cardboard money
they have round here.
Burns easier.
Cheaper than coal.

2. M1 Seascape near Hoyland: er it's a rough day

They huddle in their coats
and the gaffer holds his gun
but only for effect. For this
photograph I am taking, I suppose.

For the interview, the gaffer
is proud: 'We have only six more
miles of motorway to roll up
and dump in the sea' he quips.

3. er Darfield Seascape

And the waves pound
against Clifton's shop
and Clifton's shop never closes.
On Christmas Day someone rushes in
for a pair of tights. She has
a bulging purse from Habitat
in the shape of a bath
filled with coal. Put it this way:
Darfield was mentioned in the Domesday Book.
Put it like this: a passing mention,
more of a mutter.

4. Little Houghton seascape er like

British Coal
sold the houses

made us live
in heads

Great big
severed heads.

Rows of heads
overlooking the sea.

Sometimes I stand
in the eyes

and I cry.
Then I burn

the tears.
Cheaper than coal.

5. *An old seadog er speaks*

First it was called NCB, you'd see it
on the boats, then British Coal, on
the wharves, then they changed the name
to British A Vase of Flowers, changed all
the boats, all the wharves, all the
signs outside the pits, then they
changed it to British Very Nice
and a month later to British Smile
and they kept repainting the boats
and wharves the fish the seaweed the

6. *er from a Learned Paper about the Seascapes*

Very few of er the South Yorkshire
Coastal Mining Settlements survive
in anything like their original

er state. Some have become islands,
some have sunk into the sea, some
have worked loose from the earth

and slither around the countryside
scaring er owls and other woodland
creatures. One was found in Harrogate

a town in North Yorkshire next to
the sea. 'It had er wings' said a local
'and was tired from much hard flying.'

7. Seaview Video, Barnsley: Er latest offers

Barnsley is Basingstoke!	£1.00 a night
Barnsley is Basingstoke 2	£1.00 a night
The Cruel Sea (Remake)	£1.00 a night
Lost Horizon (Remake)	£1.00 a night
Barnsley is Japan!	£1.00 a night
Barnsley is Japan 2!	£1.00 a night

8. Seascape could er be anywhere around here

Only the water, solid
and glinting. Only
the noise of the water,

and the noise of the moon
slowly deflating, and
only the noise of the stars

being sold, clinking,
keeps me awake
all day.

Just the Facts, Just the

In the play room
Dean won't eat his cabbage.
His mother whispers to him,
'Look, I know you don't like cabbage...'
His dad, who has been exchanging shy smiles
with me all weekend, says,
'Tha dun't like cabbage, all reight,
tha dun't...'

We sit around on the small chairs
encouraging. Enormous toys
line the walls like prefects,
two huge snails lick themselves
up the side of the glass case,
thirty-seven fish move in a tank.

We are on the eighth floor. Six
floors down, my mother settles
herself painfully into a new hip.
On the eighth floor, my daughter
spoons mush into her mouth. Tonight
the doctor will tell her to go home.
I close my eyes and see her jerking
about on the settee, bright red,
making little cardboard cries.

Cardboard cries? Pull together yourself.
Just the facts, just the

Late at night, driving between Barnburgh
and Goldthorpe, a couple making love
in a ditch, caught in the light of the
car lights, looking like a brightly
coloured bird or a brightly coloured
animal.

Yes, I guess
you are right.
Any facts will do.

Pit Closure as Art

In the centre of
the major retrospective
there is a door
which you open.

As you open it
certain nerves
in the face
are jangled
artificially:
you smile.

The smile becomes
the property of
The Artist.

Beyond the door
is a room
and another door.

You walk over to the door.

The catalogue says
'The door will not be locked'
but the catalogue also
is part of The Art.

The door is locked.
The door you came through
is locked. The Artist
has served The Art well.

As you stand there
certain nerves
in the eyes
are jangled
artificially:
you weep.

The tears become
the property of
The Artist

You dig to keep warm.
The Artist arrests you for digging.
The Artist smashes your head
for pounding on the door.

The Artist prevents you
from walking to the door.

All this is part of The Art.
The Artist has refined The Art well.

MICHAEL HOFMANN

Guanajuato Two Times

I could keep returning to the same few places
till I turned blue; till I turned into
José José
on the sleeve of his new record album
What is Love?;
wearing a pleasant frown and predistressed denims;
reading the double page spread ('The Trouble with José José')
on his drink problem,
comparing his picture 'Before' and 'After'...
I could slowly become a ghost, slowly familiar,
slowly invisible, amiable, obtuse...
I could say 'Remember me?' to the blank bellhop,
and myself remember
the septet in the bandstand playing 'Winchester Cathedral',
and the clown coming in for coffee
and to count his takings and take off his face...
I could take on all my former beds for size.
Meander knowingly through twelve towns with twelve street names
              between them.
Sit on both sides of the municipal kissing seats,
shaking my head at the blanket men
and the hammock men, in their humorous desperation
offering me hammocks for four, for five, for six...
I could learn the Spanish for
'I shall have returned' or 'Hullo, it's me again!'
and get the hang of the double handshake,
first the palms, then the locked thumbs.
My dreams would moulder and swell and hang off me
like pawpaws. I could stand and sway like a palm,
or rooted like a campanile, crumbling slightly
each time the bells tolled, not real bells
but recordings of former bells,
and never for me.

'Shivery Stomp'
(i.m. Malcolm Lowry)

To see the trees spilled, the sap stanched with sawdust,
the ground flap open like a grave. The crippled raven,
conductor of souls, squatting by on a concrete pile,
cawing. The daytime moon (naturally) gibbous.

It produces a strange adjacency,
to have visited so many of your sites, Ripe and Rye,
Cuernavaca and Cambridge, and, by fifty-nine days,
never to have done time – a term – together.

Late Lowry in towelling shirt, rucksack and duck pants.
Thirty years late Lowry. Thirty years to name the jazzer's beard,
and the talents, forever falling short of professions,
like the naming of jazz numbers and combos.

The having usurped you thirty years –
down to sitting in an overwindowed 1940s lounge,
the mousy seaside furniture, the natural gas, the Home Service,
the long 14th, the links course, the South Coast.

The whole town turned out by the same brickworks,
one tailor and one sunset bolt of cloth.
Brick and lichen, pruned willow, prunes and the W.I.
The England you fled and died in.

The bodiless wren, a tail and a teaspoon,
dipping down the street of cottage hospitals.
The Pied Piper fried food van
belting out *Greensleeves* in a poor estate.

The gulls floating and gorging on the coley-coloured water.
The hunkering on the rocks in my herringbone coat,
watching the fishermen swing their boats round
and point them back down the beach, ready for Tuesday.

The field, so comprehensively settled with starlings,
the farmer might have sown them there, starling
seeds, something perhaps like the frozen dew
I chip ahead of me in the light rough.

Las Casas

I leaned round the corner in a Gold Rush town –
fortunate, apprehensive and somewhat surprised to be there.
The wind was one hazard, and so were the ramps
and unevennesses on the pavements, and the streetsellers
with their *montóns* of oranges. The kerbs were high,
almost a foot, as though anticipating a flood or blizzard.
Everyone seemed to have come from somewhere else,
the gringos from Europe and North America, the Ladinos,
once, ditto, the Indians from their outlying villages.
Everyone was a source of money to everyone else.
Who had it: the pink- or blue-burned and -burnoused
Indians; the women, in their bosoms with their babies;
the kerchiefed figures bussed in on the back of *camións*;
the ugly, leggy, insouciant foreign girls;
or the Ladinos, of whom the Indians said
they were begotten by a Ladina and a dog
at the side of the road, 'the Ladina helping'...?
It was a raw town. The shoe shops sold mincing machines,
hats and aluminium buckets shared a shelf, paper and iron
went together – for the staking of claims, perhaps?
A town of radio shops and funeral parlours –
the dead travelled to the aquamarine graveyard
in station wagons, horizontal, to music;
the living, upright, on pickups, also to music.
Of well-lit drink shops. Of illustrated marriage magazines
and spot-the-beachball shots in Kodak shops.
Of *Secrets of a Nunnery*, and two churches
facing each other on two hills, holding a lofty dialogue.
(One was a ruin.) Of patio-and-parapet housing,
and pastel shacks whose quick spread swallowed the airport.
Of unpaved streets, away from the centre.
Of everyone off the streets, paved or not, by eight o'clock.
Of the all-day screech of tortilla machines
and the scrape of rockets up the sky, a flash in the pan,
a percussive crash, a surprisingly durable cloud.
Jubilation, and no eyes raised.

Entr'acte

The enemies of democracy were back supporting it.
Soldiers went in fear of their MPs, looked slippy
on the parade ground, tumbling from their personnel carriers,
parleyed in groups of two and three with girls at the gate.

I sat and picnicked on my balcony, no picnic,
eyeing the tarmac through the rusty gridiron underfoot,
flicking ash and wincing at my pips going lickety-split,
hitting the deck fifty feet down, among the sentries ...

Inside, the wall met neither floor nor ceiling.
Two stripes of light reached into my room from next door,
where I heard an American girl – mezzo, ardent –
crying, 'Don't come, sweet Jesus, not yet.'

Nighthawks
(for James Lasdun)

Time isn't money, at our age, it's water.
You couldn't say we cupped our hands very tightly...
We missed the second-last train, and find ourselves
at the station with half an hour to kill.

The derelicts queue twice round the tearoom.
Outside, the controlled prostitutes move smoothly
through the shoals of men laughing off their fear.
The street-lamps are a dull coral, snakes' heads.

Earlier, I watched a couple over your shoulder.
She was thin, bone-chested, dressed in black lace,
her best feature vines of hair. Blatant, ravenous,
post-coital, they greased their fingers as they ate.

I met a dim acquaintance, a man with the manner
of a laughing-gas victim, rich, frightened and jovial.
Why doesn't everyone wear pink, he squeaked.
Only a couple of blocks are safe in his world.

Now we've arrived at this hamburger heaven,
a bright hole walled with mirrors where our faces show
pale and evacuated in the neon. We spoon our sundaes
from a metal dish. The chopped nuts are poison.

We've been six straight hours together, my friend,
sitting in a shroud of earnestness and misgiving.
Swarthy, big-lipped, suffering, tubercular,
your hollow darkness survives even in this place...

The branch-line is under the axe, but it still runs,
rattling and screeching, between the hospital
lit like a toy, and the castellated factory –
a *folie de grandeur* of late capitalism.

My Father at Fifty

Your mysterious economy blows the buttons
off your shirts, and permits overdrafts
at several foreign banks. – It must cost the earth.

Once I thought of you virtually as a savage,
atavistic, well-aligned, without frailties.
A man of strong appetites, governed by instinct.

You never cleaned your teeth, but they were perfect anyway
from a diet of undercooked meat; you gnawed the bones;
anything sweet you considered frivolous.

Your marvellous, single-minded regime, kept up
for years, of getting up at four or five,
and writing a few pages 'on an empty stomach',

before exposing yourself to words – whether
on the radio, in books or newspapers,
or just your own from the day before...

Things are different now. Your male discriminations
– meat and work – have lost their edge.
Your teeth are filled, an omnivorous sign.

Wherever you are, there is a barrage of noise:
your difficult breathing, or the blaring radio –
as thoughtless and necessary as breathing.

You have gone to seed like Third World dictators,
fat heads of state suffering horribly
from Western diseases whose name is Legion...

Your concentration is gone: every twenty minutes,
you go to the kitchen, or you call your wife
over some trifle. Bad-tempered and irritable,

you sedate yourself to save the energy
of an outburst. Your kidneys hurt, there is even
a red band of eczema starring your chest.

Your beard – the friend of the writer who doesn't smoke –
is shot with white...A Christmas card arrives
to ask why you don't have any grandchildren.

In the Realm of the Senses

One perfunctory fuck on our first night,
then nothing for ever... only jokes and hard lines,
cold water, mushy soap and sleep that never comes.
We hurt with tiredness, and are abashed by our dirt.

We fall further behind the days, our overnighted systems
struggle with smoke and sights and *consommations*.
The yellow Citroën sits up and fills its lungs,
a black and white green-backed mongrel sees us off.

The road skirts the airport like a stray runway.
Incoming planes make as if to pick us off.
Sometimes it divides: one half runs along the ground,
the other makes a sudden hump – my fear of flyovers.

A little further, I read the simple-minded vertical lettering
on *Ariane*, the unmanned European rocket, the harmless beige
skin-tone of *café au lait*, falling back to earth
in eighty seconds, no use even to the weatherman...

We return late at night, my eyes are on stalks,
the breeze whips them into stiff peaks of inflammation
as they stare and stare at the city lights, *Gruppensex,*
Massage Bar, the breasts a woman bared to cool...

Our cat has sprayed the house to greet us.
Lust hurts him into eloquence, almost speech –
like the rabble-rousing live music on the record player,
cynical, manipulative, knowing where it wants to go.

Too tense for sex, too slow to kill, nothing
is as loud as the throbbing duet of the pigeons
in their bay on the roof, as the hours he spent
trapped in a thorn-bush, inhaling a local beauty.

Hausfrauenchor

'She's younger than I am, almost certainly
blonde, and he sleeps with her once a year...
The occasion is the office-party – alcohol,
music, and their formal routine collaboration
suddenly becomes something else. – All over
the country, wives write to the agony columns
for advice. One letter covers thousands
of cases. Of course, you want to allow him
his bit of fun; after working all year for
Germany's *Wirtschaftswunder* and your own.
And it's probably more than you can provide
with your cooking, your meat-and-two-veg sex,
the occasional *Sauerbraten*...He deserves it.
The rest of the time, he's faithful to you.
But when he comes home at some godforsaken hour,
lipstuck and dishevelled, drunk as a god, his
dried sperm crackling and flaking in his pants,
then you feel differently about it. You wish
you'd gone to the party and kept an eye on him.
– But then the newspapers don't recommend that:
husbands resent it – what's your business
in an office where you never set foot otherwise?'

They tell you the only course is to declare
a general amnesty for this particular offence.
A mass-exemption, like the students of '68,
who no longer have a "past", and instead hold
positions in the Civil Service: vetting radicals;
checking over photographs of demonstrations,
signatories on petitions; looking for traces
of the ineradicable red paint that is sprayed
over crowds of Communists to identify them...
So the best way is to kill them with kindness.
– And it isn't any easier for the secretary:
because she doesn't want to be a cock-teaser,
she gets into trouble with her boyfriend...
A week or two later, she gives my husband a tie
for Christmas. The whole family (himself
included) make fun of it, a silly pattern,
awful colours, what a useless garment anyway...
But then he wears it all the following year.'

STEPHEN ROMER

Higher Things

I wish I could, like Søren Kierkegaard,
be absolute and let her face recede

until it is an island in the water
he called memory. Nothing impure

could touch his lasting image of Régine.
Only in memory is love immune

from longing to be with her all the time.
He kept a candle burning in each room,

unfinished manuscript on every desk.
I shall need all his courage for the task

of settling firmly to the sublime;
there is only her face to start from.

News of Her

Because the world is wider than my thought
and reasonable voices tell me I'll forget

tonight I paid attention to the news.
Another tanker's stuck off the Azores

where I'm told it 'foundered' and 'caught fire'.
How much of my sympathy can this require

if the captain has been rescued with his crew
and the blaze will be dead by tomorrow?

But if one poor soul had been left on board
he would have made me pray (my thought is broad)

for the many who founder and catch fire,
for the few still burning, six months later.

Brasserie Lipp

The back of my head in an angled mirror.
Unflinching self-regard starts here,

with a disappointing skull. It falls away
from the crown, quite unceremoniously

finished off, behind a good façade.
There could be worse, something overbred,

the line of least resistance...To a girl
who's just sat down, I bare my Aztec profile.

Her skull is shapely but her lips are tight,
her eyes disdainful, but on the lookout;

imagine my surprise when she caressed
so tenderly the waiter's hairy wrist

bent like a croupier's to rake her money in.
It's a problem of interpretation.

Her gesture darts into four bright angles,
– infinite self-advertisement? Or else,

but there's a rhetoric to this as well,
'the shocking loneliness of the beautiful'.

Adult Single

As if a diary redeemed the time
I bring it up to date in a solemn

trivial rite, as if the recent past
were mastered like the latest

headlines, as if, once and for all,
I could get things under control

by jotting them down on this hurtling train
and disembark, born again

– but the appetite dies for reforming prose...
Papers fall from our hands, my neighbours

and I succumb
to warmth, myopia, constant rhythm

where fog has blotted out the landscape.
Cradled to sleep

I'm settling like contents in transit,
my head slips further down the seat,

my thought into solipsism, a sealed shell
of privacies, lulled from level

to level down a fault in the ocean floor.
I'm travelling back, through millennia

of evolution to the whiskered fish,
on the black stream of my single wish

to linger in perpetual motion
behind blue windows and the lash of rain.

Work

When shall we ever begin?
Swept mercilessly clean

there's a billion billion stars
in the skylight, and our chairs

make their strict companionable arc
with the fire. We're ready for work,

it's the moment we've been waiting for.
After a day of trial and error,

triumph and tantrum,
our baby's down and milky calm.

Our stubborn house
is nearly at peace,

as tamed as it ever will be.
We're dosed with tobacco and Irish tea,

there's a wall of books to be read,
hours of encircled lamplight ahead,

cimmerian voices crying to come in.
Now if ever we might begin

when the cold is eerie but it's warm in here
and we sit without moving, drunk on the idea.

ELIZABETH GARRETT

History Goes to Work

The soft-boiled egg is emptied
But makes a humpty-dumpty head
Reversed. Numbskull! Bald pate!
You know the spoon's importunate
Knock knock will wake the dead.

The silver spoon lies on its back
And spoons the room all up-
Side-down but never spills a drop:
The ovoid walls adapt their laws
And never show a crack.

The egg lies in the silver spoon
And yolkless words lie on the tongue
And all that's in the spoon-shaped room
Swears it is square; no books
Were cooked. The egg is done.

Remorse rests in its velvet drawer
Lapped in the sleep of metaphor,
The soul rests in the open palm
And will not put its shell back on,
And calmly waits for more.

Moules à la Marinière

We scoured the secret places of the creek,
Parting blistered fronds of bladder-wrack
To find the concupiscent clusters, rocked
In their granite crêche. Jack-knives prised
The molluscs out. Slick blue-blacks bruised
Slowly dull; and the sea expunged our tracks.

Bouquet of Muscadet, bouquet garni recall
The tuck and chuckle of mussels in a bucket
Behind the door. Damp and aromatic,
Steam insinuates itself into all
The kitchen clefts, and clings in briny beads
Above the flame where mussels chirp and wheeze.

I pour on wine; it seems they beg for more,
The beaked shells yearning wide as if in song –
Yet dumb – and lewdly lolling parrot-tongues.
Cream licks the back of a spoon and drawls a slur
Of unctuous benediction for this feast.
We smooth our cassocks; bow our heads; and eat.

It rained all night as though to wash away
A brininess that tanged the atmosphere:
Dreams – of forbidden fruit, of *fruits de mer*
Wrenched from their secret beds, of tastes that lay
Like sea's after-sting on the tongue. Still lingers
A trace of guilt. I wash my salty fingers.

DERMOT BOLGER

Snuff Movies

The wind shuffles through the cracked glass and the floorboards rot.
It has been eight days since I stepped outside this filthy flat
where I've sat watching and four times my vigil has been rewarded:
four times I have hung within the limbo of the static from the tube,
longing for release and yet not daring to believe it could happen,
and four times the picture hasn't jerked back on to advertisements –
my throat has dried up and my body trembled as I watched
the figure thrown naked into the room and the beating begin.
Whole days wither stagnantly in this flat and nothing happens,
days when I'm stuck like an insect on fly paper unable to move,
trapped within the metallic hiss of that ocean of static,
and I wait and pray that the advertisements will not continue
as over and over the slogans repeat without commentary or pity,
hammering out messages at those remaining sealed in their rooms.
Once we walked down streets and worked in throbbing factories,
I remember oil on my overalls and the smell of sweat without fear,
but then the coalitions collapsed and regrouped and were submerged
by the corporations who had learnt how to survive without us.
Just four times the knife has flashed like an old matador's
and youngsters raised their heads although blinded by the hood.
There is no way of knowing how many of my workmates are left,
caged up before crackling boxes terrified to miss the murders.
Last month I saw a man run with a plastic bag through the litter,
apart from him all streets to the superstore were deserted.
I breathe safely – I am too old for anybody's attention,
they will never come and shove me hooded into that studio,
I will never strain my head forward in expectation of the blow.
From this final refuge I can spy and be involved in their agony,
the flesh wincing and that final anonymous moan of pain;
and afterwards I breathe again in my renewed triumph of living.
Nobody knows any longer when the curfew begins or ends
but one evening I heard them come for somebody on the street.
I never knew which hooded neighbour I might have once passed
kept the whole of Ireland contained for a day with their death.
I know they are killing me too in this war of nerves I survive in,
it's been years since I've not slept sitting upright in this chair
dreaming of blood and waking fretfully to advertisements,

and yet I still cling on, speaking to nobody in the superstore,
running home frantic that I will miss a final glimpse of life.
Long ago I believed in God – now I believe what I am told:
there is no heaven except that instant when the set comes alive,
no purgatory except the infinite static bombarding the screen,
hell could only be if they came for the television or for me.

ROBERT CRAWFORD

The Saltcoats Structuralists
(for Douglas Cairns)

They found the world's new structure was a binary
Gleaming opposition of two rails

That never crossed but ran on parallel
Straight out of Cairo. From small boys

On Platform One who listened to the great
Schola cantorum of connecting rods

Dreamed-up by Scots-tongued engineers, they went on
To tame the desert, importing locomotives

From a distant Firth. New wives came out, and one,
Shipwrecked off Ailsa Craig, returned to Glasgow,

Caught the next boat; her servants had her wardrobe
Replaced in just four hours from the city shops.

Scotsmen among colonial expats
They learned RP, embarrassing their families

In Ayrshire villages where they talked non-stop
About biggah boilahs, crankshawfts. Nicknamed 'The Pharaohs',

They never understood the deconstruction
Visited on Empire when their reign in Egypt

Ran out of steam. They first-classed back to Saltcoats,
Post-Nasser; on slow commuter diesels

They passed the bare brick shells of loco-sheds
Like great robbed tombs. They eyed the proud slave faces

Of laid-off engineering workers, lost
In the electronics revolution. Along the prom

They'd holidayed on in childhood, with exotic walking sticks,
History in Residence, they moved

In Sophoclean raincoats. People laughed
At a world still made from girders, an Iron Age

Of Queen Elizabeths, pea-soupers, footplates,
And huge black toilet cisterns named 'St Mungo'.

Kids zapped the videogames in big arcades
Opposite Arran. Local people found

New energy sources, poems didn't rhyme.
The Pharaohs' grandchildren's accents sounded to them

Wee hell-taught ploughmen's. In slow seafront caffs
They felt poststructuralism, tanged with salt.

Scotland

Semiconductor country, land crammed with intimate expanses,
Your cities are superlattices, heterojunctive
Graphed from the air, your cropmarked farmlands
Are epitaxies of tweed.

All night motorways carry your signal, swept
To East Kilbride or Dunfermline. A brightness off low headlands
Beams-in the dawn to Fife's interstices,
Optoelectronics of hay.

Micro-nation. So small you cannot be forgotten,
Bible inscribed on a ricegrain, hi-tech's key
Locked into the earth, your televised Glasgows
Are broadcast in Rio. Among circuitboard crowsteps

To be miniaturised is not small-minded.
To love you needs more details than the Book of Kells –
Your harbours, your photography, your democratic intellect
Still boundless, chip of a nation.

Alba Einstein

When proof of Einstein's Glaswegian birth
First hit the media everything else was dropped:
Logie Baird, Dundee painters, David Hume – all
Got the big E. Physics documentaries
Became peak-viewing; Scots publishers hurled awa
MacDiarmid like an overbaked potato, and swooped
On the memorabilia: *Einstein Used My Fruitshop,*
Einstein in Old Postcards, Einstein's Bearsden Relatives.
Hot on their heels came the A.E. Fun Park,
Quantum Court, Glen Einstein Highland Malt.
Glasgow was booming. Scotland rose to its feet
At Albert Suppers where The Toast to the General Theory
Was given by footballers, panto-dames, or restaurateurs.
In the U.S. an ageing lab-technician recorded
How the Great Man when excited showed a telltale glottal stop.
He'd loved fiddlers' rallies. His favourite sport was curling.
Thanks to this, Scottish business expanded
Endlessly. His head grew toby-jug-shaped,
Ideal for keyrings. He'd always worn brogues.
Ate bannocks in exile. As a wee boy he'd read *The Beano.*
His name brought new energy: our culture was solidly based
On pride in our hero, The Universal Scot.

Customs

'*The Golden Bough* has been abridged
For the convenience of smugglers. It now fits a lady's handbag.
In any future plots against Sir James,
His works can be carried across national frontiers
To be buried in secret hiding places
He himself has chosen: the shores of the Lake of Nemi;
The sacred grove, Uppsala; the Braes of Balquhidder;
The Babar Archipelago.' So Lady Frazer
To The Brotherhood of the Golden Bough.

Sir James smiles. Blind as a seer
From Homeric times, he has encoded
His secret hates among the Fellows of Trinity
In the minutiae of the abridged edition
Alongside the names of girls from Helensburgh
He once wanted to sleep with: Helen Mackellar,
Fiona Simpson, Henrietta Walker.
He writes the words 'a dreamy voluptuous cult'.
Nobody has discovered them yet.

Lady Frazer learns masonic handshakes.
Her daughter dreams that she is Alan Breck
Lying silent, parched on top of a high rock,
With the redcoat soldiers below.
'Memories of the sister who sleeps in the land
Of Adonis never again to waken',
Sir James pauses and dips his pen
Into a mephitic pool of Quink,
'With the anemones and the roses.'

At night Lady Frazer flits like an owl
Among the rooftops of Cambridge, carrying her ear-trumpet,
Too-wooing to the sleepers, 'All of England shall pass'.
Sir James listens to the rustling skirts
Of his newest secretary, 'religious emotions
Of this sensuous, visionary sort', silky
Warm air currents waft from her legs, sending him
Like those young men at Kitty Hawk, North Carolina,
Gradually into the clouds.

He remembers his parents, his father compiling
A history of pens and paper. He remembers leading
The bull Mnevis of Heliopolis
Along East Argyle Street, tethering him to the porch.
He remembers climbing among the clump of trees
Where he perfected the ritual slaughter
Of Free Church elders, their dark, oozing blood
Staining and enriching all of Dunbartonshire,
Spirits of the Corn and the Wild.

There are similar practices in Orkney and Bavaria.
Adonis is an analogue of Rupert Brooke. Standing to address
Anthropologists in London, his eyes red over with blood,
He clutches his enormous napkin and falls.
Lady Frazer's electric hearing apparatus
Picks up signals from the Third Programme,
Broadcasting the vicious Stravinski. She grabs a steak-knife
And plunges it deep into the President
Of the Royal Society. 'Mussolini! Stalin!'

She yells, 'Come into this grove! Kill them
In the name of Sir James!' Officials
Rush towards the dinner table, dragging her screaming away.
Secretaries are dialling 999,
Demanding news-blackouts. Presbyterian hymns
Waft on the shore-wind, mixed with the peal of bells.
She writes pamphlets requiring the re-institution
Of seasonal killings and sacred prostitution.
She writes a history of the British Empire's

Cultivation of bloodsports. She is declared insane, locked up,
Lives several lifetimes, embraces the thought of Michel Foucault
Synthesised with the doctrine of reincarnation,
Claiming to be in constant astral contact
With Sir James himself, who is still dictating
Extra volumes of *The Golden Bough* which deal
With frontiers and warfare, the Oxbridge system,
Sir Walter Scott's sacrifice of Border virgins,
Television's ritual banality.

The rights of these books are all bought up
By titled people, media tycoons.
Not a word is ever published.
She reads and re-reads her husband's works:
'Ta-uz, who is no other than Tammuz, is here
Like Burns's John Barleycorn.' She cries
Over *Tristes Tropiques*. She writes the story
Of herself as she would have been if Compton Mackenzie
Had not invented visas as a method of surveillance,

If the Judeao-Christian tradition and Newtonian physics
Had not attempted to normalise and censor
Human behaviour, if poststructuralism
Had formed the basis of all human cuisine, and if Byron
Had been a woman, reincarnated as Lady Frazer.
When she dies at a secret location
(Her official obituary having been published
Years before), the children of the children
Of the Personhood of the Golden Bough

Keep alive her memory in sibylline sayings,
Videos and verses that can be unscrambled
By initiates only, hidden in sacred groves,
Chanting in unison in an age when wow and flutter
Have utterly gone, in a marketable future
In countries whose frontiers have been sanitised
Against all subversive thinking, on a planet safe for nostalgia.
Where zoom lenses lie glutted on the crewcut grass
You can hear crackly chanting on bootleg tapes:

'She places live hummingbirds in the tubes for duty-free cigars.
She is not caught.'

'She carries rare seedlings in her moist spongebag.
She is not caught.'

'She picks the mortar out of retaining walls.
She is not caught.'

'She leads the wind, nourishing it, into the crevices
Of dry-stane dykes. She is not caught.'

'She forges visas. She is not caught.'

'She emerges fully-formed from the head of Zeus.
She is not caught.'

'God smuggles Christ into her womb.
She is not caught.'

'She treasures the customs of all the peoples.
She passes through customs, bearing the seed of the new.
She smuggles towards us as we wait for her by the shore.
She croons in Gaelic "I have nothing to declare."'

FRED D'AGUIAR

Mama Dot Warns Against an Easter Rising

Doan raise no kite is good friday
but is out he went out an fly it
us thinkin maybe dere wont be a breeze
strong enouf an widout any a we to hole it
fo him he'd neva manage to get it high-up
to de tree top ware de wind kissin
de ripess sweetess fruit we cawn reach
but he let out some string bit by bit
tuggin de face into de breeze
coaxin it up all de time takin a few steps back
an it did rise up bit by bit till de lang tail
din't touch de groun an we grip de palin
we head squeeze between to watch him
an trace its rise rise rise up up up in de sky
we all want to fly in like bird but can only kite
fly an he step back juss as we beginnin
to smile fo him envy him his easter risin
when bap he let out a scream leggo string
an de kite drop outta de sky like a bird
a sail down to de nex field an we runnin to him
fogetting de kite we uncle dem mek days ago
fram wood shave light as bird bone
paper tin like fedder an de tongue o kite
fo singin in de sky like a bird an de tail
fo balance string in de mout like it pullin
de longess worm an he a hole him foot
an a bawl we could a see seven inch a greenhart
gone in at de heel runnin up him leg
like a vein he groanin all de way to de haspital
on de cross-bar a bike ridden by a uncle
she not sayin a word but we hearin her
fo de ress a dat day an evry year since
doan raise no kite is good friday
an de sky was a birdless kiteless wait fo her word

Airy Hall Isotope

Consider our man in a hovel
With no windows, a shack our missiles
Sail through; cracks that do not interrupt
The flow of moonlight or sunlight,
Seen here washing or baking his floor.

Consider too, our woman, reputed to fly
At night on the very broom that sweeps
Her yard printless; the same broom
Used to swipe Dog eyeing Hen's egg,
Noisily announced by Hen, drooled over
By Dog that is hungry, hungry;
Dreaming the one dream starring Hen.

Consider last, any boy convalescing
In a house crucified between those two
(How he was among the first to fling
Sand stones), spreadeagled
In her mud hut, she massages him
After two days in a pain she alone
Kills with her curious touch.

Consider these and you have a life,
Several lives lapping the one sun,
Casting the same lengthening shadows
From a moon so strapping, the children
Play bat and ball and make clean catches.

Only The President's Eggs are Yellow

Everyone else's resembles
Condensed milk; 'sunny-side up'
Offered as a snipe alternative.

All desires boil down to a visa,
A queue, longer than the electorate,
Half the national football team
Jumped, disappearing on tour.

The electric grid scrimps at half-strength.
Videos wait, doubling as bases for plants;
Televisions reflect exactly what is around them;
Fridges like empty coffins have a wise patience,
Keeping stale air stale at sauna-temperature.

A hundred-year tree the country's new main road
Circumnavigated either side to pass,
Spontaneously uprooted; my first cousin
Planted a nimble offshoot in its place;
In a tropics where the rains are simply due,
Its youth showed, wilting in the heat.

This democracy is forced-ripe, for what?
You can tell by how newer and newer conscripts
Dismiss being dunked, feet-up in water-barrels;
How they carry themselves as if smelling
Responsibilities far above their stations;
How they dash grudging salutes at civilians
Earmarked for nursed rounds of ammunition

(Bursting with too much importance to notice).
The American Embassy tends all their street's
Litter and trees, painted in brilliant stockings;
Shutters angled to see out, not in;
A private generator to cook cold air and ice.
I had to crawl for a visa to enter the country;

Not because I'm an undesirable, it's unwritten
Policy in line with giant economies.
A clerk supplements a low salary anyhow;
Washing one shirt every night; without
Deodorants, a skunk an hour into the day.

A strapping man, about my age, with bare feet
Begged me for any loose change I could spare.
I emptied all the tinny noise in my pockets
Into his cupped hands: 'Thanks, English.'

By twelve o'clock egg and sun look alike:
Whole office blocks are warped LPs;
A gross tremor threatening the real.

FROM Letter from Mama Dot

II

You are a traveller to them.
A West Indian working in England;
A Friday, Tonto, or Punkawallah;
Sponging off the state. Our languages
Remain pidgin, like our dark, third,
Underdeveloped, world. I mean, their need
To see our children cow-eyed, pot-bellied,
Grouped or alone in photos and naked,
The light darkened between their thighs.
And charity's all they give: the cheque,
Once in a blue moon (when guilt's
A private monsoon), posted to a remote
Part of the planet they can't pronounce.
They'd like to keep us there.
Not next door, your house propping-up
Theirs; your sunflowers craning over
The fence, towards a sun falling
On their side; begonias that belong
To them shouldering through its tight
Staves; the roots of both mingling.
So when they skin lips to bare teeth
At you, remember it could be a grimace
In another setting: the final sleep
More and more of us meet in our prime,
(Your New Cross fire comes to mind);
Who dream nowadays of peace.
You know England, born there, you live
To die there, roots put down once
And for all. Drop me a line soon,
You know me. *Neva see come fo see.*

Airy Hall Nightmare

You sleep little and light
In a bed made for two big people.
Now the springs are brands;
Now electric rings;
Now nails stacked close as bristles.

You are in this bed on the open sea
Strapped under bedding tucked in tight,
Without the strength to lift your arm,
The one with a thousand needles
Or stripped of all nerves, it's not yours.

Nose down in a pillow,
How can you shift the boulder
That is your likeness,
Greying by the second?
With sheer will? How indeed.

The Cow *Perseverance*

I

Here I am writing you on old newspaper against a tide of print,
In the regular spaces between lines (there are no more trees).
I've turned it upside-down to widen the gap bordering sense and
        nonsense,
For what I must say might very well sound as if it were topsy-turvy.
I put myself in your shoes (unable to recall when I last set eyes on
        a pair).
You read everything twice, then to be doubly sure, aloud,
Testing their soundness: *we wash cow's dung for its grain*,
And I feel your stomach turn; it's not much unlike collecting it for
        fuel,
Or mixed with clay to daub cracks in our shelters and renew door-
        mounds
That free us of rain, insects and spirits. They no longer drop the milk
We let them live for; their nights spent indoors for safe keep,
Their days tethered to a nearby post. People eye them so, they are fast
Becoming our cross; you'd think they'd fallen out of the sky.

II

Hunger has filled them with what I can only call compassion.
Such bulbous, watery eyes blame us for the lack of grass and worse,
Expect us to do something; tails that held the edge of windscreen
        wipers
In better days, swishing the merest irritant, a feather's even,
Let flies congregate until the stretched, pockmarked hide is them.
That's why, when you asked how things were, I didn't have to look
        far,
I thought, *Let the cow explain, its leathery tongue has run this geography*
Many times over, how milk turns, unseen, all at once, so lush pastures
Threw up savannahs. The storms are pure dust or deep inside the
        rowdiest
Among us, virtually dead and rowdy because they know it, they're
        not sure
What else to do. You fathom why, when a cow croons, we offer it
What we can't as a bribe for it to stop: *silence is perseverance.*

III

We watch its wait on meagre haunches, ruminating on what must be
Imperishable leather, some secret mantra, our dear buddha, for the
        miracle
We need; and us, with nowhere to turn, find we believe. God knows
It's a case of choosing which pot-hole in the road to ride; knowing
We export the asphalt that could fill them; knowing too the one
        thing
We make these days that is expressly ours is whipped in malarial
        water
And forced down our throats for daring to open our mouths.
Give us the cow's complicity anyday: its perfect art of being left
In peace; its till-now effortless conversion of chewy grass to milk;
And its daft hoof-print, ignored for so long though clearly
        trespassing.
Then and then alone, we too can jump over the moon, without
        bloodshed.
Its raised-head and craned-neck attempt to furnish an exact account
Is a tale you and I are bound to finish, in flesh or spirit.

W.N. HERBERT

FROM **The Testament of The Reverend Thomas Dick**

1. *Astronomy dominie*

No irony could touch the telescopic length
of your desire to explicate space.
You sent theoretic steam engines to the stars
at twenty miles per hour, taking nearly
four thousand years to make your point
and reach Uranus. You
were our MacGonagall of science, who
inspired David Livingstone to
plunge through Africa's dark galaxy,
spreading news of your Future State:
a Heaven of astronomers.
Livingstone, whose only convert lapsed,
who buried his wife en route
to nowhere, whose message got
sucked into his heart's black hole.

Not even the fourteen foot erection
in pink granite to your memory
in St Aidan's Churchyard, Broughty Ferry,
so much thinks of wrinkling back
from that frozen bath of darkness,
eternity as space not time, that your mind
colonised for the Redeemed
as our afterlife's estate. And so
we learn the pupil size
of the average Mercurian eye
is, logically, one-fiftieth of an inch,
nor did you flinch from telling us
the population of the rings of Saturn was,
probably, eight billion souls,
half topsy, half turvy: all very alien.

I christen your engine *Dick's Rocket.*
I watch it climb its gaunt arc
of track, perhaps past the moon
by now, with Livingstone as Casey Jones
and Stanley for a fireman.

A few saucers buzz round, curious,
as from the carriage dragged behind
you pump out psalms
on the Harmonium of the Spheres
to a Martian chorus,
tone-deaf of course, but not,
even to angelic ears,
not, by God, inglorious.

9. *The justified astronomer*

Not for you an eternity of tambourines,
of surreptitiously notching the millennia
on the corner of your harp. Nor yet
the fozy recreation of an urbane life;
municipal Heaven, with
each generation assigned its own
translation of the 'many mansions',
attending Mozart's millionth piano concerto
or Dante's divine sit-commedia. All
trivia, litigation, dog-walking, tea-
sipping, falconry, and the wearing
of fashionable garments, would henceforth cease.
Only astronomy would really be encouraged.

Christ, when not knocking out the framework
for another 'aerial reflector' (your design),
would gather to him Herschel and Galileo,
Tycho Brahe and Ptolemy and the gang,
and instruct them on the nature
of another previously unknown star,
its planets and their orbits,
its populations and their position (1-10)
on a scale of ultimate goodness.
Their eyes would focus on the orbs concerned
better than any lens they'd ever ground,
pierce its atmosphere, and contemplate
its temples and its raw 'moral scenery'.

Then all the countless mothy souls
would mob softly at the doors
of great public observatories;
amphitheatres with a single lens

for their roofs, that could be turned to face
any corner of the heavens – Earth itself
could be moved, on special request,
to observe rare events
in the cosmological calendar – and these
were all the temples God required,
and this was all the worship, because
the totality of physical matter, as
you guessed, is equal to the mass of the Deity.

Mappamundi

Eh've wurkt oot a poetic map o thi warld.

Vass tracts o land ur penntit reid tae shaw
Englan kens naethin aboot um. Ireland's
bin shuftit tae London, whaur
oafficis o thi Poetry Sock occupeh fehv
squerr mile. Seamus Heaney occupehs three
o thon. Th'anerly ithir bits in Britain
ur Oaxfurd an Hull. Thi Pool, Scoatlan,
an Bisley, Stroud, ur cut ti cuttilbanes in
America, which issa grecht big burdcage wi
a tartan rug owre ut, tae shaw
Roabirt Lowell. Chile disnae exist.
Argentina's bin beat. Hungary and Russia
haena visas. Africa's editid doon ti
a column in *Poetry Verruca*,
whaur Okigbo's gote thi ghaist
o Roy Campbill hingin owre um. Thi Faur East's
faan aff – aa but China: thon's renemmed
Ezra Poond an pit in thi croncit cage.
France disnae get a luke-in:
accoardin tae Geoffrey Hill, plucky wee
Charles Péguy is wrasslin wi
this big deid parrot caad 'Surrealism' fur
thi throne o Absinthe Sorbet.

In this scenario Eh'm a bittern stoarm aff Ulm.

A Portrait of Allen Ginsberg stranded
on the fire escape, 1948

Dinna skreik oan thon irin balcony!
Eh canna dae wi this black bluit
   lyk a glowrin ower groins –
Eh've cum back tae masel eftir
lossin ma cuits
                  Eh cuttum aff inna daurk wuid
                  an chuckt thum inna glog-hole's
                  platinumb ee,
Eh gote a taxi here.

No allowt tae trummil Eh shak lyk an ingine,
cannae stey ti stare at thi nichtingaltree
wheeplan i thi Broad
wi a fuchtir o spinniloscura bowes.

Thi lamplicht faas oan thi sang
as tho thru different times
                  a frozen smirr oan heids
                  centuries apairt
                  beaman frae
      some final Jerusalem, uts
carbunkilt licht plunkt thru time
in crystal epiphanies
that slit oor fleesh unkent
as we trachil aboot, drunkenboukit lyk
                           escapees fae
                           operatin theaturs:
wuv aa gote fou tae fiss
thi greasy chups
wur goannae pit inside us,
wir stummacks' cauld creak i thi mornin.

      Hoo can Eh credit this
laivin me paralysit wi
a parabola o scaurs that canna be seen
      lyk dernit cameras' een?
Cum awa frae thon
fire escape an lat

thi scrapirs drap thir reek upwirts ti thi lift:
Eh'm shoart o
         an oozin o
                bremerie here.

skreik: scream; *cuits*: ankles; *glog-hole*: well; *wheeplan*: emitting birdsong; *fuchtir*: agitated movement; *smirr*: fine rain; *trachil*: trail; *drunkenboukit:* with bodies full of alcohol; *dernit*: concealed; *reek*: smoke; *lift*: sky; *bremerie*: courage.

A Two Year Ode

I. *To Gorbachev* (1991)

> '*For now in the flower and iron of the truth*
> *To you we turn…*'
>   HUGH MacDIARMID,
>   First Hymn to Lenin

Thi cat sits at ma French windies,
irrepressibil, stupit, lyk thi licht
that maun cam in, she moans.

Ut's a cauld dey, thi waurmth oan ma herr,
lyk hir affeckshun, anerly exists
atween thi gless an me. Ootwith

ut aa blaws loose as meh attenshun
when Eh lat hur in. She waants
aa o me or oot again. Eh sit an feel

licht fill thi hooses in Fife
an the cheek banes o Tay's waves,
Eh rowl wi ut lyk thi cat owre

thi Baltic. Eh'm oan a trenn o licht
speedin fur Moscow, bearin Pasternak
back, shovelt oot o Zhivago's snaa-cell.

Eh'm oan a trenn o licht speedin
atween thi gless an thi sel,
enterin Russia oan a cat's shouthirs.

Eh'm fu o thi eisenin that wad stoap time
i thi middil o thi page, an force
uts maist donsy passengir

oot, tae dance upon thi snaw. Dance,
Liberty, dance! spleet yir sark an
melt a permafrost wi yir reid wame!

But Liberty nivir fed onywan. An Christ's
poke, tho unca deep, wisna designd
tae clear thi queues, 'Thi puir ur aye wi us.'

Thi licht mairches thru Leningrad streets
back frae Afghanistan, fae Germany.
Thi licht wad faa oan onywan.

Ut pleys wi ma herr, burns ma nape,
ut passis thru ma banes an laives spores
therr o daurkniss ayont aa dawins.

Thi cat dwaums o parlaments
o heidliss mice. Eh'm lukein thru'ur
intil thon nicht ayont bombs, ayont money,

whaur fowk stoap oan brigs owre thi Clyde,
thi Neva, an waatch thi licht arrive
fae extink stars, an wait fur thi licht

fae thi stars yet tae come.

II. *To Yeltsin* (1992)

> *'I am dead, but you are living.'*
> BORIS PÁSTERNAK,
> Doctor Zhivago

As thi furst bids arrehv fur Lenin's banes
twa blimps ascend abune Red Square:
yin says *Pola*, thi ithir *Cola*. Ilkane

costs saxty thoosan dollars. Thi date
is May thi Furst, but nae tanks gee thanks
tae you, as ye maun've calculatit

lang syne. Thi furst buds push thru
this English gairdin lyk fingirtips:
Eh wundir gin Eh tuke thir prints

wad Eh get sodgers, husbands, Man-
delstam? An yet ye hud tae repress
thon camsteery core o celebrants

o Stalin's burthday – sae Freudian
an act ut wad be tactless tae add
thi Capitalist's platitude

concernin thi Unearnin's gratitude
gin ye didnae sae brawly deserve ut
fur duntin yir last heid-bummir oot,

wha wadna hasten Russia's race
tae buy hur freedom frae thi West
when serfitude wiz aa yi could

invest. Eh waatch thi dentylions
brent thru thi southren simmer green
lyk black mairt brollies, bairgain boambs,

or jist thi plooks oan thi Urse's hide
as seen frae space by Krikalev,
thon cosmonaut that sat ootside

aa cheenge, angelickly-aware
thru radio hams o coup an you,
o Commonwealth an thon's despair,

thi last tae ride thi yirthly crest,
thi first tae cross owre concepts; no
thi achronic birl o dogma's collar.

Eh think o Scoatlan, still stapt ticht
in uts disunity, lyk Auld Nick's
three-heidit doag in wan slip leash;

and Dante wiz sae subtly richt
tae tell himsel tae nivir retour,
no jist tae Florence, his past hame,

but tae thi past in Florentine heids,
thir indecisive noo. Dundee
wad be lyk landin fae thon heicht,

breathan thi Steppes' uncheengin air.

maun: must; *anerly*: only; *eisenin*: desire; *donsy*: lovely, vigorous; *sark*: under-garment; *poke*: pouch; *dawin*: dawn; *dwaums*: dreams; *abune*: above; *camsteery*: fierce, perverse; *core*: roup; *heid-bummir*: leader; *dentylion*s: dandelions; *black mairt*: black market; *urse*: bear; *stapt*: rammed; *retour*: return.

JACKIE KAY

Maybe that's why I don't like
all this talk about her being black,
I brought her up as my own
as I would any other child
colour matters to the nutters;
but she says my daughter says
it matters to her

I suppose there would have been things
I couldn't understand with any child,
we knew she was coloured.
They told us they had no babies at first
and I chanced it didn't matter what colour it was
and they said *oh well are you sure*
in that case we have a baby for you –
to think she wasn't even thought of as a baby,
my baby, my baby

I chase his *Sambo Sambo* all the way from the school gate.
A fistful of anorak – What did you call me? Say that again.
Sam-bo. He plays the word like a bouncing ball
but his eyes move fast as ping pong.
I shove him up against the wall,
say that again you wee shite. *Sambo, sambo*, he's crying now

I knee him in the balls. What was that?
My fist is steel; I punch and punch his gut.
Sorry I didn't hear you? His tears drip like wax.
Nothing he heaves *I didn't say nothing.*
I let him go. He is a rat running. He turns
and shouts *Dirty Darkie* I chase him again.
Blond hairs in my hand. Excuse me!
This teacher from primary 7 stops us.
Names? I'll report you to the headmaster tomorrow.
But Miss. Save it for Mr Thompson she says

My teacher's face cracks into a thin smile
Her long nails scratch the note well well
I see you were fighting yesterday, again.
In a few years time you'll be a juvenile delinquent.
Do you know what that is? Look it up in the dictionary.
She spells each letter with slow pleasure.
Read it out to the class.
Thug. Vandal. Hooligan. Speak up. Have you lost your tongue?

To be honest I hardly ever think about it
except if something happens, you know
daft talk about darkies. Racialism.
Mothers ringing my bell with their kids
crying *You tell. You tell. You tell.*
– *No.* You tell your little girl to stop calling
my little girl names and I'll tell my little girl
to stop giving your little girl a doing.

We're practising for the school show
I'm trying to do the Cha Cha and the Black Bottom
but I can't get the steps right
my right foot's left and my left foot's right
my teacher shouts from the bottom
of the class Come on, show

us what you can do I thought
you people had it in your blood.
My skin is hot as burning coal
like that time she said Darkies are like coal
in front of the whole class – my blood
what does she mean? I thought

she'd stopped all that after the last time
my dad talked to her on parents' night
the other kids are all right till she starts;
my feet step out of time, my heart starts
to miss beats like when I can't sleep at night –
What Is In My Blood? The bell rings, it is time.

Sometimes it is hard to know what to say
that will comfort. Us two in the armchair;
me holding her breath, 'they're ignorant
let's have some tea and cake, forget them'

Maybe it's really Bette Davis I want
to be the good twin or even better the bad
one or a nanny who drowns a baby in a bath.
I'm not sure maybe I'd prefer Katharine
Hepburn tossing my red hair, having a hot
temper. I says to my teacher Can't I be
Elizabeth Taylor, drunk and fat and she
just laughed, not much chance of that.
I went for an audition for *The Prime
of Miss Jean Brodie*. I didn't get a part
even thought I've been acting longer
than Beverley Innes. So I have. Honest.

Olubayo was the colour of peat
when we walked out heads turned
like horses, folk stood like trees
their eyes fixed on us – it made me
burn, that hot glare; my hand
would sweat down to his bone.
Finally, alone, we'd melt
nothing, nothing would matter

He never saw her. I looked for him in her;
for a second it was as if he was there
in that glass cot looking back through her.

On my bedroom wall is a big poster
of Angela Davis who is in prison
right now for nothing at all
except she wouldn't put up with stuff.
My mum says she is *only* 26
which seems really old to me
but my mum says it is young
just imagine, she says, being on

America's Ten Most Wanted People's List at 26!
I can't.
Angela Davis is the only female person
I've seen (except for a nurse on TV)
who looks like me. She had big hair like mine
that grows out instead of down.
My mum says it's called an *Afro*.
If I could be as brave as her when I get older
I'll be OK.
Last night I kissed her goodnight again
and wondered if she could feel the kisses
in prison all the way from Scotland.
Her skin is the same too you know.
I can see my skin is that colour
but most of the time I forget,
so sometimes when I look in the mirror
I give myself a bit of a shock
and say to myself *Do you really look like this?*
as if I'm somebody else. I wonder if she does that.

I don't believe she killed anybody.
It is all a load of phoney lies.
My dad says it's a set up.
I asked him if she'll get the electric chair
like them Roseberries he was telling me about.
No he says the world is on her side.
Well how come she's in there then I thinks.
I worry she's going to get the chair.
I worry she's worrying about the chair.
My dad says she'll be putting on a brave face.
He brought me a badge home which I wore
to school. It says FREE ANGELA DAVIS.
And all my pals says 'Who's she?'

In Jackie Kay's *The Adoption Papers* sequence, the voices of
the three speakers are distinguished typographically:

DAUGHTER: Palatino typeface
ADOPTIVE MOTHER: Gill typeface
BIRTH MOTHER: Bodoni typeface

Pounding Rain

News of us spreads like a storm.
The top of our town to the bottom.
We stand behind curtains
parted like hoods; watch each other's eyes.

We talk of moving to the west end,
this bit has always been a shoe box
tied with string; but then again
your father still lives in that house
where we warmed up spaghetti bolognese
in lunch hours and danced to Louis Armstrong,
his gramophone loud as our two heart beats
going boom diddy boom diddy boom.

Did you know then? I started dating Davy;
when I bumped into you I'd just say Hi.
I tucked his photo booth smile into my satchel
brought him out for my pals in the intervals.

A while later I heard you married Trevor Campbell.
Each night I walked into the school dinner hall
stark naked, till I woke to Miss, Miss Miss
every minute. Then, I bumped into you at the Cross.

You haven't changed you said; that reassurance.
Nor you; your laugh still crosses the street.
I trace you back, beaming, till –
Why don't you come round, Trevor would love it.

He wasn't in. I don't know how it happened.
We didn't bother with a string of do you remembers.
I ran my fingers through the beads in your hair.
Your hair's nice I said stupidly, nice, suits you.

We sat and stared till our eyes filled
like a glass of wine. I did it, the thing
I'd dreamt a million times. I undressed you
slowly, each item of clothing fell
with a sigh. I stroked your silk skin
until we were back in the Campsies, running
down the hills in the pounding rain,
screaming and laughing; soaked right through.

GERARD WOODWARD

To a Power Station

I

You simmer your allotted districts,
Bringing a city's kettles to the boil,
Switched on with index fingers.

Your set of six vases, each of a size
To make me a tablecloth fly walking
In fear of elbows, are overgrown

With steam, like the flasks
Of film scientists who have discovered
The transformational brew.

II

You are strong under my stairs.
When the fuse blew
And we switched to candles

I played cats' cradle with you;
Threading your silver hair
I sewed you back together again.

(The wet raincoat dripped in the hall.)
I flicked the switch by the door
And watched you walk the bulb's tightrope.

III

The pylons crackle like sellotape unwinding.
The power station is tearing its hair out,
Threatening to overheat, turn its bricks red

And scatter them, like a child
Tired of its old toys
And wanting attention.

Then we are thankful for the cooling towers
As the power station takes a long
Draught from each and wipes its brow.

IV

Steam is the ghost of water
And rain the ghost of steam
As a flower is the ghost of a seed,

Honey the ghost of flowers
And bees the ghosts of honey.
This then is a ghost house.

I would boil myself if I had a big enough pan,
A Diogenes of the stove, knees to chin, turning
The rings full on, I would happily evaporate.

V

There is a village under wraps,
The church cloaked with oilcloth,
Windows newspapered, only the gardens vulnerable.

Cooling towers, your death is a television event.
I watched it on a day when strong winds
Filled the streets with reading matter.

Christmas arrived early in the village.
The cooling towers fell like gloves,
The thick weather made sills and flowers fat with dust.

Mevagissey Bakery

The doughnut with its red heart
Has come alive like the fish skeletons
Whose guts are rebuilt of mud.

Jamheart, mudheart, reflect each other
As the bakery window reflects the sea
Like a huge transparent postcard

And sees the town's stone mouth
Drink a mixture of tide and boats
Who spear themselves in the mud.

And childhood evolves here for each
Boat is a cupboard of toys,
Balloons, footballs, flags, windmills

Attaching themselves to wooden castles.
In this mud playground
Crabs are knitting

Like the men up on the walls
Where the quay becomes a haberdashery of linens
As though the stone had spawned seed to drift

Like old man's beard.
And the fine nets pull the sea into the town
Where the salt pulse transforms each shop

Into an imitation of itself,
The butcher's with its sawdust floor
Is a tiny beach bathed in blood

And the bakery whose yeast rises like the tide
Evolves cakes in spirals like sea snails,
Decorates its fancies with tiny sugar seahorses.

The bakery throbs with jam and yeast,
It is the town's warm heart
And feeds the journey from childhood to death

From harbour to graveyard
Where each death is marked by a fish bone;
Where, in their mud voyage

In wooden submarines, human bones
Are rebuilt of mud and through their
White periscopes sniff a mixture of salt and yeast.

Mandrax

I

In my dreams
The museum mouse
Came up the path,

The black glass
Fallen from his eyes,
Two tiny button holes.

I remember his friends;
The fox who had
A tongue of wax,

An owl, ghastly
In fixed flight,
His wings fingers of silk

And the kingfisher
Who lived in a cupboard,
His jaws dripping sap

As he fetched up
One tasteless fish
From his pool of glass.

They all shared
A forest entirely white,
Behind glass

And lit by neon;
Their feeble bodies
Packed with twine

Wound tight in knots,
Weak, unmuscular,
Their skulls quite empty

As was this mouse's head
As he crept into the house,
His eyes in his pink hands.

II

My mother's sleep was made
Of chalk. Round, white pills
That fixed her suddenly

In a peaceful paralysis.
Her egg, half hollowed-out,
Becoming dry and cold.

I imagined her
Inside the glass
Of her pill jar

Fixed in some transparent
Solution that was all
The sugars of the world

Crushed to one perfect
Mammoth ice
So sweet it burned.

Her book open
At every page.
Her glasses crooked.

She would go to bed
On all fours, her specs
Clatter on the carpet.

LAVINIA GREENLAW

Galileo's Wife

He can bring down stars.
They are paper in my hands
and the night is dark.

He knows why stone falls and smoke rises,
why the sand on the shore in the morning
is gone in the afternoon.

He gobbles larks' tongues from Tuscany
and honey from Crete. If only he could
measure me and find my secrets.

*

I have dropped pebbles into water
six hundred times this morning.
The average speed of descent

was three pulsebeats with a half-beat variable,
allowing for the different angle and force
with which each pebble hit the water.

Galileo wants me to explain my results.
He lectures on naval engineering
at the university tonight.

*

There has been a fire.
Our children were trapped in a tower.
He watched them fall, a feather, a stone,

and land together. He dictated notes
and ordered their bodies weighed before burial.
I sleep among their clothes.

I must leave Pisa.
He says I am to locate the edge of the world.
Galileo must complete the map.

He has a pair of velvet slippers.
It takes half an hour to lace my boots.
I like to keep my feet on the ground.

*

There is a cloud over Dalmatia.
It is the colour of my wedding dress.
Shadows burn stone.

The bears in Natolia
follow me to the marketplace
and carry food to the houses of the poor.

In Persia I walk east all day
across a desert. I look back at sunset.
The desert is a sea of orchids.

Tartaria is cold. Horses dance
on the path down the ravine. I fall
and the frozen air catches me.

In China I come to a walled city
where they know how to make a powder
that turns the sky to thunder and gold.

In the land of paper houses, a tidal wave
carries me up into the mountains.
I feed children with the fish in my pockets.

I fall asleep beside the ocean
and wake up in the New World
where my footsteps split yellow rock wide open.

A wind I refuse to name carries me home.
Galileo opens the door. I draw a circle
and he closes my eye with a single blow.

*

He says my boots have kept him awake
for the fifteen years I've been away.
He gives me pebbles and water.

Every night he is at the university
proving the existence of the edge of the world.
His students sleep and applaud.

I leave the truth among his papers
and thank the bears of Natolia
that I never taught him how to write.

From Scattered Blue
(for Lesley Davies)

I drive back along the river
like I always do, not noticing.
Something in the light tears open
the smoke from the power-station chimney,

each twist and fold, the construction
of its slow muscular eventual rise
and there, right at the edge of it,
a continual breaking up into sky.

And that's another thing, the sky.
How the mist captures what's left of sunset,
the sodium orange and granite pink
distilled from scattered blue.

The choreography of air-traffic control
and the cranes nested downstream are part of it,
like the bridge and its sugar coat
of broken fairylight. The time of year

when every bird is a brushstroke and the trees
are revealed in a lack of colour. It reminds me
of how we used to talk; how we want sometimes
to do more than just live it.

Night Parrot

The feathers were taken from the front wheel of a juggernaut.
All the colours of a winter morning, hinged with pink and bone.
The driver sensed that here was something he had stolen
and had to hide in a box at the back of an empty cupboard

in the attic of an almost empty house. The night parrot.
He had heard some story, a reason not to enter the forest after dark.
And it came true, this curse he couldn't quite remember,
for whatever he now held left him empty-handed,
and he could not sleep for the weight of what it felt like,
the air filled with the impossibility of its cries.

The Man Whose Smile Made Medical History

On dead afternoons my brother would borrow
rubber gloves and wellington boots
to chance the electrics of the ancient projector.

We would interrupt fifty-year-old summers where
a woman I now know in nappies and a walking frame
played leapfrog on a beach in West Wales

with a man whose smile made medical history.
The First World War revealed the infinite
possibilities of the human form,

so when in '16 he was sent back from France
without his top lip, the army doctors
decided to try and grow him a new one.

They selected the stomach as the ideal place
from which to tease a flap of skin
into a handle that could be stretched

and sewn to what was left of his mouth.
This additional feature was surgically removed
once it had fed the regeneration

of a thankfully familiar shape.
All I can find in my grandfather's face
to record the birth of plastic surgery

is the tight shyness he pulls into a grin,
unaware that scientific progress
which had saved his reflection could do nothing

to save his life. A doctor, aged thirty-four,
he died of viral pneumonia,
having recently heard of antibiotics.

MAGGIE HANNAN

Dr Roget's Bedside Manner

Peter Mark Roget worked as a doctor. He compiled his 'thesaurus'
because he felt that if he widened his vocabulary he would be able
to communicate more successfully with his patients.

1. *Abstract Relations*

Odd pawk this that's
laid her up for good:

copper helix like a
fiddlehead's lovelock

in her womb. The aborted
little tiny, future

bantling's all in driblets;
limb from limb and

bit by bit.
Semi, hemi, aliquot.

2. *Space*

Abysm, from which there
is an exodus of keck and

gurk, and pardon, ouch
excuse me. This one's

really shotten herring:
feed with skilly, brewis,

brose. Until tomorrow,
collywobbly. Operation

pending.
P.S. Appendix

3. *Matter*

Doomed. There is a point
at which the pap appears

to reach its critical
mass. When it comes to

the push: agues, grief.
The word is cancer.

There is no hope:
the patient's now *in*

articulo mortis, swansong:
crunk, pule, pip. Croak.

4. *Intellect*

Idioglossia, so to speak,
is blether and blat. Tics:

multi- and poly-. Politic
to isolate – not, to wit,

to woo disaster through
folie à deux. Look out!

Incarcerate the madman,
in bedlam, the bin; he'll

hornswoggle, clack –
queer fish, *ad infinitum.*

5. *Volition*

About as independent
as a hog on ice. His

last days were a
shilly-shally between

going and staying.
What it came down to

was a rope, a chair.
Lesions. *Post Mortem.*

Result of action:
suicide, a lesser evil.

6. *Affections*

Sob-stuff, you think?
Well, I knew this rip,

got his comeuppance;
too much moll and mopsy,

I'd guess, or demi-rep.
Debagged, putrescent,

in my office, I told
him *syphilis.* Expect

fistula. Ooze.
Ultimately, loss of face.

Environment

1. *Elsewhere*

Having arrived, the first
and last thing you

acquire is a taste
for absolutes; as if

you know you have become
a part of the slip-meet

at the fell's foot,
scratchings, and Hush.

Water travels elsewhere,
under-running Dowgang

and Redwing, leaving
a clench of rust

on rubble. You note
the dead roots, forests

shitting slowly out
of kilter and into

other. Whatever leaves,
returns, or stays

the eye is wile:
tail-flick or leaf-fall,

to harry, pass or dream
time: this dispossession.

2. *Hoardings*

So so-so, this accumulation
of odds and ends, refuse

the digger will bank into
skips. The dog – days

hungry – knows the nub
of the matter is being

able to minnow the gap
between concrete and wire,

make off through the no-go,
past metal, metal and blinding,

to become made dust:
cumulonimbus rising

out of the dip of the track.
Out of the dip of the track,

the horizon is visible:
rooftops, cables, chimneys

you would hammer down
like tacks, people

grouped under the hoardings;
ads for bitter or Multiscreen:

*The Final Nightmare, For the Boys,
Die Hard, Truly, Madly, Deeply.*

3. *Provincial*

Here, and here again
through the region's

knap and sink
of anywhere, seen

from any window:
this door, that street –

not, but not
far from the diktat

of knack, of knowing that
where the weather is *fine*

the people are also
without astonishment

at birdsong or the memory
of it, the migrant

nuance of alarm,
to which, in the gardens,

the municipal tulip
is anathema, emblem

of radical boredom.
Here, and here again

*you know gan be gyp
to the ditto, if doggo.*

The Vanishing Point

> *Human Beings like you are very rare in the world. You act as a prism.*
> *You are Sagawa, who ate a human being.*
> – Interviewer to ISSEI SAGAWA, who killed and ate his girlfriend.

1. *Framed*

On the ground were the two bodies, entwined
and, presently, still... Listen. This is what

you expect; there are two ways of seeing
things. 1. *On the ground were the two bodies,*

entwined and, presently, still. His eyes shut
as if to kiss, his mouth was fast against

the mouth... See? The radio is talking
dirty... *his mouth was fast against the mouth...*

But listen. 2. (This is not what you think...)
...against the mouth of the wound... You want me

to continue?... *the wound where the bullet*
had entered her body... Then you come to

the eyewitness... *where her head had been was*
framed with blood, like... rupturing the speaker.

2. *You are Sagawa*

You are Sagawa, who ate a human being
Sagawa, whose voice is a hawkmoth.

You are Sagawa, who ate a human being
Sagawa. Small. Sphagnum-tongued.

Sagawa, who ate a human being?
Shithead. Meatbrain. Sagawa.

You are Sagawa
Fish-gilled, breathing blood.

Sagawa, you ate a human being
Sagawa dreaming. Waking.

Sagawa

Mother and father of appetites, I am
Sagawa, who'll kiss you, for starters.

Who acts as a prism?
Sagawa the hammer, the pane of glass.

3. The Prism

It will be as the light • wings across you •
there will be • a woman • water flowing •
into water • intimate as water •
appetent and eye • for you are touching •
the world with your skin • strange and ablaze she •
will be held • gently so gently • you will •
weep sweet come • in the sweet palm of your hand •

It will be. As the light wings across you,
there will be a woman; water flowing
into water, intimate as water.
Appetent and eye, for you are touching
the world. With your skin strange and ablaze, she
will be held gently. So gently you will
weep. Sweet come in the sweet palm of your hand.

4. Chat Show

2351 hrs.   (APPLAUSE) *Good evening Issei Sagawa!*
2352 hrs.   Check out the idiot boards.
2353 hrs.   Walk across the floor of the TV studio.
2354 hrs.   Answer the question about taste. (APPLAUSE)
2355 hrs.   The host appeals for a volunteer, a woman.
2356 hrs.   *Issei Sagawa...the host says...what do you think*
2357 hrs.   *of the girl we have here for you?* (APPLAUSE)
2358 hrs.   *Oh, I say, I love big girls.* Then leaning forward
2359 hrs.   like an uncle to touch her cheek, I say
0000 hrs.   *You are so nice I could eat you.* (EXIT/LAUGHS)

KATHLEEN JAMIE

The way we live

Pass the tambourine, let me bash out praises
to the Lord God of movement, to Absolute
non-friction, flight, and the scarey side:
death by avalanche, birth by failed contraception.
Of chicken tandoori and reggae, loud, from tenements,
commitment, driving fast and unswerving
friendship. Of tee-shirts on pulleys, giros and Bombay,
barmen, dreaming waitresses with many fake-gold
bangles. Of airports, impulse, and waking to uncertainty,
to strip-lights, motorways, or that pantheon –
the mountains. To overdrafts and grafting

and the fit slow pulse of wipers as you're
creeping over Rannoch, while the God of moorland
walks abroad with his entourage of freezing fog,
his bodyguard of snow.
Of endless gloaming in the North, of Asiatic swelter,
to launderettes, anecdotes, passions and exhaustion,
Final Demands and dead men, the skeletal grip
of government. To misery and elation; mixed,
the sod and caprice of landlords.
To the way it fits, the way it is, the way it seems
to be: let me bash out praises – pass the tambourine.

Julian of Norwich

Everything I do I do for you.
Brute. You inform the dark
inside of stones, the winds draughting in

from this world and that to come,
but never touch me.
You took me on

but dart like a rabbit into holes
from the edges of my sense
when I turn, walk, turn.

*

I am the hermit whom you keep
at the garden's end, but I wander.
I am wandering in your acres

where every step, were I
attuned to sense them,
would crush a thousand flowers.

(Hush, that's not the attitude)
I keep prepared a room and no one comes.
(Love is the attitude)

*

Canary that I am, caged and hung
from the eaves of the world
to trill your praise.

He will not come.
Poor bloodless hands, unclasp.
Stiffened, stone-cold knees, bear me up.

(And yet, and yet, I am suspended
in his joy, huge and helpless
as the harvest moon in a summer sky.)

Outreach

With a stick in the hot dust
I draw a tenement, a plane, a church:
my country we have no
family fields, In a smoke-choked hut
where a barren wife gave birth
they pat the sackcloth, *sit!*
while hens peck around the sleeping kids
and someone coughs, coughs. *What your family?*

Hunkered in the mean shade
of our compound walls: *Your tits
not big!* Our yard grows
nothing, their constant feet.
At noon, the murderous heat,
I clang the gate: *come back tomorrow.*
Perhaps in my heart of hearts
I lack compassion. I lie

hot nights on a straight bed,
watch crowded stars through mosquito mesh
and talk to Jesus. Moonlight strikes
our metal gate like a silent gong.
Sometimes I wake
to a dog's yelp, a screech of owl,
sometimes, a wide-eyed girl
hugely wrapped in shawls. *What your husband?*

I walk a fine line with the headman,
write home: *One day I'll build a church*;
because I believe in these Lazarus' huts
are secret believers;
and listen in village lanes
of bones and dung for Jesus' name
among the shouts, the bleating goats,
the bursts of dirty laughter.

Mother-May-I

Mother-May-I
go down the bottom of the lane,
to the yellow-headed piss-the-beds,
hunker at the may-hedge, skirts
fanned out in the dirt and
see the dump
where we're not allowed;
twisty trees, the burn, and say
all sweetie breath:

> *they are the woods*
> *where men*
> > *lift up your skirt*
> *and take down your pants*
> *even though you're crying.*
> Mother may I?

> > > Play at Man-hunt, just
> in the scheme Mother may I
> tell small lies *we were sot*
> in the lane, sat on garage ramps,
> picking harling
> with bitten nails, as myths
> rose thick as swamp mist
> from the woods behind the dump
> > > > where hitch-hikers rot
> in the curling roots of trees,
> and men
> leave tight rolled up
> dirty magazines. Mother may we

> pull our soft backsides
> through the jagged may's
> white blossom, run across the stinky dump
> and muck about
> at the woods and burn
> dead pleased
> to see the white dye
> of our gym-rubbers seep downstream.

GLYN MAXWELL

Helene and Heloise

So swim in the embassy pool in a tinkling breeze
The sisters, *mes cousines*, they are blonde-haired
    Helene and Heloise,
One for the fifth time up to the diving board,
The other, in her quiet shut-eye sidestroke
Slowly away from me though I sip and look.

From in the palace of shades, inscrutable, cool,
I watch exactly what I want to watch
    From by this swimming pool,
Helene's shimmer and moss of a costume, each
Soaking pony-tailing of the dark
And light mane of the littler one as they walk;

And the splash that bottles my whole life to today,
The spray fanning to dry on the porous sides,
    What these breathtakers say
In their, which is my, language but their words:
These are the shots the sun could fire and fires,
Is paid and drapes across the stretching years.

Now Heloise will dive, the delicate slimmer,
Calling Helene to turn who turns to see
    One disappearing swimmer
Only and nods, leans languorously away
To prop on the sides before me and cup her wet
Face before me near where I'd pictured it.

I was about to say I barely know them. –
I turn away because and hear of course
    Her push away. I see them
In my rose grotto of thought, and it's not a guess,
How they are, out of the water, out
In the International School they lie about,

What they can buy in the town, or the only quarters
Blondes can be seen alighting in, and only
    As guided shaded daughters
Into an acre of golden shop. 'Lonely?'
Who told me this had told me: 'They have no lives.
They will be children. Then they will be wives.'

Helene shrieks and is sorry – I don't think – my
Ankles cool with the splash of her sister's dive:
    I wave and smile and sigh.
Thus the happiest falling man alive,
And twenty-five, and the wetness and the brown
Hairs of my shin can agree, and I settle down.

'Already the eldest – suddenly – the problems.
The other draws, writes things.' I had heard
    Staccato horrid tantrums
Between earshot and the doorbell, held and read
Heloise's letters in chancery
Script to her dead grandmother, to me,

To nobody. They have a mother and father,
And love the largest pandas in the whole
    World of Toys. The other
Sister rang from Italy and was well,
But wouldn't come this time. 'She'll never come.
She has a home. They do not have a home.'

Stretching out in her shiny gold from the pool,
Heloise swivels, and sits and kicks
    Then reaches back to towel
Her skinny shoulders tanned in a U of lux-
Uriant material. Helene
Goes slowly to the board, and hops again

Into the dazzle and splosh and the quiet. Say,
Two, three miles from here there are heaps of what,
    Living things, decay,
The blind and inoculated dead, and a squad
Of infuriated coldly eyeing sons
Kicking the screaming oath out of anyone's.

Cauchemar. – We will be clear if of course apart,
To London again me, they to their next
            Exotic important spot,
Their chink and pace of Gloucestershire, Surrey, fixed
Into the jungles, ports or the petrol deserts.
I try but don't see another of these visits,

As I see Helene drying, Heloise dry,
The dark unavoidable servant seeming to have
            Some urgency today
And my book blank in my hands. What I can love
I love encircled, trapped and I love free.
That happens to, and happens to be, me,

But this is something else. Outside the fence,
It could – it's the opposite – be a paradise
            Peopled with innocents,
Each endowed with a light inimitable voice,
Fruit abundant, guns like dragons and giants
Disbelieved, sheer tolerance a science –

Still, I'd think of Helene, of Heloise
Moving harmless, shieldless into a dull
            And dangerous hot breeze,
With nothing but hopes to please, delight, fulfil
Some male as desperate and as foul as this is,
Who'd not hurt them for all their limited kisses.

Love Made Yeah

First and zillionth my eyes meet eyes
Unturnable from, unstarable in.
Whoever was marched from the Square of my reason
And to what court, I don't give a hyphen.
            Va t'en to the King!

Our drapeaux are waving and what's in the offing
But tears, tribunals and unwelcome aid?
Nothing but glorious, jealous, incredulous,
Bibulous, fabulous, devil'll-envy-us
            Love made, love made!

Yeah and you say with the press of this planet
Look how it ends up: the heroes felled
In the upshot, the oiliest climb of the customary
Bourgeois fuckers as easy as muttering
    Argent. Ackers. Geld.

Uh-huh, sans doute. But here at the heart
Of the movement I trust my hand in another!
So ABC tell me I'm odds-on to cop it.
That ain't news, guys, I did arrive here
    Via a mother.

No, when the Square is dead again – but
For some oligarchy or puppet or shah,
And I'm banged up and on trial in slippers
For following, wishing on, crediting, catching
    Her my star:

Don't do the pity. Okay, do the pity,
But that won't happen, believe it from me:
Her eyes are as hot as one needs to ignite
The cave in the human guy. I am hers,
    Friends, I am history!

Tale of the Mayor's Son

The Mayor's son had options. One was death,
    and one a black and stylish trilby hat
he wore instead, when thinking this: I Love.

The town was not elaborate. The sky
    was white collisions of no special interest
but look at the Mayor's son, at the bazaar!

'I've seen her once before...' Her name was this:
    Elizabeth. The Mayor's son was eighteen,
– his mind older than that but his mouth not.

And had no options. 'Hey, Elizabeth!'
    I could say what was sold in the bazaar,
I could be clearer on the time of day,

I could define Elizabeth. I will:
    Every girl you ever wanted, but
can't have 'cause I want. She was twenty-one.

'Hi, –' the name of the Mayor's son? Anything.
    'Let's get something together!' someone said.
'The Mayor's son out with Lisa!' someone gossiped.

The afternoon, about to be misspent,
    stirred coffee with its three remaining fingers:
'They are sugar-crazy, they are milk-lovers,

and they won't last.' Some things about the town:
    blue-printed in the days of brown and white
and laid down one fine evening, late July.

Musicians lived there; painters; people who
    did murders but deliberated first;
town-councillors for other towns; widows

of chip-eating, soap-using carcasses
    who still watch television on occasions;
ex-famous people too, well one or two,

ex-people, come to think of it; some mates
    of mine, no friends of yours, not you, not me;
a prostitute or two policemen or

a cabbage-patch doll buying a new home;
    a band of Stuart Pretenders; a fire-hose
on motorbikes, frequenting clubs and stuff;

a catholic, a protestant, a bloke;
    insurance clerks, accountants, a red horse
belonging to my cousin, and of course

the man himself. No, strike him, he just left.
    Divide the town into eleven parts,
throw ten of them away, and look at this:

They skated on the ice at the ice-rink,
    Elizabeth and a black-trilbied boy
who kept his hat on. I'd have hated that

had I seen it. I hate people who
    make such alert decisions to impress.
I'd have him on his arse. Oh good, he is.

Elizabeth, white-skirted, – no more clues –
    swooped to pick the Mayor's son off the ice,
and pterodactyl-like he shook himself.

Hat elsewhere, hat kicked on by a small bully
    and ruined by the bully's friend. Once,
that would have shelled and reddened my idea,

to see such fun. But nowadays I just
    cram it in with all the other eggs
for omelette. Skate, skate, you're crap at it,

whatever your name is, you Mayor's son.
    The Mayor's son and Elizabeth, oh my!
The middles of my afternoons in England.

Three simultaneous occurrences:
    a hump, a testimonial, a bomb.
Back to the ice-rink, just in time, we –

– There they are! Their two bicycles propped
    for vandals who'll show up in half an hour,
and off they go towards the library.

Conveniences everywhere, a town
    complete with detail, and the gardens so –
green and, and – and there! This is a poem

of love, but the boy had to urinate
    and did so, while Elizabeth began
to make a Christmas list, and left him out.

The air began to gather, pointilliste,
    and the first lamp went to a sorry pink
that wouldn't last, was a phenomenon.

They crossed roads, Beauty Gloved and the Mayor's Son,
    they made split-second choices that saved lives.
The library was all a welcome cube.

The library was full of walruses.
   Or people who resembled walruses.
Or – no. Let's say: People who would bear

comparisons with walruses, and might
   confess it was a modern poet thing,
post-Tennyson: Irish perhaps, or French.

Outside the library, the skinhead world
   dropped litter, picked up girls, and spat, and wasn't
literate, and walruses, elsewhere,

moaned in the sea and didn't give a fuck.
   So much for images. The library
was full of books. The books were like more books.

Some books were overdue. A man called Smith
   had borrowed Dante's *Purgatorio*
but not the other two. I had them both.

A man called Dorman had a book on trees,
   which nobody had mentioned recently
though it was ages overdue. A girl

who'd stripped the library of Sailing books
   had drowned recently, and was so slow
to answer warnings that they'd phoned her up

to ask politely for their library books.
   A dictionary had gone missing too
but the Mayor's son had other things in mind!

How do we know? We don't, but he had options,
   and watched Elizabeth watching the books
on Archaeology, and calling them

'Unusually specific.' The Mayor's boy
   nodded his head of ordinary hair
and felt Love working with the utensils

he generally called his heart and soul.
   'Well this is it,' she said, 'but it's too short.'
The sky was mauve, no other colour, mauve –

the walruses, the ice-skaters, the books!
  The Mayor himself was coming home to dinner,
and I was splitting up with Alison.

I think it was that day, about half-six.
  The bully, meanwhile, read about a bike
and mentioned it to his pathetic dad

as a potential Christmas present. I –
  sometimes I hope he gets it, sometimes I
devoutly hope it kills him. Anyway,

'The Library is closing now.' The Mayor
  expected his son home. Elizabeth
expected that as well, didn't expect

what happened next as they waited for the cars
  to lose their nerve and stop. He put his hand
behind the head of this Elizabeth

and bruised her with a kiss, a mad one! He
  receded and she reappeared, a girl
with somebody to marry, and not him,

her mouth politicised indignity,
  her eyes becoming tyrants, après-coup:
'How dare you?' What a question. How dare *you*?

Because we don't know what – because we do –
  Irrelevant! Elizabeth was off.
The traffic-lights were either green or red –

it doesn't matter. Look at the Mayor's son,
  no girl, no hat, under the sodium-
lamps of his home town. (Elizabeth

was born here too. Actually, so was I,
  but Alison moved here in '83.)
Change, traffic-lights! Go, hatchbacks of the time,

the buses, and the other cars! Next year
  the Mayor – who now eats veal with his wife
and son, fills a second glass with Soave

and tells a joke, and the son laughs – the Mayor
    will be deposed next year: his son will choose
a university, *it* will say no

to him but take Elizabeth, for Maths
    not Archaeology, and Alison
will suddenly, one day, in a Maths class,

befriend Elizabeth, and find that their
    acquaintances are mutual, like me
and the Mayor's son, and in a stand-up bar

all evening they'll be there. Meanwhile the books
    will pile up in my world, and someone's hat
will find its way to me and I will wear it.

Sport Story of a Winner

He was a great ambassador for the game.
                    He had a simple name.
His name was known in households other than ours.
                    But we knew other stars.
We could recall as many finalists
                    as many panellists.
But when they said this was his Waterloo,
                    we said it was ours too.

His native village claimed him as its own,
                    as did his native town,
adopted city and preferred retreat.
                    So did our own street.
When his brave back was up against the wall,
                    our televisions all
got us shouting, and that did the trick.
                    Pretty damn quick.

His colours were his secret, and his warm-up
                        raindance, and his time up
Flagfell in the Hook District, and his diet
                        of herbal ice, and his quiet
day-to-day existence, and his training,
                        and never once explaining
his secret was his secret too, and his book,
                        and what on earth he took

that meant-to-be-magic night in mid-November.
                        You must remember.
His game crumbled, he saw something somewhere.
                        He pointed over there.
The referees soothed him, had to hold things up.
                        The ribbons on the Cup
were all his colour, but the Romanoff
                        sadly tugged them off.

We saw it coming, didn't we. We knew
                        something he didn't know.
It wasn't the first time a lad was shown
                        basically bone.
Another one will come, and he'll do better.
                        I see him now – he'll set a
never-to-be-beaten time that'll last forever!
                        Won't he. Trevor.

The Eater

Top of the morning, Dogfood Family!
How's the chicken? How's the chicken?
Haven't you grown? Or have you grown,
here in the average kitchen at noontime
        down in the home, at all?

Bang outside, the bank officials
are conga-dancing and in their pinstripe
this is the life! But it isn't your life
out in the swarming city at crushhour
        dodging humans, is it?

Vacant city – where did they find it?
Blossom of litter as the only car
for a man goes by. When the man goes by
his girl will sulkily catch your eye:
     will you catch hers?

Snow-white shop – how do they do that?
Lamb-white medical knowing and gentle
man, advise her, assure and ask her:
do you desire the best for your children
     and theirs? Well do you?

Take that journey, delight in chocolate,
you won't find anyone else in the world,
lady, only the man, the sweet man
opening doors and suggesting later
     something – what thing?

Short time no see, Dogfood Family!
How's the chicken? How's the chicken?
How have you done it? Have you done it
with love, regardless of time and income
     and me? Who am I?

I am the eater and I am the eater.
These are my seconds and these are my seconds.
Do you understand that? Do you get that,
you out there where the good things grow
     and rot? Or not?

SIMON ARMITAGE

Parable of the Dead Donkey

Instructions arrived by registered post
under cover of separate envelopes:
directions first
to pinpoint the place
in the shape of maps and compass bearings;
those, then forms and stamps for loss of earnings.
So much was paid
to diggers of graves
by keepers or nearest of kin, per leg,
(which made for the dumping of quadrupeds),
sixteen quid
to send off a pig
or sink a pit for a dog or pony.
But less to plant a man than a donkey.
Cheaper by half
for a pregnant horse
that died with all four hooves inside her
than one with a stillborn foal beside her.
And this was a bind,
being duty bound
where the ownership was unestablished.
We filled the flasks and loaded the Transit,
then set out, making
for the undertaking.

Facing north, he was dead at three o'clock
in a ring of meadow grass, closely cropped,
where a metal chain
on a wooden stake
had stopped him ambling off at an angle,
worn him down in a perfect circle.
We burrowed in
right next to him
through firm white soil. An hour's hard labour
took us five feet down – and then the weather:
thunder biting
the heels of lightning,

a cloudburst drawing a curtain of rain
across us, filling the bath of the grave,
and we waded in it
for one more minute,
dredged and shovelled as the tide was rising,
bailed out for fear of drowning, capsizing.
Back on top
we weighed him up,
gave some thought to this beast of the Bible:
the nose and muzzle, the teeth, the eyeballs,
the rump, the hindquarters,
the flanks, the shoulders,
everything soothed in the oil of the rain –
the eel of his tongue, the keel of his spine,
the rope of his tail,
the weeds of his mane.
Then we turned him round and slipped his anchor,
eased him out of the noose of his tether,
and rolled him in
and started to dig.

But even with donkey, water and soil
there wasn't enough to level the hole
after what was washed away
or turned into clay
or trodden in, so we opened the earth
and started in on a second trench for dirt
to fill the first.
Which left a taste
of starting something that wouldn't finish:
a covered grave with a donkey in it,
a donkey-size hole
within a stone's throw
without a single bone to drop in it
or a handful of dust to toss on top of it.

The van wouldn't start, and we wandered home
in the dark, without supper or profit.

You May Turn Over and Begin

'Which of these films was Dirk Bogarde
not in? One hundredweight of bauxite

makes how much aluminium?
How many tales in *The Decameron*?'

General Studies, the upper sixth, a doddle, a cinch
for anyone with an ounce of common sense

or a calculator
with a memory feature.

Having galloped through but not caring enough
to check or double-check, I was dreaming of

milk-white breasts and nakedness, or more specifically
virginity.

That term – everybody felt the heat
but the girls were having none of it:

long and cool like cocktails,
out of reach, their buns and pigtails

only let out for older guys with studded jackets
and motorbikes and spare helmets.

One jot of consolation
was the tall spindly girl riding pillion

on her man's new Honda
who, with the lights at amber,

put down both feet and stood to stretch her limbs,
to lift the visor and push back her fringe

and to smooth her tight jeans.
As he pulled off down the street

she stood there like a wishbone,
high and dry, her legs wide open,

and rumour has it he didn't notice
till he came round in the ambulance

having underbalanced on a tight left-hander.
A Taste of Honey. Now I remember.

Zoom!

It begins as a house, an end terrace
in this case
    but it will not stop there. Soon it is
an avenue
    which cambers arrogantly past the Mechanics' Institute,
turns left
    at the main road without even looking
and quickly it is
    a town with all four major clearing banks,
a daily paper
    and a football team pushing for promotion.

On it goes, oblivious of the Planning Acts,
the green belts,
    and before we know it it is out of our hands:
city, nation,
    hemisphere, universe, hammering out in all directions
until suddenly,
    mercifully, it is drawn aside through the eye
of a black hole
    and bulleted into a neighbouring galaxy, emerging
smaller and smoother
    than a billiard ball but weighing more than Saturn.

People stop me in the street, badger me
in the check-out queue
    and ask 'What is this, this that is so small
and so very smooth
    but whose mass is greater than the ringed planet?'
It's just words
    I assure them. But they will not have it.

Gooseberry Season

Which reminds me. He appeared
at noon, asking for water. He'd walked from town
after losing his job, leaving a note for his wife and his brother
and locking his dog in the coal bunker.
We made him a bed

and he slept till Monday.
A week went by and he hung up his coat.
Then a month, and not a stroke of work, a word of thanks,
a farthing of rent or a sign of him leaving.
One evening he mentioned a recipe

for smooth, seedless gooseberry sorbet
but by then I was tired of him: taking pocket money
from my boy at cards, sucking up to my wife and on his last night
sizing up my daughter. He was smoking my pipe
as we stirred his supper.

Where does the hand become the wrist?
Where does the neck become the shoulder. The watershed
and then the weight, whatever turns up and tips us over that
        razor's edge
between something and nothing, between
one and the other.

I could have told him this
but didn't bother. We ran him a bath
and held him under, dried him off and dressed him
and loaded him into the back of the pick-up.
Then we drove without headlights

to the county boundary,
dropped the tailgate, and after my boy
had been through his pockets we dragged him like a mattress
across the meadow and on the count of four
threw him over the border.

This is not general knowledge, except
in gooseberry season, which reminds me, and at the table
I have been known to raise an eyebrow, or scoop the sorbet
into five equal portions, for the hell of it.
I mention this for a good reason.

Night Shift

Once again I have missed you by moments;
steam hugs the rim of the just-boiled kettle,

water in the pipes finds its own level.
In another room there are other signs

of someone having left: dust, unsettled
by the sweep of the curtains; the clockwork

contractions of the paraffin heater.
For weeks now we have come and gone, woken

in acres of empty bedding, written
lipstick love-notes on the bathroom mirror

and in this space we have worked and paid for
we have found ourselves, but lost each other.

Upstairs, at least, there is understanding
in things more telling than lipstick kisses:

the air, still hung with spores of your hairspray;
body-heat stowed in the crumpled duvet.

At Sea

It is not through weeping,
but all evening the pale blue eye
on your most photogenic side has kept
its own unfathomable tide. Like the boy
at the dyke I have been there:

held out a huge finger,
lifted atoms of dust with the point
of a tissue and imagined slivers of hair
in the oil on the cornea. We are both
in the dark, but I go on

drawing the eyelid up by its lashes,
folding it almost inside-out, then finding
and hiding every mirror in the house
as the iris, besieged with the ink
of blood rolls back

into its own orbit. Nothing
will help it. Through until dawn
you dream the true story of the boy
who hooked out his eye and ate it,
so by six in the morning

I am steadying the ointment
that will bite like an onion, piping
a line of cream while avoiding the pupil
and in no time it is glued shut
like a bad mussel.

Friends call round
and mean well. They wait
and whisper in the air-lock of the lobby
with patches, eyewash, the truth
about mascara.

Even the cats are on to it;
they bring in starlings, and because their feathers
are the colours of oil on water in sunlight
they are a sign of something.
In the long hours

beyond us, irritations heal
into arguments. For the eighteenth time
it comes to this: the length of your leg sliding out
from the covers, the ball of your foot
like a fist on the carpet

while downstairs
I cannot bring myself to hear it.
Words have been spoken; things that were bottled
have burst open and to walk in now
would be to walk in

on the ocean.

Very Simply Topping Up the Brake Fluid

Yes, love, that's why the warning light comes on. Don't
panic. Fetch some universal brake-fluid
and a five-eighths screwdriver from your toolkit
then prop the bonnet open. Go on, it won't

eat you. Now, without slicing through the fan-belt
try and slide the sharp end of the screwdriver
under the lid and push the spade connector
through its bed, go on, that's it. Now you're all right

to unscrew, no, clockwise, you see it's Russian
love, back to front, that's it. You see, it's empty.
Now, gently with your hand and I mean gently,
try and create a bit of space by pushing

the float-chamber sideways so there's room to pour,
gently does it, that's it. Try not to spill it, it's
corrosive: rusts, you know, and fill it till it's
level with the notch on the clutch reservoir.

Lovely. There's some Swarfega in the office
if you want a wash and some soft roll above
the cistern for, you know. Oh don't mind him, love,
he doesn't bite. Come here and sit down Prince. Prince!

Now, where's that bloody alternator? Managed?
Oh any time, love. I'll not charge you for that
because it's nothing of a job. If you want
us again we're in the book. Tell your husband.

BIOGRAPHICAL NOTES

Simon Armitage was born in 1963 in Huddersfield. He works as a probation officer in Oldham, near Manchester, and lives in Marsden, West Yorkshire. His publications include: *Zoom!* (Bloodaxe, 1989), *Xanadu: a poem-film for television* (Bloodaxe, 1992), *Kid* (Faber, 1992) and *Book of Matches* (Faber, 1993).

John Ash was born in 1948 in Manchester. He lives in New York. His collections include *Casino* (1978) and *The Bed* (1981) from Oasis Books, and *The Goodbyes* (1982), *The Branching Stairs* (1984), *Disbelief* (1987) and *The Burnt Pages* (1991) from Carcanet.

Sebastian Barry was born in 1955 in Dublin. Since 1977 he has lived in France, England, Greece and Switzerland, and now lives in Ireland, where he writes primarily as a dramatist. His fiction includes *The Engine of Owl-Light* (Paladin/Carcanet, 1988); his poetry, *The Water-Colourist* (Dolmen, 1983), *The Rhetorical Town* (Dolmen, 1985) and *Fanny Hawke Goes to the Mainland Forever* (Raven, 1989); his plays, *Boss Grady's Boys* and *Prayers of Sherkin* (both Methuen).

Sujata Bhatt was born in 1956 in Ahmedabad, India, and educated in the USA. She lives in Bremen with her husband, the German writer Michael Augustin, where she translates Gujarati poetry into English. She has published two collections with Carcanet, *Brunizem* (1988) and *Monkey Shadows* (1991).

Eavan Boland was born in 1944 in Dublin. She is a reviewer and lecturer, and lives in Dublin with her husband, novelist Kevin Casey, and their two daughters. Her books include *The War Horse* (1975), *In Her Own Image* (1980) and *Night Feed* (1982) from Arlen House, and *The Journey* (1987), *Selected Poems* (1989) and *Outside History* (1990) from Carcanet.

Dermot Bolger was born in 1959 in Dublin. He founded Raven Arts Press, and its successor New Island Books. His publications include *Finglas Lilies* (Raven, 1981) and *Internal Exiles* (Dolmen, 1986), and the novels *Night Shift* (1985), *The Woman's Daughter* (1987/1991), *The Journey Home* (1990) and *Emily's Shoes* (1992) all from Penguin, who have published his plays as *A Dublin Quartet*.

Charles Boyle was born in 1951 in Leeds. After teaching in Egypt and travelling widely in North Africa he returned to Britain to work in publishing, first for Time-Life and currently for Faber. He has published four collections with Carcanet: *Affinities* (1977), *House of Cards* (1982), *Sleeping Rough* (1987) and *The Very Man* (1993).

John Burnside was born in 1955 in Dunfermline, Fife, and lives in Surrey. He has published three collections: *The hoop* (Carcanet, 1988), *Common Knowledge* (Secker, 1991) and *Feast Days* (Secker, 1992).

Duncan Bush was born in 1946 in Cardiff. He teaches writing at Gwent College, and divides his time between Wales and Luxembourg. His books include: *Black Faces Red Mouths* (Bedrock Press, 1985); a novel, *Glass Shot* (Secker, 1992); and three collections with Poetry Wales Press, *Aquarium* (1983), *Salt* (1985) and *The Genre of Silence* (1988), the latter a presentation of the life and work of a fictional Russian poet, Victor Bal.

Ciaran Carson was born in 1948 in Belfast. He is a writer and musician, and lives in Belfast, where he works as an arts officer. His *Pocket Guide to Irish Traditional Music* was published in 1986. He has published three books of poems: *The New Estate* (Blackstaff, 1976; Gallery, 1988), *The Irish for No* (Gallery, 1987; Bloodaxe, 1988) and *Belfast Confetti* (Gallery, 1989; Bloodaxe, 1990).

Harry Clifton was born in 1952 in Dublin. He has lived in Ireland between stays in West Africa, where he was a teacher; in Thailand, where he administered aid programmes; in Italy, and now in London. He has published five books of poems with Gallery, *The Walls of Carthage* (1977), *Office of the Salt Merchant* (1979), *Comparative Lives* (1982), *The Liberal Cage* (1988), and *The Desert Route: Selected Poems* (1992), the latter published in Britain by Bloodaxe.

David Constantine was born in 1944 in Salford. He lives in Oxford where he is Fellow in German at the Queen's College. He has published eight books with Bloodaxe: his novel *Davies* (1985); his collections *A Brightness to Cast Shadows* (1980), *Watching for Dolphins* (1983), and *Madder* (1988) – published in French as *Sorlingues* (1992); his *Selected Poems* (1991); and his translations of Friedrich Hölderlin (1990), Henri Michaux (with Helen Constantine, 1992) and Philippe Jaccottet (with Mark Treharne, 1993). His other books include *Early Greek Travellers and the Hellenic Ideal* (CUP, 1984) and a critical introduction to the poetry of Hölderlin (OUP, 1988).

Robert Crawford was born in 1959 in Bellshill, near Glasgow. He teaches at the University of St Andrews, where he co-edits the magazine *Verse*. He has published two collections with Chatto, *A Scottish Assembly* (1990) and *Talkies* (1992), a collection shared with W.N. Herbert, *Sharawaggi* (Polygon, 1990), and two critical studies with Oxford University Press, *The Savage and the City in the Work of T.S. Eliot* (1987) and *Devolving English Literature* (1992).

Tony Curtis was born in 1946 in Carmarthen. He lives in Barry, and teaches at the University of Glamorgan. He has published several books with Poetry Wales Press/Seren Books, including his collections *Preparations* (1980), *Letting Go* (1983), *Selected Poems 1970-1985* (1986), *The Last Candles* (1989) and *Taken for Pearls* (1993), his critical anthologies *The Art of Seamus Heaney* (3rd ed, 1993) and *Wales: The Imagined Nation* (1986); and his anthologies *The Poetry of Pembrokeshire* and *The Poetry of Snowdonia* (1989), and *Love from Wales* (with Sian James, 1990). His other books include *Poems: Selected and New* (Storyline Press, USA, 1986), *Dannie Abse* (University of Wales Press, 1985) and *How to Study Modern Poetry* (Macmillan, 1990).

David Dabydeen was born in 1957 in Guyana. He lives in Coventry and teaches at the University of Warwick. He has published two poetry collections, *Slave Song* (Dangaroo Press, 1984), winner of the Commonwealth Poetry Prize, and *Coolie Odyssey* (Hansib/Dangaroo, 1988); two novels, *The Intended* (1991) and *Disappearance* (1993), both from Secker; and two critical studies, *Hogarth's Blacks: Images of Blacks in Eighteenth Century Art* and (with Nana Wilson-Tagoe) *A Reader's Guide to West Indian and Black British Literature*.

Fred D'Aguiar was born in 1960 in London of Guyanese parents, and grew up in Guyana. He lives in London, and is currently teaching at Amherst College, Massachusetts. He has published three collections of poems, *Mama Dot* (Chatto, 1985), *Airy Hall* (Chatto, 1989) and *British Subjects* (Bloodaxe, 1993). He edited the Black British section of *The New British Poetry* (Paladin, 1988). His plays include *High Life* and *A Jamaican Airman Foresees His Death*.

Nuala Ní Dhomhnaill was born in 1952 in Lancashire, and grew up in the West Kerry Gaeltacht (Irish-speaking area). She lives in Dublin with her Turkish husband and four children. She has published three Irish-language collections: *An Dealg Droighin* (Mercier Press, 1981), *Féar Suaithinseach* (An Sagart, 1984) and *Feis* (An Sagart, 1993); and three bilingual editions: *Selected Poems/Rogha Dánta* (translated by Michael Hartnett, Raven Arts, 1986), *Pharoah's Daughter* (various translators, Gallery Press, 1990) and *The Astrakhan Cloak* (translated by Paul Muldoon, Gallery Press, 1992).

Peter Didsbury was born in 1946 in Fleetwood, Lancashire, and grew up in Hull. He works as an archaeologist in Hull. He has published three collections with Bloodaxe, *The Butchers of Hull* (1982), *The Classical Farm* (1987) and *That Old-Time Religion* (1994), and a pamphlet, *Common Property* (Carnivorous Arpeggio, 1992).

Michael Donaghy was born in 1954 in the USA and has lived in New York and Chicago. He was poetry editor of the *Chicago Review* for several years. He lives in north London. His collections include *Shibboleth* (1988) and *Errata* (1993), both from OUP.

Carol Ann Duffy was born in 1955 in Glasgow. She grew up in Staffordshire, later moved to Liverpool, and now lives in London, where she is a freelance writer. She edited the Kestrel anthology *I Wouldn't Thank You for a Valentine* (Viking, 1992), and has published four collections with Anvil: *Standing Female Nude* (1985), *Selling Manhattan* (1987), *The Other Country* (1990) and *Mean Time* (1993).

Ian Duhig was born in 1954 in Hammersmith, London, of Irish parents. He has worked in homelessness projects in London, Belfast and Yorkshire, and now lives in Leeds. His first collection *The Bradford Count* was published by Bloodaxe in 1991.

Helen Dunmore was born in 1952 in Beverley, Yorkshire, and lives in Bristol. She works as a freelance writer of poetry, short stories, poems for children and novels. Her publications include: four collections from Bloodaxe, *The Apple Fall* (1983), *The Sea Skater* (1986), *The Raw Garden* (1988) and *Short Days, Long Nights: New & Selected Poems* (1991); a novel published by Viking, *Zennor in Darkness* (1993); two novels for young people from Julia MacRae Books, *Going to Egypt* (1992) and *In the Money* (1993); and a book of children's poems, *Secrets* (Bodley Head, 1994).

Paul Durcan was born in 1944 in Dublin. He has given poetry readings around the world, and is a member of Aosdána. His publications include: three collections with Raven Arts Press, *Jesus, Break His Fall* (1980), *Ark of the North* (1982) and *Jumping the Train Tracks with Angela* (1983), the latter published in Britain by Carcanet; a book of poems from paintings, *Crazy About Women* (National Gallery of Ireland, 1991); five books with Blackstaff, *The Selected Paul Durcan* (1982), *The Berlin Wall Café* (1985), *Going Home to Russia* (1987), *Jesus and Angela* (1988), and *Daddy, Daddy* (1988); and *A Snail in My Prime: New & Selected Poems* (Harvill, 1993).

John Ennis was born in 1944 in Co. Westmeath, Ireland, and lives in Co. Waterford, where he is Head of Humanities at Waterford Regional College. He has published four books with Gallery Press, *Night on Hibernia* (1975), *Dolmen Hill* (1977), *A Drink of Spring* (1979) and *The Burren Days* (1985), and two with Dedalus Press, *Arboretum* (1990) and *In a Green Shade* (1991).

Elizabeth Garrett was born in 1958 in London, and grew up in the Channel Islands. She lives in Oxford, where she works for the Voltaire Foundation. She has published a pamphlet, *The Mortal Light* (Mandeville Press, 1990), and a book of poems, *The Rule of Three* (Bloodaxe, 1991).

Lavinia Greenlaw was born in 1962. She grew up in Essex, and in London where she lives. She has worked in publishing as an editor and now works for the London Arts Board. Her publications include *The Cost of Getting Lost in Space* (Turret, 1991), *Love from a Foreign City* (Slow Dancer, 1992) and *Night Photograph* (Faber, 1993).

Maggie Hannan was born in 1962 in Wiltshire and lived in Derbyshire and Cumbria before moving to Hull. Her poems have appeared in *The Gregory Anthology* (Hutchinson, 1990) and *The New Lake Poets* (Bloodaxe, 1991), and she is now working on her first book.

David Hartnett was born in 1952. He lives in Sussex, and co-edits the literary magazine Poetry Durham. His collections include *A Signalled Love* (Anvil, 1985), *House of Moon* (Secker, 1988) and *Dark Ages* (Secker, 1992). He also writes short fiction.

Geoff Hattersley was born in 1956 in Wombwell, South Yorkshire. He lived in Huddersfield before moving to Barnsley where he edits the magazine and press, *The Wide Skirt*. His many small press collections include *The Deep End* (Echo Room Press, 1987), *Slouching Towards Rotherham* (Wide Skirt, 1987), *Port of Entry* (Littlewood, 1989) and *Split Shift* (Smith/Doorstop, 1990), the best poems from these collected in *Don't Worry* (Bloodaxe, 1994).

W.N. Herbert was born in 1961 in Dundee. He lives in Oxford where he has worked as a teacher, and is currently writer-in-residence in Dumfries and Galloway. He co-edits the Scots literary magazine *Gairfish*. His publications include *Sharawaggi* (with Robert Crawford, Polygon, 1990), *Dundee Doldrums* (Galliard, 1991), *Anither Music* (Vennel Press, 1991), *The Testament of the Reverend Thomas Dick* (Littlewood Arc, 1993) and *Forked Tongue* (Bloodaxe, 1994), and a critical book, *To Circumjack MacDiarmid* (OUP, 1992).

Selima Hill was born in 1945, and lives in Dorset. She won the Arvon/*Observer* International Poetry Competition in 1988 with part of her book-length poem *The Accumulation of Small Acts of Kindness* (Chatto, 1989). Her other books of poetry are *Saying Hello at the Station* (Chatto, 1985), *My Darling Camel* (Chatto, 1988) and *A Little Book of Meat* (Bloodaxe, 1993).

Michael Hofmann was born in 1957 in Germany, the son of the German novelist Gert Hofmann. He lives in London, where he works as a freelance writer and translator. He has published two collections with Faber, *Nights in the Iron Hotel* (1983) and *Acrimony* (1986); a third, *Corona, Corona*, is forthcoming.

Michael Hulse was born in 1957 in Stoke-on-Trent. He lives in Cologne, where he works for Deutsche Welle TV, as a freelance writer and translator, and as director of the Cologne International Literature Festival. He has published four books of poems: *Knowing and Forgetting* (1981) and *Propaganda* (1985) from Secker, *Eating Strawberries in the Necropolis* (Harvill, 1991) and *Mother of Battles* (Littlewood Arc, 1991). He has translated German literature (Goethe, Wasserman, Jelinek), literary criticism and art criticism.

Kathleen Jamie was born in 1962 in Renfrewshire, grew up in Midlothian, and now lives in Fife, where is a freelance writer. She has travelled around the East, the fruits of which include two poetry books from Bloodaxe, *The Way We Live* (1987) and *The Autonomous Region* (with Sean Mayne Smith, 1993), and a travel book, *The Golden Peak* (Virago 1992). She has also published *A Flame in Your Heart* (Bloodaxe, 1986), a book of poems set in the summer of 1940, written with Andrew Greig.

Linton Kwesi Johnson was born in 1952 in Jamaica, and came to London in 1963. He has been a pioneering figure in black poetry and music, with six dub poetry and reggae LPs. His selected poems *Tings an Times* (Bloodaxe, 1991) includes work from his previous collections *Voices of the Living and the Dead* (1974), *Dread Beat An' Blood* (1975) and *Inglan Is a Bitch* (1980).

Jackie Kay was born in 1961 in Edinburgh, grew up in Glasgow, and now lives with her son in London, where she is a freelance writer. She has written three plays, two poetry collections, *The Adoption Papers* (Bloodaxe, 1991) and *Other Lovers* (Bloodaxe, 1993), and a collection of poetry for children, *Two's Company* (Blackie, 1992). Her poem-film *Twice Through the Heart* was shown in the BBC 2 *Words on Film* series in 1992.

David Kennedy was born in 1959 in Leicester. He lives in Sheffield where he works as a senior manager in manufacturing industry. He is a poet and critic, and a regular reviewer for the *Times Literary Supplement, Poetry Review, PN Review* and other journals in the UK, US and Australia.

Frank Kuppner was born in 1951 in Glasgow and has lived there ever since. He has published a novel, *Life on a Dead Planet* (Polygon, 1993), and three poetry books with Carcanet, *A Bad Day for the Sung Dynasty* (1984), *The Intelligent Observation of Naked Women* (1987) and *Ridiculous! Absurd! Disgusting!* (Carcanet, 1989).

Tom Leonard was born in 1944 in Glasgow, and still lives there. His publications include two poetry books from Galloping Dog Press, *Intimate Voices: Selected Work 1965-1983* (1984) and *Situations Theoretical and Contemporary* (1986), and a biography of James Thomson, *Places of the Mind* (Cape, 1993).

Liz Lochhead was born in 1947 in Motherwell, Lanarkshire, and apart from two years in America has spent most of her adult life in Glasgow. Her publications include *The Grimm Sisters* (Next Editions, 1981), *Dreaming Frankenstein and Collected Poems* (Polygon, 1982), *True Confessions and New Clichés*, a set of monologues and theatre pieces (Polygon, 1985), and *Bagpipe Muzak* (Penguin, 1991). She has written several plays for stage, radio and television.

Ian McMillan was born in 1956 in Barnsley, and lives in Darfield, South Yorkshire. He is a freelance writer, broadcaster and performer. His publications include *Selected Poems* (Carcanet, 1987), *Unselected Poems* (Wide Skirt, 1988), *More Poems Please, Waiter, And Quickly* (Sow's Ear, 1989), *A Chin?* (Wide Skirt, 1991), and *Dad, The Donkey's On Fire* (Carcanet, 1993).

Glyn Maxwell was born in 1962 in Welwyn Garden City, Hertfordshire. He works as a freelance writer and reviewer. He has published two collections with Bloodaxe, *Tale of the Mayor's Son* (1990) and *Out of the Rain* (1992), and a book of three verse plays, *Gnyss the Magnificent* (Chatto, 1993).

Paula Meehan was born in 1955 in Dublin. She runs workshops in prisons, schools, universities and with community groups throughout Ireland. She has published three collections of poetry, *Return and No Blame* (1984) and *Reading the Sky* (1986) from Beaver Row, and *The Man Who Was Marked by Winter* (Gallery Press, 1991).

David Morley was born in 1964 in Blackpool. He lives in Sheffield, where he works as a writer, editor and scientist. His books include *Releasing Stone* (Nanholme, 1989), *A Belfast Kiss* (Smith/Doorstop, 1990); *Mandelstam Variations* (Littlewood Arc, 1991/Exile Editions, Canada, 1993), and *Under the Rainbow: Writers and Artists in Schools* (Northern Arts/Bloodaxe, 1991).

Grace Nichols was born in 1950 in Guyana, where she was a journalist. She moved to Britain in 1977, and works as a freelance writer in Sussex. Her publications include three poetry collections, *i is a long memoried woman* (Karnac House, 1983), *The Fat Black Woman's Poems* (Virago, 1984) and *Lazy Thoughts of a Lazy Woman* (Virago, 1989), several children's books, a novel and a black poetry anthology.

Sean O'Brien was born in 1952 in London, and grew up in Hull. He lives in Newcastle, where he works as a writer and reviewer. His poetry books include *The Indoor Park* (Bloodaxe, 1983), *The Frighteners* (Bloodaxe, 1987) and *HMS Glasshouse* (OUP, 1991). He is now writing a critical study of contemporary poetry for Bloodaxe.

Bernard O'Donoghue was born in 1945 in Cullen, Co. Cork. He lives in Oxford, where he teaches at Magdalen College. His poetry books include *Poaching Rights* (Gallery Press, 1987), *The Absent Signifier* (Mandeville Press, 1990) and *The Weakness* (Chatto, 1991). He has also published books on medieval literature.

Peter Reading was born in 1946, and trained as a painter. He lives in Shropshire, where he worked for many years in a feedmill. He has published twelve collections with Secker: *For the Municipality's Elderly* (1974), *The Prison Cell & Barrel Mystery* (1976), *Nothing for Anyone* (1977), *Fiction* (1979), *Tom o'Bedlam's Beauties* (1981), *Diplopic* (1983), *C* (1984), *Ukulele Music/Going On* (1985), *Essential Reading* (1986), *Stet* (1986), *Final Demands* (1988) and *Perduta Gente* (1989); as well as one with Ceolfrith, *5x5x5x5x5* (1984), and two with Chatto, *Three in One* (1992) and *Evagatory* (1992).

Michèle Roberts was born in 1949 in England, and is half French. She lives and works in London, primarily as a novelist, and has been poetry editor of *Spare Rib* and *City Limits*. Her publications include two books of poems from Methuen, *The mirror of the mother* (1986) and *Psyche and the hurricane* (1990), and six novels, *A Piece of the Night* (1978), *The Visitation* (1983), *The Wild Girl* (1984), *The Book of Mrs Noah* (1987), *In the Red Kitchen* (1990), and *Daughters of the House* (1992), which was shortlisted for the 1992 Booker Prize. She also co-edited *Northern Stories Four* (Littlewood Arc, 1993).

Stephen Romer was born in 1957. He lives in Nazelles, France, and teaches at the University of Tours. He has published two collections with OUP, *Idols* (1986) and *Plato's Ladder* (1992), the latter including work prompted by his stay in Poland in 1989-90. He co-translated Jacques Dupin's *Selected Poems* (Bloodaxe, 1992) with Paul Auster and David Shapiro.

Jo Shapcott was born in 1953 in London. She has been an English lecturer, an education officer, and currently works for the Arts Council in London. She has published two books of poems, *Electroplating the Baby* (Bloodaxe, 1988) and *Phrase Book* (OUP, 1992).

Pauline Stainer was born in 1941. Before taking an M.Phil. at Southampton University, she worked in a mental hospital, a pub and a library. She is married with four children, and lives at Little Easton, Dunmow, Essex. She has published two collections with Bloodaxe, *The Honeycomb* (1989) and *Sighting the Slave Ship* (1992).

Matthew Sweeney was born in 1952 in Donegal. After living for some time in Germany, he moved to London where he is a freelance writer. His collections include *A Round House* (1983) and *The Lame Waltzer* (1985) from Allison & Busby/Raven Arts, *Blue Shoes* (1989) and *Cacti* (1992) from Secker, and a children's poetry book from Faber, *The Flying Spring Onion* (1992).

George Szirtes was born in Budapest in 1948 and fled to England in 1956. He trained as a painter, and lives in Hitchin, Hertfordshire. He has published four collections with Secker, *The Slant Door* (1979), *November and May* (1981), *Short Wave* (1983) and *The Photographer in Winter* (1986), two with OUP, *Metro* (1988) and *Bridge Passages* (1991), and an edition of the Hungarian poet Ottó Orbán, *The Blood Song of the Walsungs* (1993) with Bloodaxe.

John Hartley Williams was born in 1942 in Cheshire, grew up in London, and worked in France, Africa and Yugoslavia. He teaches at the Free University in Berlin, where he has lived for the past 15 years. His books include *Hidden Identities* (1982) from Chatto, and *Bright River Yonder* (1987), *Cornerless People* (1990) and *Double* (1994) from Bloodaxe.

Gerard Woodward was born in 1961 in north London. He trained as a painter, studied anthropology, and lived in Falmouth and Manchester before moving to Kent. He has published two collections, *The Unwriter* (Sycamore Press, 1989) and *Householder* (Chatto, 1991).

Kit Wright was born in 1944 in Kent, and lives in north London. He is a poet, children's writer, editor and broadcaster. He published one book, *The Bear Looked Over the Mountain* (1974), with Salamander Imprint, and four with Hutchinson, *The Day Room* (1977), *Bump-starting the Hearse* (1983), *Poems 1974-1983* (1988) and *Short Afternoons* (1989). His children's books include *Rabbiting On, Arthur's Family, Hot Dog, Professor Potts in Africa* and *Cat Among the Pigeons*.

ACKNOWLEDGEMENTS

Thanks are due to the following copyright holders for permission to publish the poems in this anthology:

Simon Armitage: To author and Bloodaxe Books Ltd for poems from *Zoom!* (1989); to author and Faber & Faber Ltd for poems from *Kid* (1992); to author for 'Parable of the Dead Donkey' from the *Times Literary Supplement*: © Simon Armitage 1989, 1992, 1993.

John Ash: To author and Carcanet Press Ltd for poems from *The Goodbyes* (1982), *The Branching Stairs* (1984), *Disbelief* (1987) and *The Burnt Pages* (1991): © John Ash 1982, 1984, 1987, 1991.

Sebastian Barry: To author for poems from *The Water-Colourist* (Dolmen, 1983) and *Fanny Hawke Goes to the Mainland Forever* (Raven Arts Press, 1989): © Sebastian Barry 1983, 1989.

Sujata Bhatt: To author and Carcanet Press Ltd for poems from *Brunizem* (1988) and *Monkey Shadows* (1991): © Sujata Bhatt 1988, 1991.

Eavan Boland: To author and Carcanet Press Ltd for poems from *The Journey* (1987) and *Outside History* (1990): © Eavan Boland 1987, 1990.

Dermot Bolger: To author for 'Snuff Movies' from *Internal Exiles* (Dolmen, 1986): © Dermot Bolger 1986.

Charles Boyle: To author and Carcanet Press Ltd for poems from *Affinities* (1977), *Sleeping Rough* (1987) and *The Very Man* (1993): © Charles Boyle 1977, 1987, 1993.

John Burnside: To author and Secker & Warburg Ltd for poems from *Common Knowledge* (1991) and *Feast Days* (1992): © John Burnside 1991, 1992.

Duncan Bush: To author and Seren Books for poems from *Salt* (1985): © Duncan Bush 1985.

Ciaran Carson: To author and The Gallery Press for poems from *The Irish for No* (Gallery, 1987; Bloodaxe, 1988): © Ciaran Carson, 1987, 1988.

Harry Clifton: To author and The Gallery Press for poems from *The Desert Route: Selected Poems* (Gallery, 1991; Bloodaxe, 1992): © Harry Clifton 1991, 1992.

David Constantine: To author and Bloodaxe Books Ltd for poems from *Selected Poems* (1991): © David Constantine 1991.

Robert Crawford: To author and Chatto & Windus Ltd for poems from *A Scottish Assembly* (1988) and *Talkies* (1991): © Robert Crawford 1988, 1991.

Tony Curtis: To author and Seren Books for 'Thoughts from the Holiday Inn' from *The Last Candles* (1989): © Tony Curtis 1989.

David Dabydeen: To author and Dangaroo Press for poems from *Slave Song* (1984) and *Coolie Odyssey* (1988): © David Dabydeen 1984, 1988.

Fred D'Aguiar: To author for poems from *Mama Dot* (Chatto, 1985); to author and Chatto & Windus Ltd for poems from *Airy Hall* (1989).

Nuala Ní Dhomhnaill: To author, translators and The Gallery Press for poems from *Pharaoh's Daughter* (1990): © Nuala Ni Dhomhnaill 1981, 1984, 1990, © Paul Muldoon and Seamus Heaney 1990.

Peter Didsbury: To author and Bloodaxe Books Ltd for poems from *The Butchers of Hull* (1982) and *The Classical Farm* (1987); to author for 'That Old-Time Religion, reprinted from *Bête Noire*: © Peter Didsbury 1982, 1987, 1993.

Michael Donaghy: To author and Oxford University Press Ltd for poems from *Shibboleth* (1988) and *Errata* (1993): © Michael Donaghy 1988, 1993.

Carol Ann Duffy: To author and Anvil Press Poetry Ltd for poems from *Selling Manhattan* (1987), *The Other Country* (1990) and *Mean Time* (1993).

Ian Duhig: To author and Bloodaxe Books Ltd for poems from *The Bradford Count* (1991); to author for 'Captain Dung Takes a Butcher's': © Ian Duhig 1991, 1993.

Helen Dunmore: To author and Bloodaxe Books Ltd for poems from *Short Days, Long Nights: New & Selected Poems* (1991): © Helen Dunmore 1991.

Paul Durcan: To author and Blackstaff Press Ltd for poems from *The Berlin Wall Café* (1985), *Going Home to Russia* (1987) and *Daddy, Daddy* (1988): © Paul Durcan 1985, 1987, 1988.

John Ennis: To author for poems from *Dolmen Hill* (Gallery Press, 1977): © John Ennis 1993.

Elizabeth Garrett: To author and Bloodaxe Books Ltd for poems from *The Rule of Three* (1991): © Elizabeth Garrett 1991.

Lavinia Greenlaw: To author for all four poems: © Lavinia Greenlaw 1993.

Maggie Hannan: To author for all three poems: © Maggie Hannan 1993.

David Hartnett: To author and Secker & Warburg Ltd for poems from *House of Moon* (1988) and *Dark Ages* (1992): © David Hartnett 1988, 1992.

Geoff Hattersley: To author for poems from *Slouching Towards Rotherham* (Wide Skirt Press, 1987), *Port of Entry* (Littlewood, 1989) and *The Good Stuff* (Wide Skirt Press, 1991) and for 'Minus Three Point Six', 'Slaughterhouse' and 'Eccentric Hair': © Geoff Hattersley 1987, 1989, 1991, 1993.

W.N. Herbert: To author and Littlewood Arc for poems from *The Testament of the Reverend Thomas Dick* (1993); to author for poems from *Anither Music* (Vennel Press, 1991) and for 'A Two Year Ode': © W.N. Herbert 1991, 1993.

Selima Hill: To author and Chatto & Windus Ltd for poems from *My Darling Camel* (1988); to author and Bloodaxe Books Ltd for poems from *A Little Book of Meat* (1993); to author for 'Orchids', reprinted from *The London Review of Books*, for 'The Tablecloths', reprinted from *The Poetry Book Society Anthology 1988-1989* (PBS/Hutchinson, 1988), and for 'Monkeys', reprinted from *Ambit*: © Selima Hill 1988, 1992, 1993.

Michael Hofmann: To author and Faber & Faber Ltd for poems from *Nights in the Iron Hotel* (1983) and *Acrimony* (1986); to author for 'Guanajuato Two Times', ' "Shivery Stomp" ' and 'Las Casas': © Michael Hofmann 1983, 1986, 1993.

Michael Hulse: To author and HarperCollins Publishers for poems from *Eating Strawberries in the Necropolis* (Harvill, 1991); to author for 'Getting a Tan' from *Knowing and Forgetting* (Secker & Warburg, 1981): © Michael Hulse 1981, 1991.

Kathleen Jamie: To author and Bloodaxe Books Ltd for poems from *The Way We Live* (1987); to author for 'Outreach' and 'Mother-May-I': © Kathleen Jamie 1987, 1993.

Linton Kwesi Johnson: To author, LKJ Music (Publishers) Ltd and Bloodaxe Books Ltd for poems from *Tings an Times: Selected Poems* (1991): © Linton Kwesi Johnson 1991.

Jackie Kay: To author and Bloodaxe Books Ltd for poems from *The Adoption Papers* (1991): © Jackie Kay 1991.

Frank Kuppner: To author and Carcanet Press Ltd for poems from *A Bad Day for the Sung Dynasty* (1984) and *Ridiculous! Absurd! Disgusting!* (1989): © Frank Kuppner 1984, 1989.

Tom Leonard: To author for poems from *Intimate Voices: Selected Work 1963-1983* (Galloping Dog Press, 1984): © Tom Leonard 1984.

Liz Lochhead: To author and Polygon Books for poems from *Dreaming Frankenstein & Collected Poems* (1982); to author and Penguin Books Ltd for poems from *Bagpipe Muzak* (1991): © Liz Lochhead 1982, 1991.

Ian McMillan: To author and Carcanet Press Ltd for 'Just the Facts, Just the' from *Selected Poems* (1987); to author for 'The Er Barnsley Seascapes' from *More Poems Please, Waiter, And Quickly* (Sow's Ear Press, 1989), and for 'Ted Hughes Is Elvis Presley' and 'Pit Closure As Art' from *A Chin* (Wide Skirt Press, 1991): © Ian McMillan 1987, 1989, 1991.

Glyn Maxwell: To author and Bloodaxe Books Ltd for poems from *Tale of the Mayor's Son* (1990) and *Out of the Rain* (1992); to author for 'Love Made Yeah': © Glyn Maxwell 1990, 1992, 1993.

Paula Meehan: To author and The Gallery Press for poems from *The Man who was Marked by Winter* (1991): © Paula Meehan 1991.

Grace Nichols: To author and Virago Press Ltd for poems from *The Fat Black Woman's Poems* (1984) and *Lazy Thoughts of a Lazy Woman* (1989); to author for 'My Northern-Sister': © Grace Nichols 1984, 1989, 1993.

Sean O'Brien: To author and Bloodaxe Books Ltd for poems from *The Indoor Park* (1983) and *The Frighteners* (1987); to author and Oxford University Press Ltd for poems from *HMS Glasshouse* (1991); to author for 'Somebody Else': © Sean O'Brien 1983, 1987, 1991, 1993.

Bernard O'Donoghue: To author and Chatto & Windus Ltd for poems from *The Weakness* (1991): © Bernard O'Donoghue 1991.

Peter Reading: To author and Secker & Warburg Ltd for poems from *Stet* (1986) and *Perduta Gente* (1989); to author and Chatto & Windus Ltd for poems from *Evagatory* (1992); to author for 'Soirée' from *The Prison Cell & Barrel Mystery* (1976), for 'Fiction' from *Fiction* (1979), for 'Song of the Bedsit Girl' from *Tom o'Bedlam's Beauties* (1981), and for poems from *C* (1984) and *Ukulele Music/Going On* (1985), all these collections previously published by Secker & Warburg: © Peter Reading 1976, 1979, 1981, 1984, 1985, 1986, 1989, 1992.

Michèle Roberts: To author and Methuen Ltd for poems from *The mirror of the mother* (1986) and *Psyche and the hurricane* (1990): © Michèle Roberts 1986, 1990.

Stephen Romer: To author and Oxford University Press Ltd for poems from *Idols* (1986) and *Plato's Ladder* (1992): Stephen Romer 1986, 1992.

Jo Shapcott: To author and Bloodaxe Books Ltd for 'The Surrealists' Summer Convention Came to Our City' from *Electroplating the Baby* (1988); to author and Oxford University Press Ltd for 'Phrase Book' from *Phrase Book* (1992): © Jo Shapcott 1988, 1992.

Pauline Stainer: To author and Bloodaxe Books Ltd for 'Sighting the Slave Ship' from *Sighting the Slave Ship* (1992); to author for 'The Ice-Pilot Speaks', reprinted from *Index on Censorship*: © Pauline Stainer 1992.

Matthew Sweeney: To author for 'Ends' from *The Lame Waltzer* (Allison & Busby/Raven Arts, 1985); to author and Secker & Warburg Ltd for poems from *Blue Shoes* (1989) and *Cacti* (1992): © Matthew Sweeney 1985, 1989, 1992.

George Szirtes: To author and Secker & Warburg Ltd for 'The Courtyards' from *The Photographer in Winter* (1986); to author for extract from 'Porch' and 'The Big Sleep': © 1986, 1993.

John Hartley Williams: To author for two poems from *Hidden Identities* (Chatto, 1982) and for 'On the Island'; to author and Bloodaxe Books Ltd for 'Dawn Beach' and 'The Ideology' from *Cornerless People* (1990): © John Hartley Williams 1982, 1990, 1993.

Gerard Woodward: To author and Chatto & Windus Ltd for poems from *Householder* (1992): © Gerard Woodward 1992.

Kit Wright: To author for poems from *Poems 1974-1983* (Hutchinson, 1988): © Kit Wright 1988.